MLS

W9-BKI-429

P.O. 23615

11-27-00

DATE DUE

MAY 1 1 2015	
	PRINTED IN U.S.A.

ABOUT ISLAND PRESS

Island Press is the only nonprofit organization in the United States whose principal purpose is the publication of books on environmental issues and natural resource management. We provide solutions-oriented information to professionals, public officials, business and community leaders, and concerned citizens who are shaping responses to environmental problems.

In 1999, Island Press celebrates its fifteenth anniversary as the leading provider of timely and practical books that take a multidisciplinary approach to critical environmental concerns. Our growing list of titles reflects our commitment to bringing the best of an expanding body of literature to the environmental community throughout North America and the world.

Support for Island Press is provided by The Jenifer Altman Foundation, The Bullitt Foundation, The Mary Flagler Cary Charitable Trust, The Nathan Cummings Foundation, The Geraldine R. Dodge Foundation, The Charles Engelhard Foundation, The Ford Foundation, The Vira I. Heinz Endowment, The W. Alton Jones Foundation, The John D. and Catherine T. MacArthur Foundation, The Andrew W. Mellon Foundation, The Charles Stewart Mott Foundation, The Curtis and Edith Munson Foundation, The National Fish and Wildlife Foundation, The National Science Foundation, The New-Land Foundation, The David and Lucile Packard Foundation, The Pew Charitable Trusts, The Surdna Foundation, The Winslow Foundation, and individual donors.

The Trade-Off Myth

THE TRADE-OFF MYTH

Fact and Fiction About Jobs and the Environment

Eban Goodstein

ISLAND PRESS

Washington, D.C. • Covelo, California

Library of Congress Cataloging-in-Publication Data
Goodstein, Eban S., 1960–
    The trade-off myth : fact and fiction about jobs and the
environment / Eban Goodstein.
        p.   cm.
    Includes bibliographical references and index.
    ISBN 1–55963–683–1 (cloth)
    1. Environmental policy—Economic aspects—United States.
    2. Industries—Environmental aspects—United States.   3. Plant
shutdown—United States.   4. Unemployment—United States.
    I. Title.
    HC110.E5G655   1999   99–33886
    331.12'042'0973—dc21   CIP

Printed on recycled, acid-free paper

Manufactured in the United States of America
10 9 8 7 6 5 4 3 2 1

To Anita Shafer Goodstein
(1929–1998)

Contents

ACKNOWLEDGMENTS

Thanks for this book start with Marc Breslow and my editor at Island Press, Todd Baldwin, who got the ball rolling. Todd, of course, kept it rolling and provided valuable guidance along the way. Laurie Johnson helped me talk through the ideas. Holly Pettit assisted with the research on timber workers in chapter 5. Marvin Goodstein, Ted Wolf, Bob Doppelt, Ernie Niemi, Skip Laitner, Jon Koomey, Dean Baker, Tom Power, Frank Ackerman, Stephen Meyer, and Jim Barrett were kind enough to read either my proposal or drafts of various chapters. I also received valuable feedback from seminar participants at the Economic Policy Institute. This book reflects many of their insights.

Much of the research supporting this book—done both by me and others—was commissioned by the Sustainable Economics Project of the Economic Policy Institute. I am also grateful for summer research support provided to me by Lewis and Clark College. Finally, thanks to Cecilia González and the production staff at Island Press for putting it all together.

Chapter 1

FICTIONS, FACTS, AND POLITICS

In 1992, I was working on the first edition of my college textbook in environmental economics. In the chapter on the costs of environmental protection, I wanted to include a section on the negative employment impacts of regulation. Like many people at the time, I assumed that the issue had been blown out of proportion by the press. Nevertheless, I fully expected that jobs–environment trade-offs would still loom large, at least at the regional level.

They don't.

Many Americans believe three things about jobs and the environment. First, at an economy-wide level, environmental protection has created long-run unemployment. Second, environmental protection has been responsible for large numbers of plant shutdowns and layoffs in manufacturing. And third, environmental protection has led many U.S. firms to flee to developing countries with lax environmental regulations—so called "pollution havens."

When you hear someone say "All economists agree," as a general rule it is best to head for the door. But stay seated for this one. Virtually all economists who have studied the jobs–environment issue agree that the three propositions identified above are false. In reality, at the economy-wide level, there has simply been no trade-off between jobs and the environment. In fact, regulation-induced plant closings and layoffs are very rare. And, despite what one hears in the media, few firms are fleeing

1

industrial countries such as the United States to take advantage of loose environmental regulations in poor countries.

These facts run so counter to the conventional wisdom that I suspect most readers, at first encounter, will not believe them. However, the research base that supports these views—and they are the strong consensus views within the economics profession—is substantial. Chapters 2 and 3 show that jobs–environment conflicts are very small in both relative and absolute terms.

Although environmental protection seldom causes large-scale layoffs, jobs–environment conflicts—particularly in coal mining or timbering towns—do pose serious hardships for some workers. Chapter 4 focuses attention on these issues. How big are the impacts, and what can government policies do to help workers adjust?

In contrast to the conventional wisdom that jobs and the environment are in conflict, a revisionist view has recently arisen that maintains that environmental protection measures can actually reduce U.S. unemployment problems. Chapter 5 evaluates several different claims about a "jobs–environment synergy." Green jobs, it turns out, cannot solve major problems of unemployment; however, under the right conditions, a shift from "dirty" to "clean" production methods can be an important element of a local economic development strategy.

Chapter 6 looks at jobs–environment trade-offs that might emerge as we attack the problem of global warming. In December 1997, the United States and other industrialized countries signed a treaty in Kyoto, Japan, whereby they agreed to reduce carbon dioxide and other greenhouse gas emissions by a combined total of 5 percent from 1990 levels, with the goal to be achieved between 2008 and 2012. However, the U.S. Senate has yet to ratify the treaty, and no enabling legislation has been passed. Opposition has been based on predictions of large-scale job loss that industry groups have floated.

In fact, the job impacts of the global warming treaty are likely to be modest, on the order of a few thousand jobs per year nationwide. But the layoffs will be concentrated on distinct groups, such as coal miners, coal-shipping railway workers, and employees at oil- and coal-fired electric utilities. Yet, despite these circumstances, the political influence of job-loss arguments is likely to loom large, perhaps large enough to scuttle the agreement itself. Predictions of widespread layoffs, no matter how unfounded, find fertile ground today despite the relatively "healthy economy" of the late 1990s. The twin forces of globalization and the declining power of organized labor unions have left American families facing an environment of intense economic insecurity. The same forces have also left the political coalition that in the past supported strong environmental regulations increasingly vulnerable. Given this, understanding and addressing the underlying concerns of workers will be key to making further progress in cleaning up the environment.

What follows, in brief, is the story.

THREE TYPES OF UNEMPLOYMENT

Economists divide unemployment into three principal categories: cyclical, structural, and frictional. *Cyclical unemployment* is caused by business cycles. During recessions, the unemployment rate in the United States will typically rise to between 7 and 9 percent of the workforce. This translates into roughly ten to eleven million unemployed workers. During booms, the unemployment rate falls into the 4 percent range, which economists define as *full employment.*

But how can we have achieved full employment if around six million people are still looking for jobs? This is what is termed *frictional unemployment*—people who are temporarily between jobs. Even when the economy is operating at full tilt, some firms will lay off workers who in a short time will find new jobs, some workers will quit to find better opportunities, and young people and new entrants into the labor market will spend time searching for a job. When the unemployment rate in a given region approaches 4 percent, most of it is frictional.

Finally, *structural unemployment* occurs when major regional shifts in production patterns leave workers stranded. The devastating and long-lasting impacts of structural unemployment were captured in Michael Moore's classic film *Roger and Me.* After General Motors pulled out of Flint, Michigan, not much was left in parts of the town besides row after row of boarded up houses and shops.

With this bit of terminology in hand, the three myths about jobs and the environment can be recast more precisely.

> *Myth 1:* At the economy-wide level, environmental regulation aggravates cyclical unemployment by deepening recessions and making it hard if not impossible to achieve full employment.

Chapter 2 addresses this charge, revealing it to be completely without foundation. Cyclical unemployment is created by economy-wide downturns; however, environmental regulation has neither caused nor deepened recessions. The real economy-wide effects of regulation are to shift the *types* of jobs, without increasing the overall level of unemployment either in booms or recessions. There are now well over two million people who work directly or indirectly in environmentally related jobs. And, surprisingly, these jobs tend to be concentrated more than proportionately in blue-collar sectors of the economy. Combined, some 31 percent of jobs that are dependent on environmental spending are in construction and manufacturing, compared with 20 percent of jobs in the economy as a whole.

> *Myth 2:* Environmental regulation has led to wide-scale plant shutdowns and layoffs, which have severely aggravated structural unemployment.

Chapter 3 tells the real story. Across the United States, well over two million workers are laid off each year due to factors such as import competition, shifts in demand, or corporate downsizings. In sharp contrast, annual layoffs in manufacturing due to environmental regulation are on the order of one to 3,000 per year. In 1997 (the last year for which data were available), regulation accounted for less than one-tenth of 1 percent of large-scale layoffs in the economy.

> *Myth 3:* Even if it has not led to massive shutdowns, environmental regulation has encouraged new manufacturing investment to flee overseas to countries with lax environmental requirements. This, in turn, has created structural unemployment.

Economists have actually been looking quite hard for exactly this effect for some twenty years. We even have a name for it: the "pollution haven hypothesis." However, as chapter 3 shows, pollution havens, while perfectly plausible in theory, are quite hard to find in practice. Beyond a couple of high profile—and highly publicized—cases, firms have not been fleeing the developed world to escape environmental regulations. The reasons? Regulatory costs, even in heavily regulated industries, are a small percentage of total sales (i.e., only rarely rising above 2 percent); costs are only one factor affecting a location decision; and much of pollution control technology is embedded in plant design. Because an oil refinery built today by a U.S. oil company in Mexico would look a lot like one built in California, the potential savings on pollution control equipment are not significantly reduced.

The point is not that environmental regulations are without cost. Any time we as a society legislate cleaner air or water, we pay for it in the form of higher prices for commodities ranging from gasoline and automobiles to food and drinking water, at least in the short run. Environmental protection often does require a trade-off, but it entails foregone consumption of some goods and services, not fewer overall jobs.

THE MYTHMAKERS

The jobs–environment debate resurfaces in the United States every time a significant piece of environmental legislation comes before Congress. Today the issue is Senate ratification of the 1997 Kyoto treaty to control greenhouse gas emissions. Before this fight, the two major recent battles were the 1990 Clean Air Act (CAA) amendments, and President Bill Clinton's 1993 Forest Plan for the Pacific Northwest. Throughout this book, I rely on examples drawn primarily from the CAA amendments, the Forest Plan, and the greenhouse debate.

The CAA amendments, which President George Bush signed into law in 1990, had two main thrusts. First, they required electric utilities to clean up their sulfur dioxide and nitrogen oxide emissions to reduce acid rain. Second, they imposed controls on the release of so-called "air toxics," or hazardous air pollutants, from chemical companies. President Clinton's Forest Plan, which was initiated in 1993, protected substantial tracts of old-growth timber on federal lands in the Pacific Northwest from logging. The primary motivation behind the plan was to preserve the habitat of the endangered spotted owl. While on the campaign trail in 1992, President Bush adamantly opposed the plan. Habitat protection, he predicted, would mean that "We'll be up to our neck in owls, and every mill worker will be out of a job." Significantly—and unfortunately—debate over both of these measures took place during the recession of the late 1980s and early 1990s. High levels of cyclical unemployment in both the eastern coal fields and western timber country left workers in both regions feeling desperate and under siege.

In the midst of the CAA battle, the *Wall Street Journal* collected an astounding poll result. In a nationwide survey, 33 percent of the respondents told pollsters that they personally felt themselves "likely" or "somewhat likely" to lose their own job as a consequence of environmental regulation. Clearly, the perception of a jobs–environment trade-off, which played out dramatically during the early 1990s on both the east and west coasts, has been deeply imbedded in the national psyche.

For the overwhelming majority of workers, these fears are completely unfounded. So how do these different job trade-off myths arise? I noted earlier that regulation is not without cost. It does mean higher prices for some of the goods and services we buy. However, in addition to raising prices, environmental regulations also cut into corporate profits. For this reason, companies often oppose regulations. Yet when they try to fight them, they face a serious dilemma. Political arguments that regulations are bad because they raise prices simply fall flat. Americans do not seem to mind generalized price increases for goods if it means a cleaner environment. And, of course, the argument that environmental regulations will reduce profits is a nonstarter. So what message could be fashioned to capture the debate?

Many corporations have responded in a way that is best summed up in one word—*jobs*. Each time a new environmental regulation is considered, the affected industries roll out second-rate studies to prove that the regulations will be "job-killers." Later in the book, we will dissect several of these analyses. The point here is that it has been this relentless, thirty-year-old media campaign—combined with rising economic insecurity and an all-too-common media preference for easy answers—that has led to the entrenchment of these three myths in the public mind.

In fact, the limited jobs impact of environmental regulation is reflected in two high-profile, worst-case scenarios that have taken place in recent years: timber workers versus old-growth forest measures in the Pacific Northwest and coal miners versus clean air efforts in the southern Appalachians. Chapter 4 looks closely at these two circumstances, however, one point is worth making here. Even in these highly publicized scenarios, the number of direct layoffs was less than 10,000 spread out over several years and across several states. Real economic pain was clearly suffered by these workers and their communities. But in terms of the jobs lost, each of these two events would be dwarfed by even a modest-sized corporate downsizing.

You wouldn't know this, however, from reading two stories that ran in the *New York Times* in the space of a week in February 1996.[1] Both stories clearly illustrate the hold that the jobs versus environment myth has on the imagination of readers and reporters. The headlines read:

"EASTERN COAL TOWNS WITHER IN THE NAME OF CLEANER AIR"

"SQUEEZING THE TEXTILE WORKERS:
TRADE AND TECHNOLOGY FORCE A NEW WAVE OF JOB CUTS"

The first article, a front-page, lead story, detailed the five-year impact of the 1990 CAA amendments on Appalachian communities as electric companies switched to low-sulfur western coal to meet tougher air pollution standards. The piece on textile workers appeared in the business section and examined the impact of trade and technology on employment in the textile industry during 1995. Care to guess the number of job losses in each case? In the coal industry, the number of layoffs was hard to pinpoint, in large part due to the fact that the industry was continually downsizing in response to shifting markets and technological advances. Although the reporter, Peter Kilborn, never directly stated as much in his article, if one reads carefully and does some math, it can be calculated that *at most* he was talking about 1,000 job losses per year over a multistate region that could possibly be attributed to regulation. By contrast, in the textile industry, the number was an astounding 100,000 layoffs in a single year.

Again, this is not to downplay the devastating impact that layoffs can have both in textile towns and coal communities. But it does beg an interesting question: Why did the *Times* feel compelled to report truly small layoff events on the front page, while burying in the business section the news about job losses that were one hundred times larger?

There are two answers. The first is the corporate world's ability to spin the media. Reporters uniformly report—often without comment—the absurdly high job-loss predictions that industry think tanks regularly churn out. More profoundly, journalists are looking for someone to blame for rising income inequality, corporate downsizing, and increasing middle-class insecurity. While the declining power of labor unions, increasing levels of import competition, and rapid pace of automation are genuine suspects, environmental regulations are apparently a more comfortable villain.

A JOBS–ENVIRONMENT SYNERGY?

Environmental protection is simply not the "job killer" it has been made out to be. What about the opposite view? Some environmentalists and policy makers claim that environmental regulation can be a "green jobs machine" that will help solve U.S. unemployment problems. Vice President Al Gore, for example, has argued that investment in new environmental technologies could provide a dramatic spark to our economic system to a degree comparable to that experienced as a result of the Marshall Plan, which followed World War II. Others have argued that reducing greenhouse gas emissions (e.g., by cutting oil imports) will create a significant number of new jobs in the United States.

If the argument is that green jobs will solve the problem of cyclical unemployment, then it is without substance. Just as regulation does not cause recessions, neither does it prevent their occurrence. (However, regulation may mitigate the depth of recessions somewhat by mandating a "stimulus" in the form of clean-up investment.)

What about structural unemployment? Under the right circumstances, a shift from a dirty to a clean technology can lead to modest gains in local jobs. This is evident from a couple of ongoing experiments in "sustainable development" close to my home in Oregon. In different arenas, environmental groups are working with businesses to promote new jobs in waste-based manufacturing and value-added natural resource products. But these kinds of employment benefits are contingent on location, time, and technology. A shift to green production is, therefore, no panacea for depressed regions. Nevertheless, it should be considered as one important tool for promoting local economic development.

JOBS AND GLOBAL WARMING

The central thesis of this book is that the employment gains or losses from environmental protection are small, gradual, and tend to balance each other out. Nevertheless, for political reasons, "jobs" will continue to loom large when new regulations are proposed. President George Bush set the tone for the current global warming debate at the Rio Earth Summit in 1992 when he defended the U.S. opposition to a strong greenhouse agreement as "protecting American jobs from environmental extremists." Since then, several major consulting firms, working on behalf of the fossil fuel and auto industries, have churned out studies that predict near-term job losses of over two and a half million.

What are the likely employment impacts if the U.S. Senate ratifies the Kyoto global warming treaty? At the economy-wide level, the likely answer is a few thousand per year, nationwide. However, specific sectors will be hard hit. In particular, attempts to reduce greenhouse gas emissions will further shrink the U.S. coal industry. Coal miners have borne the brunt of environmental regulation before. Under the CAA amendments of 1990, adjustment assistance programs were set up that have since served several thousand eastern coal miners over the last few years.

However, the keystone of the adjustment program for coal miners—which is an extension of the job training program that is available to workers who are dislocated by trade and defense downsizing—has been, to put it politely, largely useless. Study after study has demonstrated that the underfunded, short-term approach to training that is available under the Job Training Partnership Act (JTPA) simply has no impact on raising the earnings potential of their graduates. Longer-term retraining has real value, however, without income support, many dislocated workers can't afford to take advantage of the longer-term options that the JTPA offers. Even good training has its limits. For coal miners, many of whom live in regions with persistent, high rates of structural unemployment, the question has become: "training for what jobs"? Also, nothing in coal counties pays like coal mining; many laid-off miners have taken income cuts of 50 percent or more.

There are better ideas out there: President Clinton's Northwest Forest Plan provided an increase in federal infrastructure and business development dollars for hard-hit timber communities. The plan also funded an innovative conversion effort. Dubbed "Jobs in the Woods," the program was originally designed to promote living-wage jobs in the forest-restoration industry. These initiatives are explored and evaluated in chapter 4. Policies such as these, combined with a serious commitment to rigorous retraining programs, as well as buyouts for older workers, could form the basis for a fair adjustment package for miners and others who do lose their jobs as a consequence of climate-change policy.

THE WORKERS' ENVIRONMENT

During the 1993 Forest Summit that was held in Portland, Oregon, 50,000 environmentalists who were bent on protecting the remaining old-growth forest, and its now-famous resident the spotted owl, attended a rally and rock concert in a riverside park. The next day, 20,000 workers from the logging industry rallied in the same park. They called on President Clinton to end logging restrictions in the old-growth forest. Buzz Eades, a sixth-generation logger, put his predicament this way: "I represent thousands of timber workers[,] . . . modern Paul Bunyans who are hiding in the car while their wife buys groceries with food stamps."[2]

Eades tells a critically important story, but one that is only tangentially about spotted owls. All across the country, the last two decades have seen the gradual disappearance of decent, family-wage jobs for high school and, increasingly, college graduates. The fiction that environmental protection creates large-scale unemployment needs to be understood in this American context of ever-increasing job insecurity and growing income inequality. Manufacturing plants are fleeing overseas, attracted not by loose environmental regulations but by low wages. Service industries, even in good times, are continually downsizing and restructuring, which has lead to layoffs that by historical standards are indeed massive. Economy-wide, inflation-adjusted hourly wages for male workers are in a twenty-year slide from which there is no evidence of recovery. And many workers who are laid off from established industries do not quickly—if ever—recover their former salaries.[3] Given these circumstance, it is no wonder that people are concerned about highly visible government policies that seem to them likely to further destabilize their communities.

Much of the concern about job loss in the case of miners and timber workers was related to the disappearance of high-paying union jobs that were available to hard-working high school graduates and that made up the backbone of the blue-collar middle class in the 1960s and 1970s. A powerful indication of this trend is that the percentage of the U.S. workforce in unions fell from 24 percent in 1979 to 14 percent in 1997. And the loss of these jobs is certainly to be mourned. America's middle class has found itself working harder and harder to maintain a constant family income. In 1996, the typical married-couple family worked over six weeks longer than in 1989 and brought home a slightly smaller paycheck.[4] Stresses at home have mounted while quality of life has declined.

Meanwhile, incomes for the top 20 percent of earners have escalated rapidly. Emblematic of this trend is that the average pay for a CEO more than doubled between 1989 and 1997 and is now more than 116 times that of the typical worker. Even the booming stock market over this same period couldn't help middle-class families, who saw their wealth actually decline by over 3 percent as stagnant incomes lead to more debt. Stock market gains did benefit one group—the richest 10 percent of U.S. households reaped over 85 percent of the run up in stock value.[5] This tremendous growth in economic inequality has led to a troubling new label for America in the 1990s: "the 80-20 society."

However, environmental regulation is not the cause of deindustrialization or of the growth of income inequality in the United States. If we, as a society, are generally concerned about rising income inequality, than one solution is to make union organizing in this country feasible again. Since the early 1980s, many American businesses have aggressively exploited loopholes in the nation's labor laws to render union organizing virtually impossible. The number of employers using five or more anti-union tactics during organizing drives (e.g., holding compulsory anti-union meetings, publicly threatening plant closure, firing organizers) has more than doubled since 1986. And the risks for workers supporting a union drive have skyrocketed. The AFL-CIO estimates that in 1995, over 11,000 workers were illegally fired during organizing campaigns. In 1980, one in twenty workers who voted for a union was illegally fired; in 1995 that number had risen to one in eight.[6]

Not surprisingly, the number of union elections dropped by over 50 percent over the same period of 1980 to 1995. Two points can be made here. One is that if Americans are concerned about the loss of jobs with decent pay for the middle class, than the solution to the problem is unlikely to lie in rolling back environmental regulations, but rather, at least partially, in labor law reform.[7] The second point is perhaps less obvious, but equally relevant. Organized labor, by helping to elect progressive Democrats, has played a pivotal role in the political coalition that is responsible for America's environmental protection laws. Without a revived political presence on the part of unions, the future for new, major environmental legislation in the United States is likely to be dim.

UNIONS, DEMOCRATS, AND THE ENVIRONMENT

In the fall of 1997, Interior Secretary Bruce Babbit was on a speaking tour drumming up public support for the Kyoto global warming treaty. Like many economists who study environmental issues, I had become persuaded that the benefits of early action to reduce greenhouse gas emissions were large and that the initial steps to address the problem could be taken at a relatively low cost. I had a chance to speak briefly with Secretary Babbit, and I urged him to tell President Clinton to negotiate a strong agreement. My political reasoning was simple: in twenty-five years the U.S. Senate has never voted down a major piece of environmental legislation once it was introduced. If Republican Presidents Nixon, Reagan, and Bush all saw major pieces of environmental legislation make it through Congress on their watch, what should Clinton have to fear? Also, the American people overwhelmingly support action on global warming. Poll results from 1997 showed that 90 percent of Americans felt that the government should limit the greenhouse gasses that businesses generate, and 72 percent said that they would pay higher utility bills to reduce greenhouse pollution from electricity plants.[8]

President Clinton did come home from Japan with a solid, first-step agreement. The Kyoto process included only the industrial nations, which was consistent with an agreement reached in Berlin in 1996. The rationale was twofold: rich countries had emitted the vast bulk of greenhouse gasses over the last century, and poor countries could not afford significant, immediate reductions. This two-step process followed the model of the successful 1987 ozone protection treaty, the Montreal Protocol. In Montreal, the developing nations were given a ten-year grace period before they were expected to reduce production of ozone destroying chlorofluorocarbons (CFCs).

But before the Kyoto Summit took place, by an astounding vote of ninety-five to zero, the U.S. Senate declared that a treaty that failed to require that developing countries adhere to the same timetable for greenhouse gas reduction as industrial countries was not acceptable. Everyone knew such a treaty would not emerge from Kyoto, and the best President Clinton could say in response was that he would obtain "significant participation" from developing countries before bringing the treaty to the Senate. Of course, the standard for significant participation was left vague. Nor is it clear whether whatever minor treaty modifications Clinton can wrangle will satisfy the Senate.

The Senate floor debate was as astounding as the vote. Not one Democrat stood up for the treaty process as it had been negotiated by President Clinton's team and agreed upon in Berlin. Democrats and Republicans alike repeated Myths 1, 2, and 3: big, economy-wide job losses would be inevitable, widespread shutdowns of manufacturing plants would be likely, and developing countries with relaxed environmental standards would steal U.S. jobs. President Clinton's economic advisor Janet Yellen had given the Senate Democrats ammunition to take down this view, arguing in the previous months that the employment impacts of Kyoto would be small. But no one was there to take up the charge. Why not?

In part, the Republican party has lost many of its environmental moderates. There is hard-core and well-organized ideological opposition to the treaty on the part of the new conservatives in the party. The debate led off with Senator Charles Hagel of Nebraska entering into the record an article from the *Wall Street Journal*'s editorial page declaring that "global warming is mostly a phantom phenomenon." This was one constant theme from the Republican side. The other theme, of course, was jobs. Reducing carbon emissions would "cripple our economy . . ." and result in the lose of 1.25 to 1.5 million jobs (Senator Mitch McConnell of Kentucky); "lead to a loss of two million jobs, most of which will actually move overseas" (Senator Trent Lott of Mississippi); and require "[i]ndividual Americans [to] pay for this treaty either in their electric bills, at the gas pump, or by losing their jobs" (Senator Hagel).

It is no news that the Republican party has moved to the right. But much more significant from an environmental perspective is a similar drift among Democrats. There are today many fewer genuine ecological voices in the Democratic party than in the 1970s, when the first wave of environmental legislation passed, or even than in the late 1980s, when the CAA amendments were enacted. Massachusetts senator John Kerry, a leading Democrat, originally opposed the anti-Kyoto resolution, calling it a "treaty killer." However, on the floor he spoke in favor of it, saying he too was concerned about the "effects on the economy" if developing countries were not part of the process at the outset. Patty Murray, Democratic senator from Washington State, parenthetically noted that she was worried about global warming, but supported the resolution because of the "concerns of American workers and industry."[9]

No Democratic senator took the floor to defend the position of environmentalists—global warming is the most critical environmental issue of the next century; developed countries, in concert, should act first; American know-how and innovation can rise to this challenge; combating climate change is an *economic opportunity*, not a crisis; and the United States has a moral obligation to claim a historic role as a world environmental leader. This kind of powerful, proenvironment rhetoric was completely absent from the Senate floor.

So who were the Democrats representing? With the exception of Senator Robert Byrd, who was arguing on behalf of West Virginia coal miners (and the coal industry), Democrats certainly were not speaking for workers. In the summer of 1997, the loud voices in the media who were protesting a possible Kyoto treaty were big business, not unions.

The AFL-CIO, while formally on record as opposing Kyoto, has not actively lobbied against the treaty, and it has sent out quiet messages that it will not do so. Since the summer of 1998, the labor federation has participated in an ongoing dialogue in Washington, D.C., with environmentalists to try to find common ground on the issue. A search of speeches, newsletters, and publications on the AFL-CIO's Website illustrates the low profile the organization has taken in opposing the treaty. The search revealed only two references to Kyoto: a buried newsletter announcement and a brief report on a West Virginia protest against the treaty by mine workers. The United Mine Workers (UMWA) has taken a vocal—and understandable—stand against controlling greenhouse gas emissions. Coal miners are the one group that is certain to suffer significant job losses. However, what makes the AFL-CIO's quiescence on the issue even more notable is the fact that Rich Trumka, former president of the UMWA, is now secretary-treasurer of the AFL-CIO.

Democrats Kerry and Murray, who both made floor speeches that expressed concern for American workers—and then voted for a "treaty killer"—were, however unintentionally, buying into the jobs–environment myth. Today's Senate liberals, few in number and lacking a clear vision, ducked the debate. They simply did not show up to deliver the clear, proenvironment message that has been the hallmark of past legislative victories in the chamber.

The Senate resolution reflects the rightward shift in the Congress over the past two decades. But the point here is that major environmental successes in the past have been spearheaded, and ultimately won, by liberal Democratic senators and representatives who, in turn, owed their electoral presence in government to the liberal coalition that emerged in the 1960s: unions, minorities, and environmentalists. Unions have played a pivotal role in this coalition by providing the bodies, the phone banks, and the working-class votes that balanced those of the conservatives.

In simplified terms, over the past thirty years, unions have been carrying much of the electoral water for environmental protection. As unions have declined, so have the number of committed progressive legislators and the support for strong environmental legislation. Table 1.1 illustrates the strong convergence of labor and environmental interests. It lists the AFL-CIO's "Top 15" senators in 1995—all of whom voted

TABLE 1.1. Labor's top fifteen senators also support the environment

Senators with greater than 90 percent lifetime labor support, 1995	Party-State	Percentage of pro-environment votes, 1995
Akaka	D-HI	86
Boxer	D-CA	100
Dodd	D-CT	100
Feingold	D-WI	100
Feinstein	D-CA	93
Inouye	D-HI	57
Kennedy	D-MA	100
Kerry	D-MA	100
Lautenberg	D-NJ	97
Levin	D-MI	100
Mikulski	D-MD	86
Murray	D-WA	100
Pell	D-RI	90
Sarbanes	D-MD	90
Wellstone	D-MN	100

Source: *AFL-CIO Report on the 1995 U.S. Congress;* League of Conservation Voters, *National Environmental Scorecard, Final 104th Congress.*

with labor 90 percent of the time or more during their Senate careers. Not surprisingly, they are all Democrats. But more significantly, with the exception of Hawaii's Daniel Inouye, the group was all strong on the environment. Eight of the fifteen received 100 percent ratings from the League of Conservation Voters. The jobs issue has clearly driven an unfortunate, and unnecessary, wedge between environmentalists and workers in America.

TAKING LABOR SERIOUSLY

The title of this book is *The Trade-Off Myth*. Myths are fictions that persist even in the face of powerful evidence to the contrary. For almost thirty years, economists have been gathering data on the employment impacts of environmental regulation, and the facts are now in. For the economy as a whole, there simply is no jobs–environment trade-off. And at the local level, in sharp contrast to the conventional wisdom, layoffs from environmental protection have been very, very small. Even in the most extreme cases, such as the protection of the spotted owl or acid rain reduction, job losses from environmental protection have been minute compared with more garden-variety layoff events.

Of course, for workers in today's economy who are laid off due to environmental regulation—or some more prevalent cause—the trade-offs are not small. This book, therefore, has a twofold purpose. The first is to examine the deep-seated, and ultimately mistaken, American belief in a widespread jobs–environment trade-off. The second is to argue that until we begin to reduce the very real economic insecurity that American workers face, new environmental initiatives will be vulnerable to the rebirth of this myth.

There are two ways to defuse the jobs–environment issue. One is to lay clear the facts, which is what this book sets out to do. The second is to take the concerns of workers seriously. Even if environmental protection is not to blame for job loss, in this era of growing employment instability the United States needs a set of policies that address, among other issues, decent job retraining and labor-law reform to help protect workers from the ravages of globalization. With such policies in place, the jobs issue will lose some of its bite in policy debates over environmental protection, as well as in the related areas of taxes and trade. However, in the absence of greater economic security for American workers, the fiction of a widespread jobs–environment trade-off will continue to reemerge as a political fact.

NOTES

1. *New York Times*, February 15, 1996, A1; and February 21, 1996, C1.
2. "Quotable," *The Spokane Spokesman-Review*, April 3, 1993.
3. Mishel et al. (1998).
4. Mishel et al. (1998).
5. Mishel et al. (1998).
6. Bronfenbrenner (1994), Jorgensen (1998).
7. Friedman et al. (1994).
8. Krosnick and Visser (1998).
9. Senate quotes are all from *The Congressional Record*, July 25, 1997.

Chapter 2

No Economy-Wide Trade-Off

In 1998, 137 million people held paying jobs in the United States. That year, the average unemployment rate dipped as low as 4.3 percent, which meant that in any given week around six million people nationwide were looking for work. Since the U.S. economy was at the peak of a business cycle, most of those people were classified as frictionally unemployed, or between jobs on a short-term basis. Given this, there was much talk in the business press about labor shortages. "Scrambling For Workers," read a front-page headline in the *Cleveland Plain Dealer*.[1]

Of course, this low nationwide average disguised some regional differences. In dozens of pockets ranging from rural upstate New York, downstate to the Bronx, parts of Detroit, some rural Mississippi counties, and the extreme eastern half of Oregon, unemployment was still over 10 percent. But these stubborn and persistent examples of structural unemployment were not much on the national mind. Most media reports on the economy were rosy; stories of hardship were rare.

However, if we turn back the clock to late 1991, when the last recessionary trough of the business cycle occurred, we find a different mood. Nationwide the unemployment rate was 7.5 percent. In communities that faced underlying structural unemployment as well as frictional unemployment, rates of over 15 percent were not uncommon. The overall *average* unemployment rate in the state of West Virginia reached 13 percent. With an extra four million people nationwide looking for jobs, all unemployed workers were having a much harder time finding work. With labor markets so competitive, pay raises largely disappeared. Stories about the hardships of unemployment were common in the media. Jobs became the defining focus of the Bush–Clinton presidential campaigns. A famous sign hung in candidate Clinton's office urged focus on one simple campaign message: "It's the Economy, Stupid."

The point is that cyclical unemployment, which leads to high rates of joblessness both regionally and nationwide, is the economic beast that frightens most of us. And in the midst of a recession, environmental regulation becomes an easy scapegoat for more fundamental economic problems. It was in the teeth of the recession of the late 1980s and early 1990s, for example, that West Virginia coal miners protested acid-rain legislation, and citizens in the Northwest were bitterly polarized over protection of the spotted owl. If environmental regulation were somehow to be implicated in the creation or aggravation of cyclical unemployment, then jobs–environment trade-offs would be serious indeed.

Fortunately, environmental regulation does not have this effect. At the economy-wide level, regulation does not increase unemployment. It leads instead to a gradual shifting of the types of jobs Americans hold. In 1970, U.S. firms, consumers, and federal, state, and local governments spent about $36 billion on environmental protection measures. This was a little less than 1 percent of total U.S. output of final goods and services, or gross domestic product (GDP), that year. These expenditures financed, among many other things, the installation of pollution-control equipment in factories, government inspections of these efforts, catalytic converters in cars, laboratory testing of new pesticides, the construction of municipal sewage plants, and the disposal of household garbage. By the year 2000, this amount is expected to rise to $219 billion, or 2.8 percent of GDP.[2]

Spending means jobs. From 1977 to 1991—the last year for which the Environmental Protection Agency (EPA) made the calculations— total employment from spending on environmental clean up climbed from 1,267,000 to 1,965,000. This 55 percent increase makes environmentally related employment one of the most dynamic growth sectors in the U.S. economy.[3] Of course if we weren't spending this money on environmental protection, we would be spending it on something else, such as health care, consumer items, or education, which would create jobs in those sectors. But it is this kind of job shifting—and not job destruction—that regulation-induced spending on the environment generates.

That there is no fundamental conflict between job growth and a cleaner environment is a conclusion that has strong consensus support in the economics profession. This was emphasized in a joint appearance at the National Press Club of Washington, D.C., by Robert Hahn of the conservative American Enterprise Institute and Paul Portney, who is president of the nation's premier environmental economics think tank, Resources for the Future. "There's no question that we can have job growth simultaneous with improved environmental protection," said Hahn. "The proof is in the last twenty years, when we've had economic growth and, in general, a lot of improved environmental quality—for instance, getting rid of a very serious pollutant, lead, in our cities' air." Portney also agreed with Hahn that if the government was managing to stimulate economic growth through its macroeconomic policies, than total job growth should not suffer from tighter environmental regulations. If new environmental protection rules cause some short-term job loss, Portney noted, "in an actively growing economy those people will be absorbed."[4]

The no trade-off conclusion has even been turned around to attack advocates of the job-creation benefits of regulation. Writing in a paper sponsored by the American Petroleum Institute, Dr. Thomas Hopkins of the Rochester Institute of Technology argues that: "If compliance with regulations spawns more jobs in pollution-control equipment firms, then such jobs are not a net benefit of the regulation. They essentially are a reshuffling of society's workforce, one that may proceed smoothly and conceivably yield higher average salaries, but not likely one that can be given credit for reducing the nation's unemployment rate."[5]

That there has been to date no economy-wide trade-off between environmental protection and jobs is the consensus view among ideologically disparate economists. But most people are not economists. For that reason, the bulk of this chapter will lay out both the basic argument and the evidence that supports the no trade-off claim.

First, recent experience clearly shows that during boom times, environmental regulation does not place any restrictions on job growth. During the sustained business-cycle peak of the 1990s, and despite the United States devoting an increasing share of GDP to environmental protection, U.S. policy makers were actually worried that employment was growing too fast. Inflationary fears led officials at the central bank to raise interest rates to slow down what was perceived as overheated job growth.

What about during recessions? Does regulation aggravate downturns in the economy? Here too the answer is "no." Evidence from both macromodeling and input–output exercises finds little support for declines in employment, and in fact suggests the possibility of modest employment gains from regulatory-induced spending.

This chapter ends with a discussion of the emerging environmental-protection sector of the economy. What types of jobs are being created by this long-run shift in the economy? Surprisingly, jobs that depend on environmental spending are disproportionately concentrated in traditional blue-collar sectors; in fact, 31 percent of environmentally related employment is in construction and manufacturing, compared to 20 percent for the economy as a whole.

IS REGULATION CONSTRAINING U.S. JOB GROWTH?

The easy way to answer this question is to simply look at the economic record from recent years. From the trough of the recession in 1991 through 1998, the U.S. economy added about fourteen million jobs.[6] In fact, by 1995, the Federal Reserve (the Fed) was concerned that job growth was *too high*. Alan Greenspan, chairman of the Fed, was worried that the economy was close to experiencing "greater than full employment." This, he feared, would fuel inflationary pressure in the economy. Greenspan's concern stemmed from the theory that once cyclical unemployment is eliminated, only frictional—largely voluntary or short-term—unemployment is left behind. Under these circumstances, employers can only attract new workers by offering higher wages (or more generous benefits). But, at some point, higher wages can lead to higher prices, as firms try to maintain profit margins. Under this scenario, an inflationary "wage–price spiral" might be triggered.

The Fed is charged by U.S. law to try to maintain both price stability and full employment. It does this by either raising or lowering interest rates. The Fed fights inflation essentially by putting people out of work. Increased interest rates mean that consumers can borrow less to build houses and buy big ticket items, such as cars or television sets. Also, higher interest rates discourage firms from undertaking new investment in plant and equipment. This decreased demand results in slower employment growth, less overtime, and actual layoffs in interest-sensitive industries, such as construction and automobile manufacturing. This direct impact then works its way through the economy via a multiplier effect as falling incomes for workers in hard-hit industries (e.g., automotive and construction) reduce their demand for other goods and services. With lowered demand across the economy, inflation subsides.

In contrast, when the economy is in a slump, the Fed tries to reverse the process by lowering interest rates. Lower rates are designed to stimulate job growth by encouraging businesses and consumers to borrow and spend.

In 1994 and 1995, in spite of spending $180 billion per year on environmental protection, the U.S. economy was growing too fast from the Fed's point of view. Too many people were employed in the United States, which was raising the specter of inflation. As a result, the Fed's Board of Governors voted several times to raise interest rates in an attempt to cool the economy down, which, in the process, meant raising unemployment rates. From 1995 to 1998, the Fed kept interest rates steady, but indicated clearly that it would not tolerate job growth that would lead to unemployment rates lower than the 4.3 percent or so experienced in 1998. Put another way, in the mid- to late 1990s, the slowing of job growth was not the result of excessive environmental regulation, but rather the firm hand of the Fed. (Some economists [myself included] would characterize it as the "excessively firm" hand of the Fed, but that is another book.)

In the 1990s, the United States was devoting a substantial portion of its economic output to environmental protection—about 2.5 percent of GDP, which was up from less than 1 percent in 1970. Also in the 1990s, one area in which the U.S. economy has excelled has been job creation. The quality of those jobs, the security that they provide, and the incomes that they pay are other issues that I will take up later in the book. The point here, however, is that at a nationwide level, unemployment rates ultimately depend on the health of the macroeconomy, which has not been impaired by environmental regulation.

DOES ENVIRONMENTAL REGULATION DEEPEN RECESSIONS?

When the sun is shining and the economy is in a boom period, the economy-wide jobs–environment question becomes irrelevant. Under these conditions, as discussed earlier, the economy is already creating jobs as fast as the inflation-fearing Fed will tolerate. But what about when the macroeconomic weather is stormier and the economy is in a recession? Will greater environmental spending retard—or promote—job growth?[7]

The argument for a negative trade-off runs like this: First, regulation will raise the price of goods and services, often in key sectors such as the automotive or electric industries, thereby reducing the quantity that consumers demand. Second, if domestic prices rise relative to imports, consumers may turn to imported products, and foreign buyers will be less interested in U.S. exports. Third, regulation will make new investment less profitable, which will lead to a reduction in new business spending. Finally, if higher prices lead to a generalized inflation, the Fed might raise interest rates. These combined factors will depress three important components of "aggregate demand": consumer demand, net export (exports minus imports) demand, and business investment demand. This reduction in demand, in turn, will cause recessions to last longer than they would if regulations, and environmental spending, were scaled back.

On the other hand (President Harry Truman once said that he wished he could find a one-handed economist to be his advisor), regulatory-induced environmental spending might actually diminish job loss in a recession. Environmental spending that occurs during a recession— either by the government or by firms—can increase employment growth by pumping up demand. For example, in the United States during the last recession of the late 1980s and early 1990s, federal, state, and local governments combined spent some $10 billion per year on the construction of new sewage-treatment facilities.[8] To the extent that these expenditures were financed by borrowing and not higher taxes, they represented new demand in the economy.

For back-of-the-envelope calculations, economists assume that $1 billion of injections of new spending will employ, in the short run, 14,000 workers. If we assume that (1) all of the government money spent on the construction of new sewage-treatment facilities was borrowed and (2) no "crowding out" of private investment as a consequence of government borrowing, conventional analysis would suggest an additional 140,000 jobs as a short-run consequence of this government spending on new sewage facilities.

One study pursued this line of argument more rigorously in the case of Greece. During the recession of the early 1980s, the Greek government borrowed a substantial amount of money to pay for projects such as municipal wastewater facilities and to improve solid-waste collection and disposal. The study found that this stimulus to aggregate demand reduced the unemployment rate in Greece by about 1 percent, bringing it down from 8.7 percent to 7.7 percent.[9]

Government-mandated private-sector spending on environmental protection may play a similar, counter-recessionary role. In a simple Keynesian view of the business cycle, recessions are driven by autonomous reductions in consumer or investment spending; once the animal spirits are in a bearish mood, the economy spirals downward. However, because environmental investment is mandated by law, firms cannot reduce such spending as much as they cut back on general investment in plant and equipment. Thus, one might hypothesize that aggregate investment spending falls less in a recession than it would in the absence of environmental regulation and that, therefore, the recession would be less severe.

During the recession of 1990–1991, for example, private-sector pollution abatement and control expenditures in the United States were around $69 billion, which represents a $34 billion increase in real terms since 1972.[10] Even if half of this $34 billion in spending constituted a net addition to business demand, the direct, short-term employment effect of regulation would be quite substantial. Of course it might not be an addition to demand. As outlined earlier, critics of regulation argue that regulation-induced environmental spending that is produced by raising costs reduces other kinds of investment, as well as consumer and export demand for U.S. products.

How can we sort out these opposing theoretical views? I will address this issue in the section that follows. However, a bit of empirical evidence can be derived from two studies conducted by Stephen Meyer at the Massachusetts Institute of Technology. Meyer's analysis relied on the fact that pollution laws and enforcement efforts can vary significantly among each state. California, New Jersey, and Minnesota devote much more attention to clean up than states such as Louisiana, Idaho, or Alabama. Meyer examined data from all fifty states and found no correlation at all between environmental regulation and job growth in general. He also found a persistent, positive, and significant correlation between growth in construction employment and the strength of statewide environmental-regulatory efforts. This may reflect spending on construction-intensive pollution-control measures, such as sewage facilities. Meyer interprets his results in the following way: "Stronger environmental regulations have not limited the pace of economic growth and development among the states over the past twenty years."[11]

MACROMODELS—TONIC OR DEPRESSANT?

One way to quantify the impact of environmental spending on unemployment over the business cycle is to use macroeconomic forecasting models. These models rely on systems of interrelated equations to predict the path of key economic variables, such as employment, inflation, and GDP growth. While adhering to some central tenets of economic theory, macroeconomic forecasting is as much art as it is science. This means, first, that even results from independent researchers must be treated skeptically. And, second, when in the hands of hired economic consultants, a few well-placed assumptions can easily drive the result in a client's preferred direction.

TABLE 2.1. Macromodels of the environment–employment link

Author	Type of study	Employment impact
Haveman (1978)	Summary of macromodel studies	Positive
U.S. EPA/DRI (1979)	Macromodel	Positive
U.S. EPA/DRI (1981)	Macromodel	Positive
Müller (1981)	Summary of 3 macromodel studies	2 Positive, 1 mixed[a]

[a] Positive short run, negative long run.
Source: DRI (1981).

Recall we are trying to weigh the strength of competing hypotheses. Does regulation, by forcing government and private investment in environmental clean up, boost aggregate demand? Or does regulation-induced spending prolong a recession by raising costs and thus slowing down activity in key sectors, such as the automotive industry? Macroeconomic models try to sort out this on-the-one-hand, on-the-other-hand argument, as well as to predict a net effect. The macroeconomic-simulation approach was popular among environmental economists in the late 1970s and early 1980s. Table 2.1 summarizes the results of the macro-modeling studies from that period, which were sponsored by relatively independent sources—either government agencies or in the academy.

Of these studies, which were conducted either in the United States or Europe, all but one suggest small positive impacts of environmental spending on job growth. The Müller study found positive short-run, but negative long-run employment implications. A 1984 summary by the Organization for Economic Cooperation and Development (OECD) characterized the results as follows: "In every case, those [employment] effects, whether positive or negative, appear to be a very small percentage of total employment."[12]

NATIONAL ASSOCIATION OF MANUFACTURERS AND ACID RAIN

By the mid-1980s, scientific analysts in the academy and in government largely abandoned macromodeling of the employment impacts of regulation. The model results were consistently suggesting that the employment effects of regulation were more or less a wash (and, if anything, slightly positive) and that not much more could be learned.

Enter the National Association of Manufacturers (NAM). In 1987, NAM paid Data Resources, Inc. (DRI, which is now DRI/McGraw-Hill), who had done earlier macrosimulations for the EPA, to evaluate proposed acid-rain-control legislation. The resulting predictions were dire indeed:

> On a cumulative basis, acid-rain legislation would cause serious and lasting damage to the economy. The causes of this damage have to do primarily with the effects of higher energy costs.
>
> First, since energy is an important input to production and a major component of production costs, there are severe output losses and employment reductions in energy-intensive sectors. The most adverse impact is in durable manufacturing and metal industries.
>
> Second, because energy prices feed through into final product prices, there are increases both in retail energy costs and the overall inflation rate.
>
> Third, because of higher inflation, interest rates increase. The rise in interest rates causes a major decline in housing starts. The result is a serious reduction in output and an increase in unemployment in housing-related industries such as construction materials. Thus, in the final analysis, a substantial share of the population will experience losses in employment opportunities, higher housing costs as reflected in higher mortgage interest rates, and higher utility bills.[13]

In conclusion, the report boldly declared:

> Initiatives such as the acid-rain legislation would, in this respect, achieve only the dubious distinction of moving the United States towards the status of a second-class industrial power by the end of the century.

Fast forward to the end of the century. Acid-rain-control legislation passed in 1990 and is now well under way. Electric utilities have reduced emissions of the acid-rain precursor sulfur-dioxide by more than half.[14] At the same time, the U.S. economy has been in a sustained upswing since the early 1990s. Unemployment rates hit their lowest level since the 1960s. In the mid-1990s, the Federal Reserve board did indeed raise interest rates, but only to put the brakes on what they considered to be an overheated economy. None of the DRI predictions have come to pass.

The NAM/DRI study represents a breed of hybrid creature, which unfortunately has come to play a dominant role in the jobs–environment debate. Economic consulting firms, featuring Ph.D. economists, are hired to produce job-loss or, less frequently, job-gain estimates. The underlying tool—in this case, a macromodel of the economy—is often legitimate enough when used in scholarly analysis or business forecasting. But when used in the realm of politics, the usefulness of the modeling exercise becomes questionable at best.

Economic models are suggestive, never conclusive. A single model tells very little, because most predictions are assumption driven. Economists make progress in understanding how the economy works by examining many different models, their underlying assumptions, and their predictions. Economists have the greatest confidence in predictions either when many different types of models yield the same general conclusions or when the results from a given model are not sensitive to plausible changes in the underlying assumptions. The problem with interest-group-sponsored research is that the focus departs from a scholarly exercise concentrated on transparency of method and assumption to the bottom line—predictions.

Did DRI tailor the assumptions of their model to generate results that pleased the client? This of course will never be known. However, what is more than likely is that if the DRI results had not gone the way the NAM wanted, they would never have seen the light of day. But what is clearly evident in the NAM/DRI report is complete disrespect for the limitations of the macroforecasting model they employed. Based on a single modeling exercise, no scholarly analyst would engage in the kind of rhetorical hyperbole (e.g., predictions of the U.S. as a "second-class industrial power") found in the report.

IGNORING INNOVATION

Macromodels operated for hire by private consulting firms have reemerged with a vengeance as players in the greenhouse debate. In fact, DRI, which is one of the big three consulting firms, is currently under contract to the coal industry and the United Mineworkers Union. I will discuss their global-warming predictions later in chapter 6. However, here it is worth emphasizing how utterly, completely, and dismally wrong DRI was on the macroeconomic consequences of acid-rain control. Also, since we will look at the model again, it is important to think a little about how it works.

In the DRI simulation during the early years of regulation, nationwide employment actually rose due to increased spending by electric utilities on sulfur scrubbers and other pollution-control equipment. However, as the summary quote of the NAM report mentioned earlier predicts, long-term increases in energy prices would result in decreasing economic growth in the long run, and thus slower recovery from a recession. Why was this supposed to have happened? Increased energy prices, the model assumed, would be passed on to consumers, which would lead to inflation. To fight inflation, the Fed would have to raise interest rates. This in turn would lead to reduced sales and layoffs in industries such as construction and automobile manufacturing. The result would be a sustained economic stagnation and higher unemployment.

One definition of an economist is someone who can give you a very good reason today why the prediction he/she made yesterday was wrong. In DRI's defense, the actual acid-rain bill that passed was predicted to be a bit less costly than the one they analyzed. DRI assumed that all electric power plants would have to reduce their emissions by a set amount. Instead, Congress adopted an innovative "marketable permit" system. A total nationwide cap was set on sulfur-dioxide emissions, and firms were issued a share of this allowed limit in the form of permits, whereby companies could then either pollute up to their permitted limit, buy permits and pollute more, or sell permits and pollute less. This added flexibility was predicted by the EPA (before the program began) to reduce the costs of the acid-rain program by between 20 and 30 percent.[15] Would this updating of DRI's assumptions have brought their predictions more in line with reality? Possibly.

Having defended NAM/DRI, let me return to reproaching them. Rather than recognize even the possibility that their assumed costs might be too high, the final paragraph of the executive summary of the report reads:

> It is to be emphasized in this context that the estimates here are conservative. They are based, as noted earlier, on government studies of the costs of this legislation. It is entirely conceivable that if the inputs to the DRI model had been based on estimates compiled by the private sector, the results would have emerged as even more deleterious. Consequently, the results of this study should not be viewed as unduly pessimistic. Rather they represent minimum estimates of the costs of the economy.

Minimum, meaning absolutely as low as possible. This kind of language is designed to reassure journalists, not persuade scientists.

Furthermore, the report was wrong again. As it turned out, the control costs for the tradeable-permit program have turned out to be much, much less than anyone—industry or the EPA—predicted. Recall that the innovative feature of the program is that the sulfur-dioxide permits are tradeable—they can be bought and sold. Given this, permit prices roughly reflect per-ton pollution-control costs. This is true because a firm generally wouldn't buy an extra permit if the cost of doing so exceeded the cost of reducing sulfur emissions by a ton in the first place.

When the tradeable-permits market was being designed in the early 1990s, credible industry estimates of permit prices (and thus control costs) were $1,500 per ton. The EPA was predicting $750 per ton. In 1997, permits were in fact selling for around $100 apiece. Part of the current low permit price is due to a higher than expected initial supply of permits, however, real compliance costs have in fact been two to four times lower than the EPA expected, as well as four to eight times below industry estimates.[16] Add this on to the EPA's 20 to 30 percent expected cost savings over the acid-rain-control costs used by DRI, and one can begin to see at least one reason why their predictions of macroeconomic disaster failed to materialize.

The acid-rain example, in which the actual monetary costs of a proposed environmental regulation were grossly overestimated, reflects a persistent pattern. In a study completed in 1997, a coauthor and I tracked down every case we could find in which credible researchers had either calculated actual regulatory costs or engaged in multiple-cost forecasts and then compared the later figures to initial cost predictions. In addition to the sulfur-dioxide trading program, we uncovered eleven such efforts, ranging from A (asbestos) to V (vinyl chloride). As table 2.2 shows, the initial estimates were at least double the actual costs in all cases but one. In the exceptional case, costs were still overestimated by 41 percent.[17]

It is no surprise that industry lobbyists wildly overestimate the overall compliance costs of proposed environmental regulations. What is less expected is that academic and government economists consistently do the same and for an equally surprising reason. When forecasting the costs of new environmental regulations, economic analysts have routinely ignored a primary economic lesson: Markets will cut costs through innovation.

For example, the much lower than expected costs for the acid-rain program can be explained in retrospect by the increased flexibility that firms were given to achieve their mandated reductions in sulfur-dioxide

TABLE 2.2. Predicted costs versus actual costs for environmental regulations

Pollutant	Initial estimate	Actual cost or revised estimate	Overestimation[a]
Asbestos	$150 million (total for manufacturing and insulation sectors)	$75 million	100%
Benzene	$350,000 per plant	Approx. $0 per plant	Infinite
CFCs	1988 estimate to reduce emissions by 50% within 10 years: $2.7 billion	1992 estimate to phase out CFCs within 8 years: $3.8 billion	41%
CFCs—Auto air conditioning	$650–$1,200 per new car	$40–$400 per new car	63%–2,900%
Coke oven emissions OSHA 1970s	$200 million–$1 billion	$160 million	29%–525%
Coke oven emissions EPA 1980s	$4 billion	$250–$400 million	900%–1,500%
Cotton dust	$700 million per year	$205 million per year	241%
Halons	1989: phase-out not possible	1993: phase-out considered technologically and economically feasible	——
Landfill leachate	mid-1980s: $14.8 billion	1990: $5.7 billion	159%
Sulfur dioxide	$4–$5 billion	——	100%–300%
Surface mining	$6–$12 per ton of coal	$0.50–$1 per ton	500–2,300%
Vinyl chloride	$109 million per year	$20 million per year	445%

[a] Column 2 divided by column 3.

Source: Goodstein and Hodges (1997) and Hodges (1997).

emissions. Rather than install expensive scrubbers (or buy extra permits), many more firms than expected have met their SO_2 targets by switching to low-sulfur coal or by developing new fuel-blending techniques. Railroad deregulation, along with economies of scale in rail transport, led to an unexpected decline in low-sulfur coal prices. And with the increased competition from this coal, scrubber manufacturers cut their prices in half from 1990 to 1995. All of this is easy to see after the fact, but would have been very hard to predict.

In summary, one explanation for the DRI model's disastrous performance is that it used government cost estimates for acid-rain control, which, in retrospect, turned out to be much too high. This is not unusual—both government and academic economists have tended to substantially overestimate compliance costs when evaluating new regulations. These facts should be kept in mind when we turn later to cost and job-loss predictions for global warming.

While regulation often costs much less than predicted, environmental regulation is not without cost. Rather, the point here is that spending on the environment creates new jobs, which leads to a gradual shift in the types of employment found in the economy. Macromodels should balance the dampening effect on aggregate demand from higher prices in regulated sectors against the direct stimulus effect of government and firm spending on environmental-protection measures. The conclusion from the academic literature is that so far these effects basically cancel each other out; if anything, the evidence suggests small employment gains during recessions.

The NAM/DRI case, by contrast, illustrates that on paper it is possible to create a macromodeling scenario in which regulation is so costly that it leads to job losses via a slowdown in economic growth or even a recession. Higher energy prices in the DRI model lead to inflation and, ultimately, higher interest rates and an economic slowdown. In the acid-rain case, DRI was very wrong on the magnitude of the actual cost increases. But suppose costs to electricity producers had gone up as much as DRI assumed. Would the model have broken down somewhere else in the lengthy assumption chain? Is the economy really that sensitive to cost increases in the energy sector? These are issues that will reemerge when we return to the discussion of the employment effects of fighting global warming.

For now, NAM/DRI's acid-rain predictions stand as a humorous monument to the failures of industry-sponsored predictions of job loss based on macroforecasting. Again, this is not to cast aspersions on the scholarly use of macromodels, which under less partisan conditions have been a useful tool for examining the "on-the-one-hand, on-the-other-hand" job impacts of environmental protection. However, since the mid-1980s, macromodeling has unfortunately become a highly politicized and lucrative private exercise. This issue is discussed further in chapter 6, where we will see that industry-sponsored macromodels uniformly predict large job losses from reducing greenhouse gas emissions.

INPUT–OUTPUT MODELS—HOW MANY JOBS PER DOLLAR?

Macromodels provide one way to think about the economy-wide effects of regulation. There is, however, another view that focuses on the employment impacts of different kinds of spending in the economy. As I noted earlier, as a back-of-the-envelope assumption, $1 billion in spending will support around 14,000 jobs. However, this aggregate figure disguises some important differences that may explain how regulation-induced spending on the environment could help reduce unemployment in recessions. Is it possible that $1 billion of spending on environmental protection creates more jobs than $1 billion spent elsewhere? The answer is "yes," assuming one of two things. If environmental spending requires goods and services that are directly and indirectly more labor-intensive and/or more "domestic-content"-intensive, then more U.S. jobs will be created for a given dollar amount of final demand.

First, some terminology. *Direct employment* from regulation-induced spending means people who are employed by the environmental expenditure itself (e.g., recycling truck drivers, workers in plants who manufacture sulfur-dioxide scrubbers, lab technicians who test new pesticides, and EPA water-pollution inspectors). *Indirect employment* supported by this first round of environmental spending would include workers in steel, automotive, chemical, and rubber plants who make the equipment that the "direct" environmental employees require. Taking it back one step, indirect employment would also include the miners and shippers who transported the coal and iron ore that are necessary to make the equipment that the direct environmental employees need. And going back yet another step, we also count as indirect employment the workers needed to make the equipment that is required to mine and transport the raw materials that are necessary to make the equipment that is needed directly in the environmental sector. This chain of jobs stretches ever backwards, ad infinitum. To evaluate whether environmental spending supports more jobs than the alternative, both direct and indirect jobs must be counted.

How can one possibly keep track of this infinite backwards chain of jobs? Economists do this by using so-called input–output models. Pioneered by Nobel Prize-winning economist Wassily Leontief, these models divide up final demand—spending by consumers, firms, governments, and foreigners—into a number of different categories. The models can then trace the quite complicated direct and indirect job impacts of a given amount of spending, as well as determine the total number of jobs required to produce a specified amount of product.

For example, a recent study done for the Department of Sanitation in New York City found that by boosting the percentage of waste that was recycled from 6 percent to 25 percent, while reducing the percentage incinerated from 76 percent to 57 percent, would result in a permanent net increase in local employment of around 400 jobs per year. This was true even when accounting for the higher taxes necessary to pay for the somewhat higher cost per ton for the recycling option. The increase in jobs arose first because recycling is labor- rather than capital-intensive, which led to a higher local payroll that created bigger indirect employment effects in the city. Second, New York City produces little of the equipment necessary to manufacture incinerators, therefore, incineration had a low "domestic" content.[18]

This input–output approach was used back in the late 1980s to study the same proposed acid-rain reduction regulations evaluated by NAM/DRI. (Again, it was a more flexible and less costly set of acid-rain regulations that actually became law as part of the Clean Air Act Amendments of 1990.) The authors found that some 95 percent of the direct expenditures on acid-rain pollution-control equipment, products, and processes—such as sulfur-dioxide scrubbers—would accrue to U.S. firms. As a result, a net increase in jobs was foreseen from the acid-rain-control policies they analyzed. Gradual job losses in high-sulfur coal mining and in electric-utility and electricity-intensive sectors would be more than balanced by pollution-control jobs that would gradually be created from the expenditure of several billion dollars per year.[19]

In these two cases, spending to improve environmental quality was predicted to increase employment either because the environmental product under consideration (e.g., recycling or sulfur-dioxide scrubbers) was either more labor- and/or domestic-content-intensive than the alternative. Is there any reason to believe that environmental spending will always win out on these fronts? In general, no. Indeed, in the case of recycling, the predicted difference of 400 jobs is not overwhelming in a city the size of New York. Moreover, it is probably within the margin of error for the model.

However, there is one area in which environmental spending will almost always create more jobs per $1 billion than the alternative, and that is investments in energy efficiency. The conventional energy sectors—coal, oil, and gas extraction, fuel refining, and gas utilities—have relatively low labor intensity compared to other sectors of the economy. In 1990, for example, oil and gas extraction supported seven jobs (both direct and indirect) per $1 million of expenditure, and coal mining thirteen. Retail trade, on the other hand, supported thirty-two, and construction twenty.[20] Moreover, much of our oil—well over 50 percent—is imported. By investing in energy efficiency, savings on fuel expenditures can be switched over to more labor-intensive and domestic-content-intensive sectors. (I should note here that labor-intensive sectors tend to pay less than capital-intensive ones. This is one but not the only or most important reason why a given amount of spending supports more jobs. For more on this issue see chapter 5.)

One input–output study, which was done for the American Council for an Energy Efficient Economy (ACEEE), argued dramatically that large-scale investments of $46 billion per year in energy efficiency could lead to over a million new jobs by 2010. A number of other studies have drawn qualitatively similar conclusions, providing strong evidence that from a jobs-per-dollar perspective, energy efficiency will almost always win out.

Counting jobs using input–output models is informative, however, the approach suffers from some analytical difficulties. Economy-wide input–output studies ask a very big question: Suppose that instead of spending tens of billions of dollars where we are already spending it, we spent it somewhere else. Then—assuming that the plant, equipment, trained workers, and transportation infrastructure are all in place to make the new stuff—how many more jobs will be created? This can be a very big assumption. For example, in the case of acid rain, the authors implicitly assumed that all the workers needed for the new scrubber industries were already living by the plants, ready and waiting for a new job. In general, input–output studies abstract away potentially large and important adjustment costs. Thus, job estimates that flow from them should be treated, at best, as upward bounds. Moreover, input–output studies are not always subject to rigorous peer review, and, as with the ACEEE study cited above, are often funded by advocacy groups, both on the environmental and industry sides. Therefore, their results should be approached with caution.

That said, the basic underlying message of input–output studies is sound. If environmental spending supports more labor-intensive production or requires fewer imports, it will, holding everything else constant, tend to boost economy-wide employment in the short run. Again, this holds true only if the economy is growing slowly and there are as a result cyclically unemployed workers who are generally available. Try to add a million jobs from energy-efficiency measures into a full-employment economy and you wouldn't get very far; the Federal Reserve, fearing inflation would raise interest rates, eliminating a million jobs somewhere else.

No Economy-Wide Trade-Off

In summary, here is the evidence supporting the consensus view that at the economy-wide level there simply is no trade-off between environmental protection and jobs. First, and most telling, it is clear that the long-term health of the U.S. macroeconomy has not been harmed by the imposition of significant environmental regulation over the last twenty years. Since 1970, annual, nationwide spending on the environment has risen to more than $180 billion. Yet, through the late 1990s the Fed's Board of Governors kept a foot on the interest rate brake in an attempt to slow down job growth.

If environmental regulation does not prevent an economy from achieving full employment, will it somehow deepen a recession? The weight of evidence says no. First, there is no correlation between environmental regulation and employment growth across the states. Second, virtually all of the disinterested macromodeling exercises have found small positive employment impacts from environmental spending. And, finally, input–output studies suggest that greater environmental spending, either because it is labor-intensive or domestic-content-intensive, can lead to higher short-run employment levels. This is especially true for energy-efficiency investments.

At the economy-wide level, environmental-protection legislation leads to greater spending on the environment and less spending on other things. This in turn generates a long-run shift in the types of jobs in the economy, not a reduction in employment. But what kind of jobs are being created? And for whom?

As an environmental economist, I owe my own job to the growth of the environmental-protection industry. Environmental economists as a distinct category didn't exist before 1970, and the market has grown tremendously over the last twenty-five years. My job is to train students to understand and participate in the process of environmental clean up, and I have also been employed as a consultant to do benefit-costs studies that evaluate proposed government regulations. Is my situation a typical one? Are the good jobs that are supported by environmental dollars exclusively high-end, white-collar jobs (e.g., lawyers, regulatory bureaucrats, or college professors)?

This is an important question. In chapter 1, I discussed the growth of the "80-20 society," in which the top fifth of the income distribution is flourishing, while the majority of families struggle to maintain their income level. While I have established in this chapter that on net environmental regulation is basically job neutral at the economy-wide level, these days any factor that promotes greater income inequality in the United States would not be welcome. Is regulation yet another factor putting the squeeze on the middle class, further closing the door to decent-paying jobs for less-skilled workers?

THE ENVIRONMENTAL-PROTECTION INDUSTRY

Until recently, there has been little official data gathered on the scope and composition of the environmental-protection industry. In an attempt to correct this gap, in 1998, the U.S. Commerce Department, in concert with the EPA, issued the first-ever "Survey of Environmental Products and Services." The government sent out surveys to 10,000 firms who were identified as likely producers of goods and services used in supplying the clean-up market. The breakdown of the businesses was made up of around 3,000 manufacturing plants, 6,350 service firms, and 650 construction companies. Plant managers were asked to estimate the value of the goods and services they produced that fit the following descriptions:

> the manufacture of products, performance of services, and the construction of projects used, or that could potentially be used, for measuring, preventing, limiting, or correcting environmental damage to air, water, and soil[,] . . . [as well as] . . . services related to the removal, transportation, storage, or abatement of waste, noise, and other contaminants.

The government used this survey data to estimate that nationwide, production in the environmental-protection industry was valued at about $102 billion in 1995. Of this amount, at least 17 percent was in the construction sector, which was more than double the economy-wide level of construction spending.[21]

Given this, it is perhaps not surprising that a more than proportionate share of the jobs created by environmental clean-up spending is in the traditional blue-collar sectors of the economy: construction and manufacturing. Researchers at the EPA have calculated both the direct and indirect employment generated by environmental spending for the year 1991. For example, the EPA estimated that around 4,000 people that year were directly employed in the manufacturing of electrical machinery used in environmental clean-up activities. But the agency also calculated that an additional 21,500 workers in the industry indirectly owed their jobs to environmental spending. This number included people who built electrical machinery that in turn was used to manufacture and transport items such as steel pipe for sewer systems, photocopying machines for environmental service companies, or trucks used to recycle solid waste. Again, economists use input–output models to keep track of these chains of job interdependencies.

Figure 2.1 illustrates how jobs related to the environmental-protection industry as calculated by the EPA breakdown across different sectors of the economy, and provides a comparison to overall U.S. employment. Environmental spending generates more than twice the average percentage number of jobs in construction (11 percent as compared to 4 percent) and one-fourth greater a proportion in manufacturing (20 percent as compared to 16 percent).

Environmental protection also induces, in relative terms, somewhat more employment in the mining and service sectors. Lawyers and professors—and most other white-collar environmental jobs—fall into this

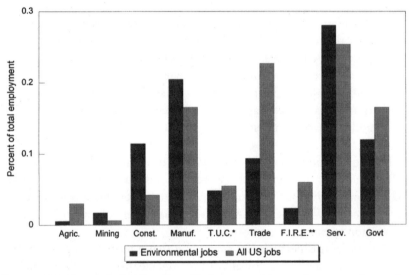

FIGURE 2.1. Sectoral distribution of jobs created by environmental spending (1991, direct and indirect jobs).
*Transportation, utilities, and communication
**Finance, insurance, and real estate

Source: Author's calculations from data generated by the input–output model used in U.S. EPA (1995). Results that confirm the blue-collar employment intensity of environmental spending, using data from a different input–output model, are reported in Goodstein (1994).

latter category. On the other hand, environmental spending creates relatively few jobs in agriculture, wholesale and retail trade, and the financial sector of the economy.

How can we account for these results? Environmental protection is a largely industrial business. In 1991, the year of the EPA study, the private sector spent $22 billion on pollution-control plants and equipment, and $43 billion on pollution-control operations, which ranged from sewage and solid-waste disposal to the purchase and maintenance of air-pollution-control devices on smokestacks and in vehicles. Federal, state, and local governments spent around $12 billion on the construction of municipal sewage facilities. These dollars, not surprisingly, supported a disproportionate number of construction and manufacturing jobs.

Perhaps the biggest surprise found in figure 2.1 is in the last column. In spite of criticisms that environmental regulation only creates jobs for pencil-pushing regulators, less than 12 percent of environmentally induced employment was at the government level, as compared to an economy-wide government employment rate of 16.5 percent. This again reflects the fact that most environmental spending occurs in the private sector. In 1991, only 2 percent of all environmental costs went to support the government's direct regulation and monitoring establishment. The EPA's total budget, including subcontracts, was less than 4 percent of all environmental spending.[22] This is not to say that environmental spending creates only high-quality, high-paying jobs. But it is clear that cleanup dollars do support more than their share of jobs in traditional blue-collar industries.

Even in heavily regulated manufacturing industries, overall job losses due to environmental regulation have been quite small. Recently, researchers at Resources for the Future, a well-known environmental economics think tank, conducted a study of the steel, petroleum, plastics, and pulp and paper industries. The analysis weighed the job losses from higher costs and reduced demand against the jobs created by direct spending on environmental protection within these industries, ignoring indirect job gains in other sectors. On balance, the net job losses in the heavily regulated industries were tiny. Extrapolating their results to the manufacturing sector as a whole, the authors found that between 1984 and 1994, on average, environmental regulation may have directly reduced employment in all regulated industries nationwide by about 470 jobs per year. The study concluded that "these results cast considerable doubt on the existence of a jobs versus the environment trade-off. While environmental spending clearly has consequences for business and labor, the idea that such spending reduces employment in key industries is at odds with the data."[23]

Economy-wide, environmental spending has provided a boost to manufacturing and construction employment. And even in the most heavily regulated industries, this increase in demand has largely offset layoffs due to higher costs. These are important facts. One of the explanations for the widespread "deindustrialization" that the United States has been experiencing over the last few decades has been a steady shift away from manufacturing into services, trade, and finance. However, as the data in this section have made clear, this trend has not been aggravated by the direct effect of increased environmental spending. Because legally mandated clean up has been construction- and manufacturing-intensive, regulation appears to have actually slowed the deindustrialization tide and created a disproportionate share of good jobs for the bottom 80 percent of workers.

In this chapter, I have presented the reasons why economists agree that environmental regulation has not aggravated cyclical unemployment in the United States. Because environmental clean-up spending has neither caused nor deepened recessions, at the economy-wide level there has simply been no trade-off between jobs and the environment. Moreover, the job-shifting process that accompanies regulation has not been one leading from a blue-collar to a white- or pink-collar economy.

However, the focus on economy-wide effects may be misleading. Even if, on net, job losses and gains cancel out, have widespread, regulation-induced layoffs at manufacturing plants and mines increased structural unemployment? Moreover, even granting that regulatory spending is construction- and manufacturing-intensive, hasn't regulation nevertheless contributed to the decline of the blue-collar economy? This could happen either if "dirty" manufacturing plants were forced to shut down on a large scale, or, barring that, if regulation promoted new investment to relocate overseas where environmental regulations were less stringent. I turn to these issues in the next chapter.

NOTES

1. *Cleveland Plain Dealer*, April 5, 1998, page 1. Unless otherwise noted, employment data in this chapter come from the U.S. Bureau of Labor Statistics.
2. Carlin (1990). All monetary figures throughout the book are in 1996 dollars, unless otherwise specified.
3. U.S. EPA (1995: Table 4). These figures include both direct and indirect employment. These terms are defined later on in this chapter.

4. "Environment Protection, Job Growth Not Necessarily Contradictory, Economists Say," *Daily Labor Report*, #236, December 10, 1993, page A-2.
5. Tietenberg (1992: 574–576); Hopkins (1992).
6. Author's calculations from U.S. Bureau of Labor Statistics data.
7. I address this issue from the point of view of macroforecasting models and input–output analysis. There is another theoretical approach concerned with the impact of regulation on long-run growth, but not unemployment over the business cycle. General equilibrium models such as Hollenbeck (1978), Jorgenson and Wilcoxen (1990), and Hazilla and Kopp (1991) generally find that regulation slows down growth over the long run. [For a critique of this conclusion, see Goodstein (1998b).] However, these models all assume full employment and so can tell us nothing about business-cycle effects.
8. Statistical Abstract of the United States (1997: Table 1180). These are current (1990) dollars.
9. Lekakis (1991); see Müller (1981) for an overview of this debate.
10. Vogan (1996).
11. See Meyer (1992) and (1993). Meyer (1992) also found a positive correlation between total employment and environmental regulation, however, this relationship was insignificant when the presence of extractive industry was considered in a framework taking into consideration multiple explanations for employment growth.
12. OECD (1984).
13. NAM (1987). The quotes that follow are on page 4 and 5, respectively.
14. Among utility facilities affected by the first phase of Title IV, emissions were reduced from a 1990 level of 10 million tons to 5.3 million tons in 1995. Burtraw (personal communication).
15. Burtraw (1996).
16. Burtraw (1996).
17. Goodstein and Hodges (1997), Hodges (1997), and Harrington et al. (1999). This is true for emission-reduction regulation. By contrast, legislation such as the Superfund, which mandates clean up of already-polluted areas, is generally much more expensive than predicted.
18. Breslow et al. (1992). Because recycling also requires capital spending on "imported" equipment, the two options did not in fact differ by a considerable amount in either their labor intensity or "domestic" content. However, the differences were large enough to translate into a net employment advantage for recycling.
19. The author's findings are based on the input–output model that is described in Wendling and Bezdek (1989). They analyze two acid-rain-control bills that were introduced in the 99th Congress, which differ somewhat from the final legislation that was passed in 1990. The authors predict net job gains of

between 100,000 and 200,000 jobs, more than 25,000 net jobs for each $1 billion spent on pollution control. These figures are almost certainly on the high side, since they assume a cost-free reassignment of resources and a ready supply of workers with the available skills. In addition, U.S. EPA (1993) found that 79 percent, rather than 95 percent, of the air-pollution-control equipment that is used in the United States is produced domestically. Finally, the acid-rain legislation that actually passed generated more fuel switching and less reliance on U.S.-made scrubbers than the one analyzed.

20. Geller, DeCicco, and Laitner (1992).
21. U.S. EPA (1998).
22. The data in this and the preceding paragraphs are from Rutledge and Leonard (1992), with monetary values in 1990 dollars.
23. Morgenstern et al. (1998a).

Chapter 3

Local Layoffs
and Pollution
Havens

At the economy-wide level, there simply has not been a jobs–environment trade-off. Knowledge of this fact, however, doesn't help workers who were laid off due to environmental regulations put food on their dinner table. Even if on net regulation leaves the job picture unchanged, it might still entail wide-scale layoffs. Such a process would be very disruptive to workers, as well as to the stability of their families and communities. Large-scale layoffs—even if matched by job gains elsewhere—would clearly justify American's strong belief in a jobs–environment trade-off. How big are regulation-induced job losses at the local level?

To answer this question, it is helpful to return to 1990, the year the Clean Air Act (CAA) amendments were under debate. The two principal goals of the legislation were the clean up of acid rain, which is created by sulfur and nitrogen-oxide emissions from fossil-fuel-fired power plants, and the reduction of hazardous "air toxics" emissions from industrial plants.

As part of their lobbying effort against the CAA, the U.S. Business Roundtable sponsored a study that made predictions regarding the likely job losses associated with the act. The authors of the analysis, Robert Hahn and Wilbur Steger, grudgingly acknowledged that economy-wide job trade-offs as a result of the CAA amendments were not inevitable:

> The short-term, negative job-loss economic effects can—on paper—be balanced, although not necessarily

completely in degree, with positive effects in other
industries and other communities. . . . [V]iewed on a
macroeconomic basis, environmental regulation might
have relatively little effect on overall employment
(except perhaps on a regional basis), as workers may lose
jobs in highly regulated industry and find jobs in others,
or it might cause some longer-term economic effects.

(The Hahn and Steger case for negative "long-term effects" on economy-wide employment was based on the National Association of
Manufacturers-sponsored, Data Resources, Inc., macromodel, whose
predictions were discussed, and revealed to be thoroughly wrong, in chapter 2.)

With the disclaimer that their focus was not on the net job impact of
the CAA amendments, Hahn and Steger went on to make their own predictions about gross job losses. Quoting from the executive summary:

There is, however, *no doubt* that, across the CAA Amendment titles studied, there are a minimum of several hundred thousands of jobs at various levels of severity of
risk—even with more moderate administration-like CAA
Amendment proposals. Furthermore, depending on the
residual risk assumptions, this study leaves little doubt
that a *minimum* of 200,000 (plus) jobs will be quickly
lost, with plants closing in dozens of states. This number
could easily exceed one million jobs—and even two million jobs—at the more extreme assumptions about residual risk (emphasis in the original).

Very scary stuff.

Within this "minimum" category of "200,000 (plus) jobs" to be
"quickly lost," the study made one firm prediction: 20,000 jobs would be
lost due to direct shutdowns by firms that were simply unable to meet the
new air-quality standards. Three-quarters of these layoffs were to come
from the closing of coke ovens in the steel industry. Hahn and Steger
viewed this as "truly a limiting, rock-bottom estimate" for several reasons. Important among them was that it considered only job losses arising from one portion of the bill—control of air toxics.

Studies such as that of Hahn and Steger clearly had an effect. A 1990
poll found that an astounding one-third of all U.S. workers thought it

likely or very likely that their own job was potentially threatened by environmental regulation. However, in spite of widespread concerns about employment impacts, the amendments did pass and were signed into law by President Bush. Regarding air toxics, the bill was in most respects *more* restrictive than the one on which the study based its 20,000 (plus) job-loss figure. The legislation also authorized retraining funds of $50 million per year for displaced workers, which provides an effective way to track job impacts.

Between 1990 and 1997, less than 7,000 workers in total received aid because their jobs were affected by the CAA amendments. The vast majority of these workers were high-sulfur, eastern coal miners who were laid off as a result of the acid-rain amendment, and not due to the air-toxics provision. (The same legislation has in fact led to a boom in the low-sulfur, western coal industry and in the railroad shipping business.) And what of the 15,000-predicted layoffs in the coke industry? Not a single worker from the coke-oven industry received adjustment assistance. In fact, between 1992 and 1995, production in the coke and (closely related) blast-furnace industries actually *increased*, from $1.74 billion to $1.95 billion.[1]

IGNORING INNOVATION, AGAIN

Hahn and Steger were consulting for industry, so it is not surprising if their numbers were packaged to appear a bit on the high side. Corporate America, when faced with new regulations, has never been shy about claiming that the sky is falling. However, these economists are no hired guns. Robert Hahn is a well-known environmental economist with very solid academic credentials, including having served on President Bush's Council of Economic Advisors. How could he and Steger have gotten it so wrong?

It turns out that Hahn and Steger's overestimation of regulatory impacts, while extreme, is not unusual. As we saw in chapter 2, both academic and government economists have a very poor record of predicting the costs of compliance with environmental regulations. This is true for two reasons. The first is that in implementation, legislation is never as draconian as it appears on paper. Timetables get stretched out, compliance dates get extended, and waivers are granted. Enforcement officials tend to go easy on firms that are having serious financial problems. Eventually the regulations do begin to bite, however, industry is usually given a fair amount of time to adjust. Yet most job-loss estimates assume high degrees of near-term compliance.

The second and related explanation is quite surprising. When doing their cost estimates, economists have tended to grossly underestimate a virtue of markets they readily preach elsewhere—flexibility. When pollution regulation makes a certain type of production more expensive, markets adjust, in fairly rapid order, by uncovering substitute methods of production and by developing cheaper clean-up technologies. This fact, while not completely ignored by economists, is seldom factored into their cost estimates. Instead, analysts tend to predict future costs as if firms would continue to use existing practices and technologies.

Hahn and Steger got their 20,000 lost jobs as a result of air-toxics regulation by following this same practice—ignoring innovative market responses. While parenthetically noting that "technological improvements could reduce the direct economic impacts," the study explicitly ignores the possibility "because of the difficulties in predicting how technology will evolve." Because available control technologies for coke ovens seemed to be quite expensive in the mid- to late 1980s, Hahn and Steger assumed that regulating air toxics would simply shut down much of the industry.

However, even as they were writing their report, the EPA's own estimates of control costs for coke ovens were plummeting. In 1987, the agency estimated that the cost of controlling hazardous air pollution from coke ovens would be roughly $4 billion. By 1991, that estimate fell to between $250 and $400 million, a decline of at least a factor of 10. Hahn and Steger may not have been aware of the EPA's more recent work. Instead, they cite an industry source to justify their claim that "there is widespread agreement that coke ovens will be required to close down, with an estimated loss of 15,000 jobs."

Peering into the future is hard work. It is, in fact, close to impossible for economists to predict the specifics of how technology will evolve. This is especially true since much of the information about potential innovations are closely held trade secrets, which industry has little incentive to reveal. But basing cost and job-loss predictions on scenarios that assume *no* evolution is guaranteed to produce gross overestimates. Innovation is indeed something at which markets are very good. When given a narrowly defined task (e.g., produce commodity *x* emitting less of pollutant *y*) short-term substitutions and long-term shifts in technology guarantee large cost reductions over current practice.

The key quote from the executive summary of the Hahn and Steger report is really worth committing to memory: "depending on the residual risk assumptions, this study leaves little doubt that a *minimum* of

200,000 (plus) jobs will be quickly lost, with plants closing in dozens of states."

The statement, complete with emphasis, is so bold, so confident, and so typical of the public debate over the job impacts of environmental regulation. It has also clearly proved to be so wrong. Yet it is this genre of the industry-sponsored report, replete with juicy sound bites, that has created and reinforced the destructive myth of a jobs–environment trade-off.

WHAT THE SURVEY DATA SHOW

The 1990 Clean Air Act experience cited earlier suggests that fears of widespread shutdowns and layoffs from regulation are dramatically overblown. The data bear out this hypothesis. Survey results from the 1970s, 1980s, and 1990s have consistently found that between 1,000 and 3,000 workers per year *nationwide* lost their job due to plant shutdowns in which environmental regulation played a significant role.

From 1987 to 1992 and from 1995 to the present, the U.S. Bureau of Labor Statistics (BLS) has surveyed firms that lay off more than fifty workers for a month or longer. Small manufacturing plants that employ fewer than fifty workers account for less than 25 percent of total manufacturing employment. In addition, small plants are concentrated in sectors of the economy that tend not to face heavy environmental regulation. The BLS survey will, therefore, recognize most shutdowns of plants that are subject to significant environmental regulation (e.g., coal mines, paper plants, oil refineries, coke ovens, metal smelters, or chemical factories). The one likely exception is in secondary wood products. Impacts on this industry are evaluated in chapter 4.

Table 3.1 lists these layoff events for recent years, showing both the number of workers laid off, as well as the employer-reported reason for the layoff. (The data for 1995 are incomplete, reflecting only the second through fourth quarters for that year.) According to employers' own estimates, from 1995 through 1997, environmental (and safety) regulation was responsible nationwide for an average of seven mass layoff events that affected an average of around 1,500 workers. This works out to between one- and two-tenths of 1 percent of all large-scale layoffs. Employers indicated environment-related reasons for a layoff less frequently than all other categories, below even natural disasters.

These survey data are, of course, not perfect. Beyond missing small plant layoffs, they rely on employer reporting of reasons for shutdowns, which may be subject to a variety of biases. For example, a manager

TABLE 3.1. Mass layoffs, 1995–1997

Reason for layoff	Layoff events			Number of people laid off		
	1995	1996	1997	1995	1996	1997
Total, all reasons	4,422	5,692	5,605	926,775	1,158,199	1,103,146
Environment related[a]	**9**	**7**	**5**	**2,816**	**1,098**	**541**
Automation	6	14	9	4,284	5,522	2,117
Bankruptcy	78	103	80	20,144	21,247	21,637
Business ownership change	120	167	121	28,482	46,425	25,141
Contract cancellation	103	87	61	18,700	19,269	11,813
Contract completion	459	557	759	100,289	124,506	175,572
Domestic relocation	63	76	76	11,059	11,323	15,241
Financial difficulty	249	263	153	58,473	56,749	39,634
Import competition	51	72	66	8,527	13,684	12,493
Labor management dispute	20	32	32	3,370	14,119	16,149
Material shortages	19	21	14	2,666	2,821	1,705
Model changeover	17	18	18	7,589	6,799	5,716
Natural disaster	7	16	5	2,117	3,599	892
Overseas relocation	14	26	38	3,713	4,326	10,435
Plant or machine repairs	31	23	19	3,867	5,169	2,362
Product line discontinued	20	35	45	4,392	6,037	9,505
Reorganization within company	384	578	482	86,331	115,669	78,324
Seasonal work	1,688	2,173	2,434	385,886	488,398	499,331
Slack work	515	831	656	78,514	112,313	90,382
Vacation period	66	69	92	14,221	11,844	13,499
Weather-related curtailment	87	97	63	10,619	9,802	8,652
Other	253	266	211	42,153	55,265	39,821
Not reported	163	161	166	28,563	22,215	22,184

[a] Includes environmental and safety-related shutdowns.
Source: U.S. Bureau of Labor Statistics, Local Area Unemployment Statistics Division.

might report that the company laid off workers because production was relocated abroad, when, in fact, the underlying reason for relocating was to escape domestic environmental regulations. On the other hand, employers might seek to make a political point and report shutdowns as environmentally related, when the true causes lay elsewhere. (An example along these lines appears in the section that follows.) However, even if the average annual layoff number of 1,500 were to be doubled, tripled, or even quadrupled, the principal point of this chapter still remains: layoffs due to environmental regulation are, relatively speaking, rare beasts.

To put this number of around 1,500 layoffs per year nationwide in context, when Al "Chainsaw" Dunlap took over as CEO of Scott Paper in 1994, he immediately announced the layoff of 11,200 employees. Overall, in 1996, "corporate restructuring" led to over 115,000 large-scale layoffs across the country.[2] The year before that, in 1995, "trade and technology" were responsible for more than 100,000 layoffs in the textile industry alone.

These recent BLS survey results regarding job losses are confirmed by the following series of comparable studies that were performed over the last twenty years, two of which included smaller firms in the sample:

- The BLS survey data from 1987 to 1992 finds a virtually identical employment impact to that shown in table 3.1.
- A survey conducted by the Oil, Chemical, and Atomic Workers Union found that of 224 permanent plant closings from 1980 to 1986, twelve of the plants, or two per year, listed environmental considerations as a *partial* motive for closure.
- The EPA estimated that from 1971 to 1981 about 3,200 workers per year lost their jobs partly in response to the costs of environmental regulation. Other prominent factors responsible for these plant closings included obsolescent equipment, declining sales, and the presence of new competitors. The EPA study looked at firms with greater than twenty-five employees.
- A Commerce Department survey that covered the years 1972 to 1978, including smaller firms, yielded similar total estimates.[3]

The data show, both in absolute and relative terms, that environmentally related shutdowns are uncommon. Given all the hype, why are regulation-induced shutdowns not more frequent? The main reason is that, for manufacturing plants, environmental compliance costs, while real, are not generally draconian. Table 3.2 shows environmental costs for the twenty most heavily regulated industries in the United States for

TABLE 3.2. The costs of pollution abatement, 1991

SIC code	Industry	Percent O&M environmental costs as a share of sales	Percent total environmental costs as a share of sales
2611	Pulp mills	3.2	7.0
2037	Frozen fruits, juices, vegetables	2.9	3.5
3274	Lime	2.9	5.5
2833	Medicinals and botanicals	2.5	4.2
2874	Phosphatic fertilizers	2.3	3.9
2621	Paper mills	2.3	4.8
2895	Carbon black	2.2	8.8
2492	Particle board	2.1	3.3
3331	Primary copper	2.1	5.4
2816	Inorganic pigments	1.9	6.4
2822	Synthetic rubber	1.9	4.1
3322	Primary lead	1.9	4.9
2823	Cellulosic manmade fibers	1.9	5.1
3241	Cement, hydraulic	1.8	4.9
2295	Coated fabrics, not rubberized	1.7	3.2
2865	Cyclic crudes and intermediates	1.7	4.5
2631	Paperboard mills	1.6	3.9
2661	Building paper and board mills	1.6	2.8
2861	Gum and wood chemicals	1.6	2.8
2869	Industrial inorganic chemicals, NEC	1.3	3.7

Note: NEC stands for "not elsewhere classified."
Source: Author's calculations from the Bureau of Economic Analysis's Pollution Abatement and Control Expenditure Survey and the Annual Survey of Manufacturers.

the year 1991. The costs are measured in two separate ways and are shown as a percentage of the industrys' total sales. The first column reveals that operating and maintenance costs (O&M) for pollution abatement top 3 percent of total sales for only one industry—pulp mills. By contrast, labor costs in manufacturing average 50 percent of total sales.

This past winter, curious about these cost data results, one of my students researched the environmental compliance costs at his father's auto-recycling business. For a small business, the company faced quite a number of different regulations that dealt with the disposal of waste oil and other fluids, as well as the need to carefully recycle freon from old air conditioners. Consistent with the numbers from table 3.2, costs for this auto-recycling firm ran just under 1 percent of sales.

Not all of the clean-up expenses that firms report are regulation induced. Even in the absence of regulation, businesses would undertake some investments in pollution control and waste disposal. Finally, bear in mind that any new environmental rules will add only a fraction of the amount that firms are already spending. Given this, the extra, or marginal, costs of regulation are very seldom big enough to break the camel's back. This is the primary explanation for the quite limited extent of environmentally related plant layoffs found in table 3.1.

IDENTIFYING THE REAL COSTS

The second cost measure in table 3.2 includes both ongoing environmental O&M, as well as irregular capital expenditures for pollution-control equipment. Even with both categories included, costs rise to above 6 percent of total sales in only three industries—pulp mills, inorganic pigments, and carbon black. I separate out O&M from capital expenditures in part because capital investments vary a lot from year to year. More importantly, however, the capital-cost category reflects an investment in plant and equipment that may have long-run benefits to the firm. In other words, capital investment imposes short-run costs, but may yield long-run paybacks.

For example, in the late 1980s, when the international phase out of ozone-destroying CFCs got under way, a company called Nortel began looking for substitutes. The company, which had used the chemicals as a cleaning agent, invested $1 million to purchase and employ new hardware. Once the redesigned system was in place, however, Nortel found that it actually saved $4 million in chemical waste-disposal costs and CFC purchases.

The CFC regulatory-compliance costs for Nortel were $1 million, however, how do we figure in the $4 million savings? Economists have long recognized that a dollar spent on environmental pollution control is not the "true" cost to society. Some have argued that the cost is in fact much higher, because environmental spending "diverts" capital investment from more productive uses.

A contrasting view has recently been introduced by Michael Porter at the Harvard Business School. Pointing to examples such as Nortel, he has argued that environmental regulations, by forcing firms to fundamentally rethink their production processes, can often lead to lower long-run production costs and thus lend a competitive advantage. This provocative argument—dubbed the "Porter Hypothesis"—has spawned significant debate and follow-up research. I will return to the issue later in this chapter when I discuss the impacts of regulation on the international competitiveness of U.S. firms.

However, one does not need to buy the entire Porter story to recognize that much of the reported costs of environmental regulation generally occur when firms invest in new capital equipment that is thoroughly redesigned to be both cleaner and more productive. But these investments, or ones like them, would have happened sooner or later anyway. So a primary effect of regulation is to speed up the investment process. This is costly to firms, because they must scrap old machinery that is not necessarily worn out. When this happens, however, much of measured compliance costs are in fact just early capital investments. This in turn implies that the reported compliance figures are higher than the real costs.

Researchers at the nation's leading environmental economics think tank, Resources for the Future, recently conducted a study that asked the question: How much does $1 spent on environmental protection really cost an industry? For some industries, specifically steel, the answer was a little more than $1, due to the diversion effect. For others, such as plastics, the industry actually saved money as productivity was boosted. On average, the study concluded, $1 spent on environmental-pollution control reflected a real expense of eighty-six cents. In general then, this new research suggests that the reported capital-cost values often overstate the true costs to the firm.[4]

This section has looked at the data on environmentally related plant shutdowns. Three decades of surveys tell a remarkably consistent story. Environmental regulation nationwide has accounted for between 1,000 and 3,000 layoffs each year. The primary reason for these low numbers is that, even in heavily regulated industries, O&M costs for pollution abatement are a small fraction of sales, seldom more than 2 percent. In addition, the capital investment in new equipment that regulation requires often yields long-term payoffs. In some industries, these benefits offset a substantial portion of the costs.

Once again, this is not to minimize the impacts on those couple of thousand laid off workers—for them the trade-off is very real. But in a nation in which well over two million workers lose their jobs each year, environmental regulation should not be appearing on anyone's radar screen as a significant job killer. And yet the myth persists. Why?

REFINING THE STORY

One reason that the myth that environmental regulation causes widescale plant shutdowns and job losses persists is simply that industry leaders have much to gain and little to lose by stressing the environmental straw when discussing the breakdown of their manufacturing camels. To illustrate this point, consider Amoco's shutdown of its oil refinery in Casper, Wyoming, in 1991. In closing the plant, which had operated on the same site since 1913, Amoco issued the following statement: "The $150 million capital investment needed for environmental projects, added to our small size, limited crude oil flexibility, and marginal performance, tipped the scales" to closure. Local supplies of the crude on which the refinery depended were also declining. In addition, the company announced that $75 million would have to be spent regardless to clean up the abandoned site. These funds helped cushion the employment blow of the plant closing to the community.

The shutdown, which idled some 200 workers, came in the midst of the ongoing, nationwide deindustrialization process. The 1980s saw a loss of some 400,000 jobs in the oil industry, as both prices and demand flattened out, crude production and exploration dropped, and automation increased. In the first half of 1992, the industry shed 40,000 jobs. Also in 1992, the year after the Casper shutdown, Amoco alone eliminated 8,500 more jobs, including at least 2,800 resulting from shutdowns of businesses deemed "nonstrategic." It seems probable that the small, "marginally" performing Casper refinery would have fallen victim to this restructuring regardless of environmental regulations.[5]

The Casper case became fodder in the national jobs-versus-the-environment debate in a generally balanced *Congressional Quarterly* article, which, in part, read:

> Air-quality standards and numerous other environmental regulations introduced since the 1970s have also taken their toll on oil-industry employment. O'Keefe [of the American Petroleum Institute] cites the case of a polluting oil refinery in Wyoming that Amoco was forced to shut down several months ago. 'That put 200 people out of work because the cost of bringing that refinery into compliance couldn't be justified,' he says.

In the same article, the author states as fact, and without evidence, that members of the American Petroleum Institute "have often found it less costly to close down polluting refineries and shift operations overseas rather than comply with environmental regulations."[6] Have air-pollution-control requirements really led to a massive or even measurable shutdown of U.S. petroleum refining capacity?

A look at import trends of petroleum products suggests not. Figure 3.1 reveals that the share of petroleum-product imports has remained remarkably constant at about 12 percent of total supply since 1975. According to the U.S. Department of Energy, "total U.S. refinery capacity has remained fairly steady" since the postrecession shakeout of 1984 to 1985. The fact that the import share of refined petroleum products has not risen is somewhat surprising for two reasons. First, the Organization of Petroleum Exporting Countries (OPEC) invested heavily in refinery capacity during the 1970s and 1980s, which ought to have boosted their exports to the United States. Second, as shown in figure 3.1, since 1985, U.S. refineries have had to rely increasingly on imported crude. A closer look at the pattern of imports suggests that OPEC members have indeed increased their share of the U.S. import total, while non-OPEC refineries lost ground.[7] Yet, U.S. refiners have not lost market share over the last twenty years. It is thus very hard to believe that petroleum companies have "often" shut down U.S. refining plants primarily as a result of environmental expenses.

Petroleum refining certainly seems like a logical place to look for regulation-induced job loss because environmental compliance costs are, in absolute terms, quite large. In the 1980s, plants in California were investing on average about $100,000 per year on new clean-up equipment and spending another $270,000 on ongoing pollution-control

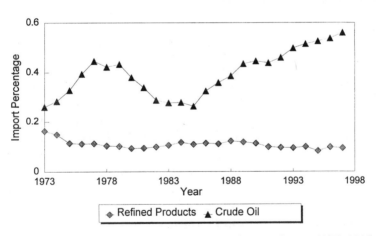

FIGURE 3.1. Import shares of refined and crude petroleum, 1975–1995.
Source: U.S. Department of Energy, *Monthly Energy Review.*

efforts. The two expenditures combined added up to about 1.5 percent of the value of sales. And so, in a 1997 study, Boston University economists Eli Berman and Linda Bui went hunting for layoffs in the refining industry.[8]

Their research found that the South Coast Air Quality Management District in Southern California, due to its severe air-pollution problems, has much more stringent air-quality regulations than does the rest of the country. Working with plant-level data from the Census Bureau, Berman and Bui examined what happened to employment in Southern California refineries, and other heavily regulated industries, after new, local regulations were introduced. To control for other factors that might be affecting employment in the industries under consideration, Berman and Bui used job levels in comparable plants in less heavily regulated parts of the country. In their words:

> Comparing changes in employment in regulating manufacturing plants in the South Coast to those of comparable plants not subject to regulation in other parts of the country yields a surprising finding: though the South Coast regulations imposed considerable abatement costs on manufacturing plants, they did not cause an appreciable loss of jobs. If anything, they increased employment slightly.

The study estimated that air-quality regulations added on net about two jobs per plant, though the estimate was not statistically significant. The results were, however, precise enough to rule out measurable job losses at regulated plants. The authors also evaluated whether jobs were lost in Southern California due to the exit or slower entry of highly regulated firms over a five-year interval. Again they were able to rule out such effects.

Commenting on the likely reasons for their findings, Berman and Bui argue that economic theory

> points to a likely explanation: the job loss from reduced sales [as regulatory costs are passed on to consumers] could be smaller than the job gain due to abatement activity at the plants. If firms sell in a local market in which all their competitors face the same regulations, the

reduction in sales [by a given firm] due to regulation may in fact be quite small. Also, for the industries most affected by air-quality regulation—petroleum refining, power generation, and, to a lesser extent, chemicals, the market is quite local, so the lack of job loss is not surprising.

The authors also found some evidence for productivity improvements—and thus monetary paybacks—accompanying the regulatory-induced abatement investment. Oil refineries in the South Coast "were subject to a series of extremely expensive regulations in the 1987–92 period that caused abatement investment to quadruple (it reached 3 percent of revenues in 1992), [which is] a much faster rate of increase than that for refineries in the rest of the United States. Preliminary results on the productivity of oil refineries indicate that, despite these increased costs, refineries actually became *more* productive during that period. In contrast, the rest of U.S. refining suffered a productivity decline."

It should be pointed out here that Berman and Bui looked at basically the same on-the-one-hand, on-the-other-hand theoretical arguments that underlay the macromodeling exercises from the late 1970s that were discussed in chapter 2: Will those jobs that are directly created by regulatory spending balance out jobs that are lost due to a decline in demand for regulated goods with higher prices? Berman and Bui's answer, which is based on a very careful, industry-specific analysis, is in fact the same answer as the one generated by the macromodels—no trade-off. They write that "In contrast to the widespread belief that environmental regulation costs jobs, the most severe episode of air-quality regulation of industry in the [United States] probably created a few jobs."

This is another quote that is worth committing to memory.

Earlier I laid out the evidence to support my claim that layoffs due to environmental regulation are quite few in number. Here I have dug a little deeper to show how a single layoff event at an old and "marginal" oil refinery in Wyoming becomes mythologized. With the unwitting help of the national media and the witting assistance of the American Petroleum Institute, the incident was transformed into a claim that oil refiners have "often" shut down and relocated overseas to escape expensive U.S. regulations. This claim simply cannot be supported by the data. U.S. refineries have held their own against imports over the last two decades. Also, Berman and Bui's study shows no evidence of job loss at existing plants or of shutdown due to regulation in plants facing high regulatory costs in Southern California.

Berman and Bui argue that one reason they did not find employment loss in refineries (and power plants) was that these industries sold in local markets; thus, all competitors faced the same general level of regulation. But many markets are becoming increasingly globalized. Having established that regulation-induced layoffs and shutdowns are small, another line of attack remains open. Does regulation reduce the competitiveness of manufacturing in the United States, and thus encourage new investment to occur in less-developed countries with lax environmental regulation?

THE POLLUTION-HAVEN HYPOTHESIS

The pollution-haven story is somewhat unique in its broad political appeal, having firm believers on both the left and right. Joshua Karliner in his book *Corporate Planet* (Sierra Club 1997) states the argument succinctly: "The widening investment opportunities generated by international agreements such as [the General Agreement on Trade and Tariffs] and [the North American Free Trade Agreement] allow corporations to play investment-hungry countries off against one another, thus engendering a 'race to the bottom' for environmental standards."[9] Business leaders sing the same tune by attacking new regulations on the grounds that the costly rules will, however reluctantly, force them to close down and move overseas. How realistic are these threats of widespread capital flight?

For some twenty-five years, economists have been trying to answer precisely this question. Until recently, our theoretical expectation has been that the costs imposed by regulation should impose some visible penalty on the competitiveness of U.S. firms, leading to the growth of pollution havens. But from the dozens of studies that have specifically looked for evidence, the support for the pollution-haven hypothesis that has emerged is, to say the least, underwhelming. In an exhaustive review of this literature, Adam Jaffe of Brandeis University and his coauthors— Steven Peterson; Paul Portney, president of Resources for the Future; and Robert Stavins of Harvard—concluded that "studies attempting to measure the effect of environmental regulations on net exports, overall trade flows, and plant-location decisions have produced estimates that are either small, statistically insignificant, or not robust to tests of model specification." In plain English, regulation has had no reliably measurable impact on the competitiveness of U.S. manufacturing, nor has it led to the growth of significant pollution havens in developing countries.

Economists have looked for pollution havens in two different ways. The first has been to examine directly the impact of regulation on plant-location decisions. In other words, do pollution-intensive industries seem to be building a disproportionate number of new factories in countries (or areas within the United States) where environmental regulation is weak? The second test of the pollution-haven hypothesis is indirect: Are exports from developing to developed countries showing an increasing percentage of "dirty" (pollution-intensive) goods? The section that follows briefly summarizes a few of the major studies that are representative of each genre. For the interested reader, Jaffe et al. (1995) provide a comprehensive overview.

DIRECT TESTS: REGULATION AND LOCATION DECISIONS

When considering international-location decisions, it is important to recall that pollution-control costs are a small portion of total business costs (for heavily regulated industries, typically 1 percent to 2 percent of sales). Moreover, costs are only one factor influencing business-location decisions. Considerations as diverse as access to markets and the quality of life are important components of business-location decisions. One recent study identified, in order of importance, market size, wages, tax rates, political stability, access to the European market, and distance to the United States as the primary determinants of U.S. investment abroad. Given these factors, most U.S. direct foreign investment continues to be in developed countries that have environmental regulations comparable to our own.[10]

Around 80 percent of all U.S. manufacturing investment abroad is in other developed countries. The country with the second highest share of U.S. investment, Germany, is also the country with the most stringent pollution-control requirements outside of the United States, as measured by the percent of Gross National Product (GNP) devoted to environmental protection. In fact, some Japanese and German air-quality regulations are more stringent than those in the United States.

All told, less-developed countries have about a 20 percent share of U.S. foreign manufacturing investment. Together, our two hemispheric neighbors, Mexico and Brazil, attract over 50 percent of American capital headed toward less-developed countries. Mexico is close to the U.S. market, while Brazil has a large internal market of its own.[11]

While manufacturing investment in poor countries remains relatively small, it is growing. For example, the share of U.S. imports originating in developing countries grew from 29 percent in 1979 to 36 percent in 1990.[12] Over this period, capital flight to low-wage countries has had a devastating impact on labor-intensive U.S. industries, such as shoes and textiles.

Has environmental regulation had a similar impact of driving dirty industry overseas? The ideal study here would involve tracking global start-ups of pollution-intensive plants to see if their location was sensitive to regulatory differences. Unfortunately, this kind of data is not easily available across international borders. As a consequence, most studies of firm-location decisions focus on births of new plants *within* the United States. There are substantial interstate and intercounty variations in the United States among both environmental regulations and enforcement efforts. If firms are willing to pack up and move from California to Mexico to escape regulations, then, because of access to markets, better infrastructure, and a familiar cultural environment, we would certainly expect them to be even more willing to move from California to Idaho.

A first generation of studies looked at the impact of different state regulations on the location decisions of pollution-intensive industry. The results reveal no reliable pattern of pollution havens within the United States. Heavily polluting firms are not fleeing states with high levels of regulation in search of lower environmental costs. Some recent work by Clark University's Wayne Gray, who has carefully studied the location choices of the paper industry, is typical. Clark and a coauthor found in one statistical specification that paper plants are somewhat more likely to locate in states where the political system is less sensitive to environmentalist interests. However, the result is quite weak, disappearing in other specifications and leading the authors to recommend caution in interpreting their "preliminary" results. Consistent with Berman and Bui's analysis discussed earlier, no impact at all in location at the state level was found for refining, which was the other industry that was studied.[13]

The absence of strong location effects, in spite of the heavy regulation facing the paper industry, is consistent with what Gray learned from extensive interviews with plant officials:

> First, a variety of factors influence plant location, the most important of which are the location of demand for the firm's product and the location of existing facilities in the firm. Wage rates, tax incentives, and other economic variables are also identified as important. Environmental regulations are important, but not among the most important factors. . . . The main influence of environmental regulations is said to come through difficulties in getting *construction* permits (emphasis added). . . . Firms are leery of tying up hundreds of millions of dollars in a new paper mill, if delays in permitting will delay the

plant's opening until the next cyclical downturn in the demand for paper. . . . Several people said they would rather have strict regulations that were clearly specified, so that they could be incorporated in the design of the new facility, raising costs somewhat but not delaying the project.[14]

With paper-industry executives caring most on the environmental front about the timely issue of construction permits, it is no wonder that economic researchers have found little consistent correlation between plant location and the state-level stringency of emission-control requirements. Summarizing the work of Gray and others, Michael Rauscher, another economist who has written widely on the subject, concludes: "Direct methods of testing the hypothesis that environmental regulation affects trade and international capital movements tend to reject such a relationship."[15]

Since 1996, however, a few new studies have looked even closer at the impact of county-level differences in regulation on new investment. In the United States, counties that fail to achieve national air-quality standards—"nonattainment" counties—must develop and implement tougher regulations to try to meet the goals. Here some evidence is beginning to emerge that these regulations are encouraging new plants in pollution-intensive industries to relocate, not to the next country, but at least to the next county.

Over the period 1982 to 1989, manufacturing employment grew somewhat slower (or fell more) in counties that failed to attain air-quality standards than in other U.S. counties. Matthew Kahn of Columbia University has studied this relationship. However, it is still not clear from his work if tougher regulation in nonattainment areas caused the manufacturing slowdown. An alternative explanation would be that nonattainment areas in general began with higher concentrations of manufacturing jobs. Between 1982 and 1989, the United States lost two and a half million manufacturing jobs due to capital flight and automation. It is not surprising that a disproportionate number of these jobs came from highly polluted areas. Indeed, as Kahn notes in a later paper, "declines in key rustbelt industries such as primary metals [were] unlikely to be caused by environmental regulation." Kahn cited instead a failure to invest in new technology.[16]

The most conclusive link between environmental regulation and new plant location was established in 1998 by Randy Becker and Vernon Henderson of Brown University. They looked at the nationwide construction of new plants in four of the most air-pollution-intensive industries in the country: industrial-organic chemicals, metal containers, plastics, and wood furniture. In the counties with the highest level of air pollution—and thus the toughest regulations—births of new pollution-intensive plants declined significantly when compared to the rest of the country after regulations began to bite. Again, we are not referring here to lay-offs, just slower growth in a few pollution-intensive sectors. This also does not mean that jobs were lost on net in these areas. Rather, as shown in an earlier study in 1996, Henderson found that total employment growth was actually slightly faster in nonattainment counties than in the rest of the country.[17]

Figure 3.2 shows data on new plant construction from the Becker and Henderson study. These data are most remarkable for what they do not show. The bars reflect the number of new plants, and the "preregulatory" period of 1967 to 1972 represents the baseline. (Major national air and water regulation got under way only in the early 1970s.) The second cluster of bars shows that there were about 30 percent more new plants that produced industrial-organic chemicals that were constructed in the period just after regulation began (1977 to 1982) than in the first period, about 50 percent more plastics plants, and so on.

Recall that the four industries shown in figure 3.2 were specifically selected by the authors as among the most air-pollution intensive in the country. Under the pollution-haven hypothesis, one would expect to see U.S. investment in these dirty industries simply dry up. Yet, even in these exceptional cases, the data on new plant construction in the postregulation era (after 1972) tell a very different story. Nationwide, the number of new plant births rose in three of the industries and fell in only one—metal containers. Clearly, no general trend of capital flight to pollution havens can be supported by these numbers.

The latest research to look at the most heavily polluted counties in the United States suggests that environmental regulation may have (1) slightly hastened the shift to services and (2) has discouraged new investment by some of the most pollution-intensive industries. This does not, of course, mean that these plants are fleeing overseas. They may well be heading to the next county. Indeed, relocation by dirty industry, if it is occurring, is generally too small to be picked up at even the interstate level. From these latest studies economists have concluded that, in general, environmental regulation is a minor factor in the decision of U.S. firms to relocate internationally. At the very least, research has ruled out all but small-scale pollution-haven effects.

But surely when the U.S. Chamber of Commerce and Greenpeace

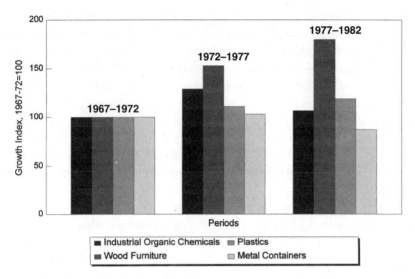

FIGURE 3.2. New plant construction in dirty industries.
Source: Becker and Henderson (1997: Table 1).

ecowarriors agree on something, there has to be a kernel of truth lurking somewhere behind the story. The pollution-haven argument saw its most forceful articulation in the 1993 debate over the North American Free Trade Act (NAFTA). And if there is a case to be made for a pollution haven, Mexico—with its lax environmental enforcement, as well as its low wages and proximity to the United States—is the perfect test case.

Even before NAFTA went into effect, the Maquiladora region of northern Mexico provided a good place to evaluate the validity of the pollution-haven hypothesis. An area within 100 kilometers of the U.S. border, the Maquiladora region has had a long-standing arrangement by which plants there have been able to import and export products freely. While these plants were required in theory to meet U.S. federal environmental standards, in practice the underfunded Mexican government has not vigorously enforced the law. As a result, air- and water-pollution problems have become quite serious in the region.[18]

Right across the border is Los Angeles. The L.A. basin has the worst air pollution in the United States and, as a nonattainment region, some of the toughest emission-control standards. This gross disparity in regulatory conditions provided the backdrop for a highly dramatic instance of plants from the wood-furniture industry moving south in the years leading up to the NAFTA debate. (Wood furniture was one of the four industries selected by Becker and Henderson in their county-level study of new investment, which was previously discussed.)

Solvent-based coatings for wood furniture evaporate easily, which contributes to smog. In 1988, regulations in the Los Angeles area mandated the phasing in of expensive collection chambers to contain the solvent emissions. As of 1990, there were *no* regulations in the Maquiladora region pertaining to the emission of solvents. An added if not primary inducement for these firms to relocate was lower wages and benefits. The average hourly wage in Los Angeles was $8.92; across the border it was $0.77. In addition, as U.S. employers, the firms were required to pay $1.75 per hour in workman's compensation. The equivalent Mexican tax was only $0.13. For furniture makers, labor *and* environmental costs were significant factors in the decision to locate in Mexico.

Based on rather sketchy evidence, the U.S. government estimated that four to five plants per year moved to the Maquiladora region over the three-year period from 1988 to 1990, partially as a result of environmental regulations. This accounted for a loss of about 350 jobs per year.[19] More generally, a 1988 survey of seventy-six Maquiladora plants found that 10 percent listed environmental factors among the main reasons for locating in Mexico.[20] These kinds of anecdotes, along with press reports of the "Border Boom's Dirty Residue," have helped form a prima facie case that northern Mexico provides a classic example of a pollution haven. However, more systematic, if indirect, evidence contradicts this impression.

INDIRECT EVIDENCE: THE FLOW OF "DIRTY" TRADE

If the Maquiladora has become a pollution haven, then we would expect that the composition of production in the region would reflect a disproportionate number of pollution-intensive industries. At the same time, exports from the Maquiladora to the United States should be dirtier than average. Princeton economists Gene Grossman and Alan Krueger tested this hypothesis using data from 1987. Compared to the composition of U.S. production as a whole, the Maquiladora did not have more pollution-intensive industries, and industries facing higher pollution-abatement costs in the United States did not have higher than average exports to the United States from the Maquiladora region. Indeed, Grossman and Krueger found the reverse relationship in one case: Mexican exports were significantly higher from industries with *lower* pollution intensity. Not surprisingly, Grossman and Krueger determined that, by far, the most important factor affecting a decision to locate in Mexico was labor costs.

The Grossman and Kreuger study is one of the better pieces of research in a broader literature on trade flows. Some studies have found shifts in the composition of trade in pollution-intensive goods, while others have not. In the former group, the results go both ways. Depending on the time frame or data set, U.S. imports have been found to become either more or less pollution intensive.[21] Adam Jaffe and his coauthors, in their 1995 survey article discussed earlier, characterize these results as "either small, statistically insignificant, or not robust to tests of model specification." Thus, in spite of looking hard, the indirect evidence of pollution havens found by economists is quite weak, ruling out any major shift of dirty industry from the North to the South.

In the past, researchers have generally had to look at the sum total of U.S. imports, regardless of country of origin. However, most imports come from industrialized countries that have environmental regulations comparable to our own. Therefore, aggregate trade-flow data might fail to pick up a rise in dirty imports from the South. Two years ago, information on country-specific imports at a highly disaggregated level became available. What is unique about these data is that they can be matched up with industry-specific pollution-control expense information. Thus, we can now look specifically at U.S. imports from developing countries to try to capture evidence for the pollution-haven hypothesis.

Table 3.3 compares the industries with the fastest growing imports from developing countries into the United States to see whether they are also ones that have faced high levels of environmental regulation. They have not. The table lists the goods-producing industries that had the fastest growth in imported products across two business cycles—1973 to 1979 and 1979 to 1989. *Environmental costs* as a share of sales were greater than average for the boldfaced entries. Of the top twenty import-growth leaders, in the first period, only three faced greater than average regulatory costs, while only one did during the second period. Not surprisingly, the list of import-growth industries are dominated by labor-intensive, and relatively clean, light manufacturing—mostly textiles.

Table 3.4 tells a similar story from another angle. Here the industries listed for each period are the top twenty in terms of *environmental regulatory costs* as a share of sales. The boldface type now indicates *import growth* that was faster than average for all manufacturing. Of the top twenty industries with the greatest environmental regulatory costs, only five had growth in imports greater than average over the years 1973 to

TABLE 3.3. Top twenty industries by increased import share from LDCs (bold entries indicate greater than average environmental costs)

1973–1979	1979–1989
Carpets, NEC	Footwear, except rubber, NEC
Rubber and plastics footwear	Women's footwear, except athletic
Leather and sheep-lined clothing	Leather and sheep-lined clothing
Waterproof outerwear	Canned and cured fish and seafood
Footwear, except rubber, NEC	Rubber and plastics footwear
Leather gloves and mittens	Footwear, cut stock
Primary nonferrous metals, NEC	**Semivitreous table and kitchenware**
Watches, clocks, and parts	Leather gloves and mittens
Pottery products, NEC	Luggage
Fabric, dress, and work gloves	Fur goods
Women's handbags and purses	Waterproof outerwear
Girls dresses and blouses	Pottery products, NEC
Women's dresses and blouses	Robes and dressing gowns
Bras, girdles, and allied garments	Apparel and accessories, NEC
Luggage	Household audio and video equipment
Edible fats and oils, NEC	Women's and children's underwear
Footwear, cut stock	Children's suits and coats
Semivitreous table and kitchenware	Women's suits and coats
Personal leather goods, NEC	Personal leather goods, NEC
Lace goods	Fabric, dress and work gloves

Note: NEC stands for "not elsewhere classified."
Source: Goodstein (1997).

1979, and only two had grown faster than average from 1979 to 1989. Random chance would show a higher correlation. In any list of industries pulled out of a hat, on average half should show import growth greater than the mean. Tables 3.3 and 3.4 suggest first that rapid import-growth industries have not been ones to face much environmental regulation, and second that industries that are highly regulated did not perform poorly vis-à-vis their international competition. This clear lack of any correlation between import growth and high levels of regulation held up when I controlled for other factors (e.g., labor intensity, profitability, and raw material intensity) that might have affected import growth.

This new data tell the convincing story that dirty imports into the United States from the developing countries did not increase their share of total imports over the period analyzed. Thus, at least as far as the United States is concerned, the trade-flow evidence confirms the

TABLE 3.4. Top twenty industries by environmental cost share (bold entries indicate greater than average import growth from less developed countries)

1973–1979	1979–1989
Primary zinc	Alkalis and chlorine
Pulp mills	Primary zinc
Primary lead	Primary copper
Nitrogenous fertilizers	Pulp mills
Primary copper	**Cement, hydraulic**
Paper mills	Industrial inorganic chemicals, NEC
Primary nonferrous metals, NEC	Primary lead
Cement, hydraulic	Gum and wood chemicals
Electrometallurgical products	Medicinals and botanicals
Industrial inorganic chemicals, NEC	Paper mills
Primary aluminum	Synthetic rubber
Blast furnaces and steel mills	Industrial inorganic chemicals, NEC
Gum and wood chemicals	Cyclic crudes and intermediates
Cyclic crudes and intermediates	Agricultural chemicals, NEC
Inorganic pigments	Explosives
Particle board	Particle board
Semivitreous table and kitchenware	Inorganic pigments
Wood products, NEC	Primary aluminum
Medicinals and botanicals	Phosphatic fertilizers
Raw cane sugar	**Electrometallurgical products**

Note: NEC stands for "not elsewhere classified."
Source: Goodstein (1997).

general result of twenty-five years of research in this area—environmental regulation has not led to the growth of pollution havens in developing countries.

However, that being the case, some firms will still relocate to poor countries to escape environmental regulations. For the United States, this is particularly true in relation to investment in Mexico, given both its wage advantage and proximity.[22] Such well publicized, if infrequent, cases, as the previously discussed decision on the part of furniture makers to locate to Mexico, help to explain the widespread fear of job loss as a result of environmental protection that many Americans seem to share. Moreover, as the grim environmental conditions in the Maquiladora demonstrate, after relocating, even firms in relatively clean industries, such as textiles, automobile assembly, or shoe production, will certainly take advantage of looser pollution standards. Indeed, in one spot check, monitors found clear violations of both U.S. and Mexican standards at one-third of the industrial sites visited.[23]

In summary, the direct evidence on firm-location decisions and the indirect evidence from the trade-flow literature find precious little support for any significant pollution-haven phenomenon. However, the idea has a lot of superficial plausibility—if businesses are profit-maximizers, why wouldn't they seek out less regulated, and thus lower-cost, production sites?

WHY NO POLLUTION HAVENS?

There are a number of answers to this question. Chief among them, as discussed earlier, is that operating- and maintenance-regulatory costs are not particularly burdensome for most industries. Moreover, capital-investment costs in cleaner, more efficient processes often generate partially offsetting benefits. And in any event, costs are only one factor in the complex nexus of a business-location decision. Proximity to markets is often a determinate issue, as evidenced in the case of the petroleum-refining industry as discussed earlier, or for heavily regulated electric utilities. Ready access to raw material supplies and low transportation costs are also important for industries such as paper and mining. These facts make many pollution-intensive industries much less footloose than the stereotypical runaway shop, which is typically labor intensive and not dependent on local raw materials or local markets.

Another reason relates to the fact that much pollution-control technology is now embedded in modern plant designs; that is, pollution control increasingly reflects fundamental process changes rather than end-of-the-pipe filters. This means that an oil refinery or chemical plant built by a multinational corporation in Seattle will in fact look a lot like one built in south China. Nancy Birdsall and David Wheeler, economists at the World Bank, interviewed executives at several large multinational pulp and paper and petrochemical firms operating in Chile. They reported that "they do not know the extra costs they incur in the form of 'cleaner' equipment; they invest in modern, efficient, clean equipment—as a package. In some cases they accept higher costs to reduce emissions and ensure that the exported product meets foreign standards; for example, paper produced with chlorine will have traces of dioxin and cannot be exported to Germany. But even where product standards can be met with dirty processes, the fact that the newest technology is clean dominates any search for lower costs."[24]

This is not to say that all firms that move South are model environmental citizens. However, the evidence suggests strongly that environmental concerns seldom rise high enough on the corporate radar screen to signal a need for relocation.

For a final possible explanation as to why U.S. trade competitiveness has not visibly suffered from environmental regulation, we can return to the Porter Hypothesis, which was introduced earlier in the chapter. Michael Porter has argued that environmental regulation, while imposing short-run costs on firms, actually enhances their long-run competitiveness. There are several ways in which this might happen. First, regulation might favor forward-looking firms that develop products in future demand. Second, when firms redesign their production processes to reduce emissions, they may wind up reducing inefficient use of energy or raw materials. Third, Porter has also argued that firms can use the redesign process to promote "outside-the-box" innovative thinking. Finally, regulation may force an expansion in research and development spending.

In combination, these three factors—relatively low costs, the "packaged" nature of clean, new technology, and procompetitive, Porter-like effects—help explain why the pollution-haven hypothesis, in spite of its superficial plausibility, has not proven out. Economic researchers can't seem to find more than a few isolated cases of manufacturing firms that have headed to countries south of the border to escape environmental regulations, and it has not been for want of trying.

VERY SMALL LOCAL TRADE-OFFS

In chapter 2, I showed that at the economy-wide level there is no trade-off between employment and a cleaner nation. This chapter has explored two different, more local propositions. Perhaps our pervasive national belief in a jobs–environment trade-off can be traced back to large-scale, regulation-induced layoffs. Even if matched by long-run job gains elsewhere, such a process would be extremely hard on workers and communities. A second underlying fear may be that regulation forces new manufacturing investment to relocate abroad, thus decimating the manufacturing base and aggravating structural unemployment, especially for low-skilled workers.

However, as was the case with concerns about economy-wide trade-offs, the facts show that such fears are unfounded. Local job losses due to environmentally related plant shutdowns are simply tiny compared to the real downsizers: technology, trade, and corporate restructuring. Nevertheless, Americans seem to feel that, as inevitably as dying and paying taxes, we simply have to sacrifice jobs, jobs, and more jobs on the altar of a clean environment. Through the magic of public relations, layoffs on the order of 1,500 per year, spread out over half a dozen plants nationwide, have transformed environmental regulation into a giant job killer.

The same holds true for the pollution-haven hypothesis. Ask any friend whether American corporations are shipping manufacturing jobs overseas to escape onerous environmental regulations. Republican or Democrat, right-wing or left-leaning, the answer will be, "Of course they are." Now ask that same friend to name three cases where this has happened, or even one. Researchers who have looked for pollution havens over the last two decades have had the same trouble.

If these are the facts, why then does a belief in a jobs–environment trade-off take hold so readily? First, as discussed in chapter 1, there is the real rise in economic insecurity faced by many middle-class workers today. Environmental regulation is an easy handle for people to grasp when trying to cope, on the one hand, with the global economic forces of trade and technology and, on the other hand, with the political agenda that has produced a steady dismantling of institutions—labor unions and regulatory constraints on business—that historically have provided some relief against those storms.

Second, the substantive jobs–environment conflicts have not been in manufacturing at all, but rather in extractive industry—logging in the Northwest, coal mining in the East, and, to a lesser extent, oil development on Alaska's North Slope. In the first two cases, we have seen high profile job losses on the order of several thousand spread throughout multistate regions. Concerns over the impact of these job losses were bigger than the relatively small numbers at stake for three main reasons. First, it was feared that whole rural communities would crumble without their "base" industry. Second, unemployed workers in rural areas knew they would find it hard to get new jobs with pay comparable to their old ones. Last, workers in these industries were already facing broad assaults on their jobs from both automation and declining demand for their product. In this context, the workers, their unions, and—for somewhat different reasons—their employers fought the regulations as hard as they could.

Jobs versus owls and coal miners versus acid rain set the national tone for our thinking about the economic effects of environmental regulation in the early 1990s. The highly politicized struggles of the timber workers and miners have apparently spilled over into a generalized—and wildly incorrect—belief in regulation-induced job loss in manufacturing. Given this, I turn in the next chapter to a closer look at jobs–environment conflicts in rural, extractive industry.

NOTES

1. Goodstein and Hodges (1997).
2. House Democratic Policy Committee (1996), and "Squeezing the Textile Workers: Trade and Technology Force a New Wave of Job Cuts," *New York Times*, C1, February 21, 1996.
3. See Goodstein (1996), U.S. EPA (1991), Kieschnick (1978), and Wykle et al. (1991).
4. The Nortel case is described in Cook and Miller (1996). Gray (1987) tells the conventional negative productivity story. For a discussion of the Porter Hypothesis, see Porter and Van der Linde (1995) and Palmer et al. (1995). The RFF cite is Morgenstern et al. (1998b).
5. See "Amoco to Close Casper Refinery" and "Impact of Refinery Closing Not Yet Known," *Casper Star-Tribune*, October 10, 1991 and November 11, 1991; "Oil Company Plans to Cut 8,500 Jobs," *Belleville (IL) News-Democrat*, July 7, 1992.
6. "Jobs Versus Environment," *Congressional Quarterly Researcher*, pp. 2–18 and 41–60, May 15, 1992. Bezdek (1993) also cites the Casper case as evidence of a jobs–environment trade-off.
7. Quote is from the Energy Information Administration's *International Energy Outlook 1992*, p. 7. Among non-OPEC countries, the losers were all islands: the Bahamas, Trinidad and Tobago, the Antilles, the Virgin Islands, and Puerto Rico. Non-OPEC countries with significant (greater than 40,000 barrels per day) increases in exports to the United States included Brazil, Mexico, Spain, and the former U.S.S.R.
8. Berman and Bui (1997).
9. Karliner (1998). In his vigorous defense of the pollution-haven hypothesis, Karliner (1997) cites only two specific cases of American plants that moved abroad in direct response to environmental regulation.
10. Koechlin (1992).
11. Pollution control expenditures are found in OECD (1991: Table 23). Direct Foreign Investment figures are from Scholl et al. (1992).
12. Scott (1997).
13. Gray and Shadbegian (1998).
14. Gray (1997).
15. Rauscher (1997). Comparable assessments of this literature can be found in Becker and Henderson (1997), as well as Jaffe et al. (1995).
16. Kahn (1997); Kahn (1998). Duffy-Deno (1992) also finds weak evidence that metropolitan areas with high pollution control expenditures in manufacturing have slightly slower manufacturing growth. But this finding may simply reflect the fact that cities dominated by older, more pollution intensive sectors had less dynamic job growth in general.

17. Becker and Henderson (1997) and Henderson (1996). In the earlier study, Henderson presents evidence for slower growth in heavily polluted counties for two other industries, steel and petroleum refining, over the period 1978–1987. Yet recall that Berman and Bui (1997) found no evidence of exit or entry differences between Southern California and the rest of the country for either refining or chemicals over a similar period.

18. "Border Boom's Dirty Residue Imperils U.S.–Mexico Trade," *New York Times*, March 31, 1991.

19. These are the mid-range estimates from the U.S. GAO (1991), based on 78 percent of employers reporting stringent air-pollution controls as one reason for moving.

20. See U.S. GAO (1991) and "A Warmer Climate for Furniture Makers," *Los Angeles Times*, May 14, 1990. The survey results are discussed in Sanchez (1990).

21. For example Kalt (1988) found that U.S. exports became less pollution intensive over the period 1967–1977; however, I show that this result is reversed in 1979–1989 [Goodstein (1997)]. Similarly, Leonard (1984) found that nonferrous metal mining suffered from serious import competition during the 1970s; however, I show that almost all of the sustained import gains came from the developed and not the developing countries. [Goodstein (1997)].

22. There is some speculation that liability under the hazardous waste regulations passed during the 1980s may become significant enough to effect location decisions. See Hettige et al. (1992).

23. Karliner (1997: 156).

24. Birdsall and Wheeler (1993). Wheeler and Martin (1992) provide more evidence supporting this point.

Chapter 4

Coal Miners, Timber Workers, and Slopers

In 1995, after twenty-one years working in the coal mines of northern West Virginia, John Beveridge was laid off. A worker with highly specialized skills, his annual salary during his last year on the job was $48,000. He told the *New York Times* in a 1996 front-page article "I'm scared to death. I'm 44 years old. I'd like to live another 50 years. What am I going to do?"

Beveridge worked in Marion County, which was hard hit by coal mine shutdowns. Marion and neighboring Monongalia counties were featured in the *Times* article. Between them, in the period between 1990 and 1997, the two counties lost two-thirds of their mining jobs, or 3,120 workers.[1] This accounted for around 6 percent of the total workforce in the counties, as well as a good proportion of the higher paying jobs. This in turn appeared to create a ripple effect. According to the *Times* article, "Marion County has lost nearly 400 retail jobs in the first half of the 1990s, and 27 of its 355 retail stores."

Coal miners in the East and timber workers in the West—these groups were on the frontlines of the two high-profile, jobs–environment conflicts of the early 1990s that have left a deep mark on the national debate. In chapters 2 and 3, I have tried to dispel two myths that have since clouded that debate. I showed first that at the economy-wide level there simply is no trade-off between jobs and the environment. Second, nationwide regulation-induced layoffs are, by any measure, very small.

71

Yet, given that, coal miners, timber workers, and their communities have absorbed a high proportion of these layoffs, and undoubtedly seen jobs sacrificed to a cleaner environment.

The West Virginia story highlights several of the key issues—middle-aged workers losing high paying union jobs; a disappearing way of life in some regions; and job losses multiplying as retail and service businesses go under.

It also begs some key questions. To what extent was the job loss in the region in fact due to environmental regulation? What other causes, such as automation, aging plants, and shifting demand, could have caused the layoffs? What actually happens to the laid off workers in the long run? Are rural economies really that sensitive to the disappearance of jobs in their so-called "base" industry—mining or logging? What kind of government programs can help mitigate the impact? This chapter focuses attention on the coal and timber cases in an attempt to develop answers to these questions.

Before beginning, however, it is worth considering an important point: What exactly was it about John Beveridge's case that merited front-page attention from the *New York Times?* The very next week, the *Times* ran a story on Martha Smith, who lost her job at a textile plant in Alabama—one of 100,000 textile workers who that year were laid off due to the nebulous workings of "trade and technology." But unlike Beveridge's story, Smith's was buried in the bottom of the business section.

Beveridge's case is indeed important, but not because he lost his job to the Clean Air Act. His fear is a very legitimate one, shared equally by Martha Smith and her coworkers at the textile plant. The outlook for so-called "dislocated" workers in America today is generally not a pretty one. Workers who lose jobs they have held for several years suffer significant and long-term earnings losses. One comprehensive study looked at dislocated workers in the early to mid-1980s who were laid off after six or more years on the job. The grim result was that the workers suffered long-term income losses on an average annual basis of 25 percent.[2] This experience was common across different sectors of the economy. In another study, workers with somewhat less seniority who were laid off in the early 1990s experienced mean wage declines of 13 percent.

Both studies documented one unsurprising point: the losses were greater if workers were laid off in regions that faced persistent structural unemployment. As we shall see, this description still fits many coal-mining communities in the East. However, former timber workers in the

Northwest have, by and large, begun their search for new careers in a more robust economy.

COAL MINERS AND CLEAN AIR

Jobs in the coal industry have been disappearing at a steady rate for almost two decades due to two factors. First, as figure 4.1 illustrates, there has been a shift in production from labor intensive, underground mines in the East, to much less labor intensive surface mines in the West. Strip mines employ between a third and a half as many workers as underground mines to generate the same coal tonnage.

Second, within the eastern mines, productivity gains have been dramatic. In 1978, the average underground miner produced just over 1 short ton per hour of labor; by 1990, that figure had risen to over 2.5 short tons per hour. These productivity gains implied that—had production stayed constant—the number of jobs would have shrunk by well over half.[3]

U.S. coal employment peaked in 1981, declining from 225,000 in that year to 131,000 jobs in 1990, when the CAA amendments passed. The drop was quite large, but less than 50 percent, because, again, as shown in figure 4.1, underground production increased over the period. However, the debate over the impact of acid-rain control and the Clean

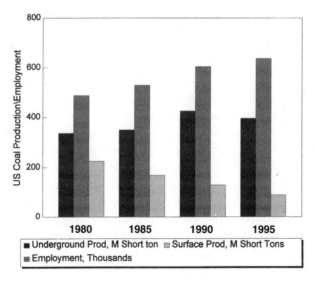

FIGURE 4.1. U.S. coal production and employment, 1980–1995.
Source: Statistical Abstract of the United States, Table 1172.

Air Act on the coal country was framed against the grimly ironic back-drop of annual mounting coal production and plummeting coal employ-ment. Harrison County, West Virginia, for example, had seen 1,000 min-ing jobs disappear during the 1980s. Coupled with the (unrelated) loss of over 2,200 manufacturing jobs, Harrison County spent much of the decade battling depression-level unemployment rates. Under these con-ditions, in 1990, coal miners and their families were being asked to shoul-der yet another burden—further job losses for the sake of acid-rain reduction.

THE ACID RAIN STORY

In the mid-1960s, freshwater fishermen in Sweden, Norway, Canada, and the Adirondack Mountains of New York State began to notice a decline in the fishery stocks of mountain lakes. By the late 1980s, Sweden was reporting 14,000 lakes that were unable to support sensitive aquatic life, with 2,200 virtually dead. In Norway, lakes covering 13,000 square kilo-meters had lost fish species. In Canada, over 14,000 lakes were strongly acidified, while in the Adirondacks over 180 lakes had lost the ability to support most native fish.

In the late 1970s, German foresters noted a rapid decline in the health of their resource; by 1985, over half the forests in the country were damaged in what was termed simply waldsterben or "forest-death." Sim-ilar, though less dramatic, reports of retarded forest growth came from North America, with particular concern focused on sugar maples and high-elevation red spruce in Canada and the Northeast, as well as pines in the Southeast and California.

Acid rain was the suspected culprit in the damage to both water and forest resources. Acid rain is formed when sulfur dioxide (which is pri-marily released when coal is burned) and nitrogen oxide (which is emit-ted from any kind of fossil-fuel combustion) are transformed while in the atmosphere into sulfuric and nitric acids. These acids return to the earth attached to rain drops, or in some cases dry dust particles. Researchers have established that acid rain is guilty of acidifying lakes and streams. In the case of forest death, no widespread link has yet been established. However, ground-level ozone (which is produced by the transformation of nitrogen oxides), possibly in combination with acid rain, has been shown to reduce forest and agricultural productivity.[4]

Acid deposition harms fish and plant life directly and can also cause indirect damage by leaching and mobilizing harmful metals such as alu-minum and lead out of soil. The impact of acid rain on ecosystem health varies from region to region depending on the base rocks underlying the area. Naturally occurring limestone or other alkaline rocks can neutralize much of the direct impact of the acid. Such rocks are not found in the primarily igneous terrain of the Adirondack Mountains of New York State, southeastern Canada or northern Europe, which explains the serious impact on aquatic environments in those regions.

In addition to damaging water and forest resources, the acids also erode buildings, bridges, and statues. Suspended sulfate particles in the air can also dramatically reduce visibility. Finally, they contribute to sickness and premature death in humans. Although human health risks were not a prime motivating factor in the acid-rain control debate of the late 1980s, in retrospect, the health benefits have turned out to be quite significant. A 1997 study found that, largely due to health and visibility benefits, the measurable benefits of acid-rain control have far exceeded the costs.[5]

Pollution from sulfur dioxide was at one time concentrated around power plants and metal refineries. The area around Copper Hill, Tennessee, for example, is so denuded of vegetation from now-closed copper-smelting operations that the underlying red-clay soil of the region is clearly visible from outer space. In an attempt to deal with these local problems, and with the encouragement of the ambient standards mandated by the Clean Air Act of 1970, smokestacks were built higher. However, dilution proved not to be a complete pollution solution. Sulfur and nitric oxides were picked up by the wind and transported hundreds of miles only to be redeposited as acid rain. The acid-rain problem in the northeastern United States and Canada was thus blamed on regional polluters—coal-fired utilities and nitrogen-oxide emitters ranging from the Midwest to the Eastern seaboard.

Solving the acid-rain problem boiled down to reducing, rather than diluting, sulfur (and nitrogen-oxide) emissions. Two strategies were available. One would have been to require all utilities to install sulfur scrubbers that trapped the sulfur before it was emitted. The other solution would have been for power plants to switch away from the use of high-sulfur coal, which is mined in the East, to low-sulfur coal, which is mined primarily, though not exclusively, in the West. The former strategy—which was discussed off on and on throughout the 1980s—would have slowed coal-mining job losses in the East. However, it was both considerably more expensive and not attractive to politicians from low-sulfur coal districts.

Thus, when the political logjam surrounding acid-rain control finally broke in 1990, Congress turned to the second approach. The CAA amendments passed that year required by the year 2000 a 10-million-ton reduction of sulfur-dioxide emissions from 1980 levels, down to an annual average of 8.95 million tons per year, as well as a 2.5-million-ton reduction of nitrogen-oxide emissions. No scrubber adoption was mandated. Instead a highly flexible approach was used that relied on the use of so-called "marketable permits." The idea behind the marketable permits system was to achieve a reduction in acid-rain pollution at the lowest possible cost.

Beginning in 1995, electric utilities were given permits based on their sulfur-dioxide emission levels ten years earlier. When the program is fully phased in, each utility will receive permits equivalent to 30 percent to 50 percent of their 1986 pollution. These permits can be bought and sold. Thus, if a firm finds it relatively cheap to reduce sulfur emissions, it can reduce its emissions to below its permitted level and sell its excess rights or permits to emit sulfur dioxide. A firm having difficulty meeting its own permitted emission levels could then buy these permits. The net effect will be a given reduction in pollution at a lower cost than if each firm had to meet an inflexible target.

To eastern coal miners, however, the relevant feature of the CAA amendments was not the fact that permits were tradeable. Rather, it was the flexibility of the system that was most threatening. Under the law, firms were allowed to meet their emission targets any way they chose. The fear was that rather than install scrubbers and stick with high-sulfur coal, many utilities would switch to low-sulfur, western coal. This fear was borne out. Moreover, railroad deregulation, as well as a subsequent decline in freight charges, independently accelerated this trend after 1990. As a consequence, about 25 percent fewer scrubbers were installed after the CAA amendments passed than were originally predicted.[6]

JOB LOSS: DIRECT EFFECTS AND THE MULTIPLIER

Job loss from acid-rain control was predicted to be fairly centralized in western Kentucky, northern West Virginia, and Illinois. These regions mined a lot of high-sulfur coal, and more than half of the coal produced was sold to electric utilities.[7] Both the U.S. EPA and the Labor Department published job-loss predictions in 1989 that suggested the likely disappearance from 1990 to 2000 of between 15,000 and 20,000 coal-mining "job slots," or an average of 1,500 to 2,000 per year. After some last minute changes to the final legislation, which provided incentives to utilities for scrubber installation, the EPA lowered its short-run estimate of job-slot losses to a range of 600 to 1,000 per year, or 3,000 to 5,000 in total by 1995. "Job slots" lost are somewhat different than "jobs" lost, since some miners employed in 1990 would have retired or left the industry for other reasons prior to the mine shutdowns.[8]

Beyond the direct job losses to miners, there was much fear of secondary job loss via a "multiplier" effect. Employment multipliers derive their theoretical legitimacy from what is known as a "base model" of economic development. Under the base model, a primary export sector (e.g., mining, agriculture, logging, or manufacturing) brings wealth into a community. Contractions in a community's export base get translated into secondary job losses in the service sector.

Seeming to bear out this theory, as noted earlier more than two dozen retail and service businesses closed their doors in Marion County in the first half of the 1990s. Predictions of secondary multiplier effects from acid-rain control came from the U.S. Labor Department study, which was performed by the omnipresent Data Resources, Inc. (DRI), the economic consulting firm we encountered in chapter 2. As one observer of the coal debates puts it: "No one disputed the multiplier estimates that each coal mining job lost would cost from one and a third to two additional jobs in the communities that are so dependent on high incomes from the mines."

This quote reflects a common misunderstanding about secondary multipliers—that all of the indirect job loss would in fact occur "in the communities that are so dependent on high incomes from the mines." Actually, secondary job-loss estimates are typically calculated on a regional basis. For example, when a coal company in rural eastern Illinois shuts down and reduces its demand for truck tires, a tire distributor in urban Chicago may have to lay off a worker. Small communities hit by primary job losses will seldom absorb much of the total ripple effect generated by direct layoffs.

But this nuance is typically lost in the debate. Instead, people think about grocery-store clerks, teachers, and beauticians in the coal- or timber-dependent communities themselves. Certainly *if* these types of large secondary multiplier effects were indeed present at a local level, coal job-slot losses would snowball, thereby generating very serious impacts on the local economy. In the coal country, as in timber-dependent regions of the Northwest, it was these secondary multiplier arguments that underlay the higher-end predictions for job loss and generated much of the apprehension on the ground.

In terms of direct job losses, the initial job-slot predictions appear to

TABLE 4.1. Coal miners claiming CAA
adjustment assistance, 1993–1998

State	Claimants
IL	1,732
IN	878
OH	384
WV	708
KY	1,066
MO	200
WV-PA-OH	1,825
TOTAL	6,793

Source: U.S. Department of Labor, Employment
and Training Administration.

have been on the high side, though not dramatically so. The predictions were 15,000 to 20,000 job slots lost over the entire decade. The actual figure for jobs looks to be under 10,000. The evidence comes from the number of coal miners who put in claims for adjustment assistance. Under the CAA amendments, job training centers or other institutions, such as labor unions, that act on behalf of coal miners who lose their jobs could apply for federal retraining dollars. Because the package included extended unemployment benefits, miners had a strong incentive to get signed up. However, due to a limited window for applications, some eligible miners did not receive benefits. Table 4.1 shows that, from the time the first grant was awarded in 1993, through the summer of 1998, federal retraining benefits of one form or another had gone out to about 6,800 workers.

By 1998, the CAA amendment-induced layoffs had slacked off. As a consequence, the number of claimants is not likely to rise much more through the end of this century. Although not all eligible miners made claims, and recognizing that some jobs were lost through attrition and not layoffs, a conservative estimate is that the total jobs lost to clean air legislation over the 1990s will be less than 10,000.

SECONDARY EFFECTS

What about the indirect job losses? Were the secondary multipliers of 1.3 to 2.0 nonmining jobs for every mining job on target? This question is impossible to answer definitively, however, a look at the two counties highlighted in the *Times* article mentioned earlier suggest not. Looking first at Marion County, retail businesses in the first half of the 1990s laid off 400 workers. Coal-mining employment over this period dropped by 620 workers. Taken alone and assuming—unrealistically—that all of the job losses in retail were due to coal-mining layoffs, these figures argue for a secondary multiplier of about 0.66. This is half the *low-end* of U.S. Labor Department/DRI estimate.

However, the numbers should not be taken alone. First, in addition to coal-mining jobs, the county also suffered 650 (unrelated) layoffs in manufacturing—the other half of the so-called "export base." Including these "primary" jobs drops the estimated secondary multiplier effect from layoffs in the "base" down to 0.33. Again, this is a worst-case scenario, since it ascribes all the shutdowns in the retail sector to declines in "base" employment. The point here is that, even in a county hit hard by both coal mine and manufacturing shutdowns, secondary-multiplier effects appear to be quite small.

Moreover, compared to layoffs in mining and manufacturing, job losses in the retail and service sectors are much less likely to lead to structural unemployment or large drops in income for workers. In most coal dependent counties, employment in the trade and service sectors continued to expand in the face of job losses in the "base." For example, at the same time that the twenty-seven retail businesses were shutting down in Marion County, others were opening. On net, the county actually gained 510 jobs in retail and wholesale trade over the period 1990 to 1995. In all sectors, in spite of large job losses in coal mining (and comparably sized, unrelated layoffs in manufacturing), the county gained about 1,000 jobs. Similarly, Monongalia County lost over 1,400 mining jobs in the first half of the 1990s, but saw increases in every other category of employment except in the other base sector—manufacturing. On net, the county gained about 5,000 jobs from 1990 to 1995.

Table 4.2 illustrates a similar job-tracking exercise for all the counties in northern West Virginia that faced coal layoffs from 1990 to 1996, and whose coal-mining employment in 1990 was greater than 1 percent of the nonfarm workforce. One of these was Harrison County, mentioned earlier, whose high unemployment rates and shrinking job base in the 1980s epitomized the dire conditions in the coal country. In spite of earning an initial "high risk" ranking for further job losses from acid-rain control, the county lost only twenty additional coal-mining jobs over the period 1990 to 1996. On net, it gained a total of over 5,000 new jobs.

Table 4.2 lists coal-mining job losses, as well as changes in manufacturing employment. (Note that not all these coal job losses can be laid at

TABLE 4.2. Coal mining layoffs and total job growth in northern West Virginia, 1990–1995

County	Coal's percentage of employment, 1990	Unem- ployment rate 1994	Change in coal employment 1990–1996	Change in manufacturing employment 1990–1996	Change in "base" employment 1990–1996	Change in total employment[a] 1990–1996
Grant	21.3	10.9	−590	270	−320	−660
Nicholas	17.8	13.4	−870	−80	−950	260
Braxton	10.5	15.8	−440	90	−350	670
Marion	9.6	11.2	−830	−710	−1,540	400
Marshall	9.5	9.2	−270	−380	−650	−50
Barbour	9.4	11.7	−90	10	−80	320
Monongalia	6.8	5.0	−1,730	−180	−1,910	5,260
Upshur	4.2	9.8	−200	−90	−290	580
Brooke	4.0	8.5	−130	−330	−460	430
Randolph	3.1	10.5	−210	410	200	1,610
Harrison	1.7	8.4	−20	410	390	5,020
Mineral	1.7	6.6	−80	−610	−690	−500
Lewis	1.2	12.0	−60	−60	−120	330
Kanawha	1.1	6.6	−30	−1,250	−1,280	12,650
TOTAL			−4,850	−2,260	−7,110	27,070

[a] Total nonfarm payroll.
Source: West Virginia Bureau of Employment.

the door of the CAA amendments. Productivity increases have proceeded at the same rapid 1980s pace throughout the 1990s.) Summing these together gives us the "export base." If a secondary multiplier is present, then one would expect to see decreases in base employment leading to even larger drops in total employment. However, comparing changes in base employment with changes in total nonagricultural employment provides very little support for secondary multiplier effects. Only three counties that experienced coal-mining shutdowns—Grant, Marshall, and Mineral—also suffered county-wide net job losses, and only in Grant County can an argument be made for a persistent secondary multiplier effect.

In Marshall and Mineral Counties, total job losses were less than losses in the base, thus, no secondary multiplier appears to be present. Tiny Grant County—with only 5,300 total workers in 1990—lost 590 coal-mining jobs between 1990 and 1996. Offsetting these losses a bit, the county did gain 270 manufacturing jobs. The net change in the "base" was thus a drop in 320 jobs. Total employment in the county fell by 660 jobs. A base model believer would see this as evidence for a secondary multiplier of just over one—340 nonmining, nonmanufacturing jobs lost for every 320 layoffs in the export base.

However, Nicholas County, which is almost as coal dependent as Grant, lost more coal jobs than did Grant, as well as some manufacturing jobs, and still saw an increase in total employment of 260 jobs. In fact, eight of the eleven counties experienced net job increases despite declines in coal mining coupled often with reductions in manufacturing employment. Moreover, six of these counties were quite small—under 10,000 workers in total.

It is undoubtedly the case that overall job growth in these counties was dampened by the mining layoffs. And it is likely that in small, coal-dependent towns within each county, secondary multiplier effects on the service sector such as those assumed by DRI were observed. However, these case studies indicate clearly that CAA amendment-induced coal-mine shutdowns have not plunged counties into local recessions, nor have they contributed much to local structural unemployment beyond the direct layoffs of coal miners. Even in rural coal counties that are specifically highlighted as vulnerable, any long-term employment secondary multipliers from coal-mining layoffs generally appear to be very close to zero.

Why is this? In the base model of economic development, service, trade, and construction activity emerge as secondary sectors, subsisting, in parasitic fashion, on the wealth generated by the export base. This is a simple story, as well as a misleading one. While exports are important to local economies, the base model fails to capture the resilient network of economic linkages found today in most of America's rural counties.

OFF-BASE WITH THE BASE MODEL

Thomas Power, an economist at the University of Montana, has argued that the "economic base" model really has the economic development story backwards. An export base is only a small part of a healthy economy and it is hardly "primary." We characterize economies that specialize in the production of export commodities as mineral or timber "dependent," and dependent economies are not developed. As Power puts it:

> 'More of the same'—expansion of an already specialized export industry—can hardly be called economic development. Economic development occurs when a complex web of locally oriented economic activities is spun, mak-

ing an area increasingly less dependent on imports, and,
as a result, not as dependent on export earnings.[9]

Moreover, Power argues that the base model ignores other important
sources of local income. Small businesses with regional sales, private
retirement income, government-transfer payments (e.g., social security
and unemployment and veterans benefits), and investment earnings all
generate an income flow into a community, even in the absence of a primary export sector. And even in rural counties traditionally considered to
be dependent on primary commodity exports, these income sources are
quite significant.

Finally, if the "complex web" of locally linked services does not exist,
then wealth brought in by an export industry will simply leak out again
and support very few local service-sector jobs. In the highly dependent
coal communities of Appalachia, this was certainly the pattern. During
the 1980s, a statewide survey showed that Kentucky coal counties had,
simultaneously, the highest level of annual earnings among employed
workers, as well as the highest level of families living in poverty.[10]

This leaves us with two possible ways to characterize a rural economy
with a mining, logging, or other primary export sector. In case one, the
local economy is reasonably well developed and resilient. Here, shutdowns induced by events such as acid-rain control, while certainly caus-
ing hardship for local service industries, would nevertheless be unlikely
to bankrupt them. In the second case, local linkages are thin and, as a
consequence, service jobs are few to begin with. Most of the money spent
by miners ends up outside of the immediate community. In either case,
secondary multiplier effects from a given layoff are likely to be small.

Armed with this theoretical insight, Power went looking for evidence
of employment secondary multiplier effects in western mining communities. He found none. In rural Salmon, Montana, for example:

> During the 1970s, a local mining operation was devel-
> oped, operated, and then shutdown. About 500 jobs were
> added to the economic base only to be lost. For a town
> of 3,000 this was a major change. But tracking what hap-
> pened to the rest of the economy (non-export sectors)
> reveals that the operation neither stimulated the other
> sectors, nor, after its collapse, inhibited their expansion.
> The rest of the economy in fact expanded more rapidly
> when the 'economic base' was in decline.[11]

Returning to acid-rain control and eastern coal-mining towns, here too secondary multiplier effects from mine layoffs are hard to find. If present, they generally are too small to be seen in county-level data, even for counties with small populations. Certainly there is no evidence supporting fears that 1.3 to 2.0 nonmining jobs would disappear for every miner laid off. Significant secondary multipliers have not materialized because the economic base model from which they are derived is mechanistic and outmoded, failing to capture the resilient network of linkages that characterize most rural economies. Of course, local and service retail industries have suffered as a result of coal-mine layoffs, and some, no doubt, have laid off workers as a consequence. Most, however, have not.

The good news from the acid-rain-control experience, therefore, is that fears of widespread job loss via a secondary multiplier effect have not been borne out. With this concern put to rest, we can focus our attention on the bad news: Coal miners have continued to lose their jobs, often in very unfriendly labor-market conditions. Structural unemployment in the eastern coalfields was high in 1990, reflecting a decade of coal-mining and manufacturing job losses, as well as only slow growth in other sectors. It remained high through the 1990s. This is evident from the data in table 4.2. While the national unemployment rate in 1994 was 6.1 percent, only three counties in the table were even close to this average. Half of the counties that were losing coal-mining jobs in the early 1990s already had unemployment rates greater than 10 percent.

Table 4.2 also reveals that West Virginia was suffering not only from coal-mine shutdowns, but from the more general U.S.-wide problem of the flight of manufacturing capital. At the same time the counties lost 4,850 coal-mining jobs, almost half as many manufacturing jobs— 2,260—also disappeared. These job losses, in turn, exacerbated long-standing problems of rural poverty and underdevelopment, especially in Appalachian mountain communities. For many laid off coal miners, attractive jobs close to their homes have been few and far between.

Adjustment Assistance

Most people in Congress acknowledged that the government owed some kind of assistance to workers who would lose their jobs from acid-rain control. But what kind? When the CAA amendments were being debated, two models of adjustment assistance were offered up for consideration. Senator Robert Byrd of West Virginia argued for a buyout. Under his plan, coal miners who lost their jobs as a result of the CAA amendments would be paid by the government a declining fraction of their base salary over three years—80 percent the first year and declining to 50 percent in the final year. This would be in lieu of unemployment benefits, but would include other traditional adjustment assistance options such as job training.

Senator Byrd's logic was that miners, who were entering a very depressed labor market, would need substantial time and resources to retrain and/or relocate. He argued that buyout precedents had been set in the past when specific federal action cost concentrated job losses in particular regions (e.g., when Redwood National Park was expanded). However, in the more conservative environment of the late 1980s, Senator Byrd's final amendment failed on a 50 to 49 vote in the Senate.

What finally emerged was a bill that tinkered with the existing U.S. system for dislocated workers—the Job Training Partnership Act (JTPA). Congress appropriated an additional $50 million per year from 1991 to 1995 to address the needs of workers who were laid off as a consequence of the CAA amendments.[12] JTPA provides dislocated workers with job-search assistance, access to classroom training, and, occasionally, subsidies for job training.

Job-search assistance is a relatively low-cost service that is widely acknowledged to benefit dislocated workers. In areas of high structural unemployment, however, the applicability of a program that facilitates the job search process is clearly limited. More valued in coal counties are genuine retraining experiences. Miners, highly skilled workers who had proven able to land the best jobs in the region, tend to be fairly well educated.[13] Even with good retraining, however, miners were virtually certain to experience significant income declines; nothing in the coal country pays like coal mining.

In addition, taking time off to retrain does not make economic sense for older workers. Since they don't have enough working years to recoup the initial investment, they are better off not foregoing a couple of years' wages to undertake retraining. Thus, if they can find work, they can do better heading directly into the labor market, even for lower pay. Many older dislocated workers find it very hard to make a transition to a different kind of work, however. In addition, they often face job discrimination. Given this, they may become discouraged and try to eke out a living one way or another until they can draw from social security or a private pension.

In general, job-training programs have a bad reputation among U.S. workers that is mostly deserved. But not because job training can't work. In his review of the impact of the JTPA, Michigan State economist

Robert LaLonde explains that the program has disappointed largely because "we got what we paid for."

After going though a job-counseling and job-search program, JTPA clients can choose either a short-term training program (typically six to eight weeks long) or enroll in community college with tuition paid for up to two years. The problem with the latter option is that JTPA generally provides no income, child care, or travel support, nor access to health insurance. Laid off workers thus have to rely on unemployment insurance (UI) benefits to pay the mortgage and the doctor bills, as well as to feed the family while they are in training. Normally, UI lasts about six months. Given that most workers will have used up a good chunk of their benefits by the time they even get into training, short-term training programs are all that they can afford.

Research has shown that dislocated workers do in fact benefit from receiving both vocational and academic community college–level courses that are relatively rigorous and demanding. On average, the benefit of an additional year of college to a worker is that it qualifies him or her for a new job with a raise in salary of about $1,800. If this is the economic return on a year's worth of full-time, fully accredited education, it should not be surprising to discover that a two- or three-month program has virtually no impact on a worker's future earnings. And this is exactly what we do find when we look at evaluations of short-term training.

According to LaLonde, all analyses of short-term JTPA training for dislocated workers find it to be ineffective. The studies compare the average post-layoff earnings of trainee graduates with "similar" laid off workers who didn't go through training. On average those "who have the option of receiving classroom instruction or on-the-job training derive *no additional benefit* from having access to those services"[14] [emphasis added]. A more recent 1996 study by the New England Federal Reserve found comparable results: "Workers who enrolled in education or training obtained jobs that *paid about the same* as those who received only basic services, after adjusting for other measurable differences in qualifications"[15] [emphasis added].

In some cases, short-term JTPA training programs undoubtedly help workers gain confidence, get a taste of new options, and get back on their feet again. However, in terms of earning potential, short-term JTPA training is simply worthless. Again, this is not because training does not work. Rather, it reflects a woefully inadequate commitment of resources to provide dislocated workers with retraining opportunities.

How did the JTPA program work for the coal miners? Under the

CAA amendments, Congress provided access to extended UI benefits. Miners who jumped through the right hoops could get income benefits (though no health insurance) for up to two years, which allowed them to pursue long-term retraining options. However, this left three big problems. First, not all eligible miners made it through the hoops, and as a consequence they were forced to settle for inadequate, short-term retraining. Second, in an environment with high and persistent structural unemployment, "training for what jobs?" emerged as a real problem. As a consequence, the job training some miners received did them little good in terms of finding work that matched their new skills. Finally, even those who succeeded in getting through a longer program and obtained work for which they were retrained often found that their incomes dramatically diminished.

In 1997, the average coal miner in Monongalia County, West Virginia, brought home $46,500 annually. In contrast, the earnings for the average worker in the county that year was only $23,000. A successful two-year investment in training by a miner might lead to a salary increase over that of about $3,000 or so per year—not much compensation for a worker who has had his paycheck cut in half. Drops in income on the order of 50 percent clearly illustrate one thing. If we ask, What group of people has sacrificed more than any other in our nation on behalf of a cleaner environment? the answer is, without a doubt, coal miners. Many of these men, and their families, have foregone well over $100,000 in net income as a consequence of environmental regulation.

From the miner's perspective, the adjustment-assistance program that was crafted by Congress has done little to either help them find new work at decent pay or to acknowledge the large losses that they have sustained on behalf of cleaner air. In communities that are facing high structural unemployment, job-search assistance helps little. Even good job retraining is of limited value, and eligibility rules kept significant numbers of miners from access to the extended UI benefits they needed to retrain. In addition, the legislation did nothing to address the needs of older workers; extended UI was only available for workers in training.

Given this, some variant on Senator Byrd's buyout plan would have been the better option to (1) help bridge older workers to retirement and (2) help the nation capitalize on what this skilled and productive group of workers had to offer. To engage in serious retraining, and possible relocation, miners needed financial support for at least a couple of years. Without it, most were doomed, as discussed in chapter 1, to follow the general path of workers who were dislocated from high-paying union jobs—a plunge, however delayed, into nonunionized, low-skill, low-wage, service-sector work.

It is worth underscoring this point not only for coal miners such as John Beveridge, who were laid off due to the acid-rain provisions of the CAA amendments, but also on behalf of the much larger number of miners who lost their jobs as a result of automation; and for the manufacturing workers who were laid off in those same northern West Virginia towns as their plants headed overseas; and for workers such as Mary Smith, who was downsized as a consequence of "trade and technology" from her textile plant job in Alabama. Retraining, when decently funded and well designed, can work. However, the U.S. system of adjustment assistance simply does not work to meet the needs of most American workers in today's economy.

TIMBER WORKERS AND OLD-GROWTH FORESTS

Like coal miners in the East, timber workers in the Northwest are quite familiar with boom and bust cycles, and throughout the 1980s they were under continual and severe job pressure from automation. Timber has been harvested commercially in the Northwest since the early 1900s. The housing boom that followed World War II, coupled with improvements in transportation and the introduction of the gas-powered chain saw, led to record cuts in the 1940s and 1950s. These harvests, however, occurred mainly on private lands. In 1950, the 1.6 billion board feet of timber harvested from national forests in Washington, Oregon, and northern California represented only 8 percent of the Pacific states' total of 20 billion board feet. However, harvests from federal lands soon accelerated, accounting by the mid 1960s for between one-third and one-half of the total.[16] And federal harvest levels stayed high through the late 1980s, as shown in figure 4.2.

Over the decades, increased mechanization in harvesting, transporting, and milling reduced the number of jobs in the timber industry for a given output level. Mills were consolidated and labor forces were reduced to increase productivity and efficiency. From the 1970s to the 1980s, the number of workers needed to cut and process 1 million board feet of lumber fell by roughly 20 percent—from 9.1 to 7.4.[17] At the same time, the bulk of new U.S. timber investment was bypassing the Northwest, leaving the region with increasingly antiquated mills. Attracted by lower labor costs and the growth of eastern markets, from 1978 to 1990, the nation's seven biggest lumber and plywood manufacturers reduced capac-

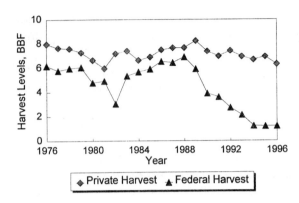

FIGURE 4.2. Private
and federal harvests
(including all federal
lands) in Washington
and Oregon,
1976–1996.
Source: Warren (1998).

ity in the Northwest by 34 percent, while increasing capacity in the South by 121 percent.[18]

On top of these two trends of mechanization at existing mills and low levels of reinvestment, the recession of the early 1980s also hit the region very hard. Figure 4.3 illustrates employment trends in the lumber- and wood-products industries for Oregon and Washington States. (Throughout this discussion, I will present data for Oregon and Washington, excluding northern California where another 15,000 workers were employed in 1990. This is because data on the timber industry for the spotted owl country in northern California alone are not readily available.[19]) From an employment peak in 1978 of 136,000, lumber- and wood-products employment in Oregon and Washington plummeted to 95,000 in the space of four years. Federal agencies responded by increasing federal harvest levels in the mid-1980s by half a billion board feet, as shown in figure 4.2.

The record timber sales spurred industry employment back up to 108,000 in 1989, however, proportional job loss due to automation continued. Recession hit again in the late 1980s, sending the industry into another tailspin: Oregon and Washington wood-products employment fell to 90,000 in three years. It was into this environment that a small, reclusive owl rose to national prominence.

As early as 1972, the northern spotted owl was argued by scientists to be closely associated with the habitat conditions of old-growth forests. Researchers began to see the owl as an indicator species, gauging the overall health of the old-growth ecosystem, 90 percent of which had already been logged. For the agencies charged with protecting the owl and its habitat, however, the task seemed politically impossible. Timber-

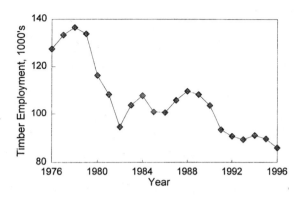

FIGURE 4.3. Lumber- and wood-products employment in Washington and Oregon, 1976–1996.
Source: Warren (1998).

dependent communities, already suffering from automation-based down-sizing, were now facing a looming recession. Setting aside enough land to give adequate protection to the owl, many believed, would mean further dramatic decreases in the timber available to these communities.

Facing these pressures, in 1987, the U.S. Fish and Wildlife Service failed to list the northern spotted owl as a threatened species under the Endangered Species Act. Environmentalists appealed the agency decision in court, and, in 1988, the first injunction was placed on federal timber sales in the region. However, timber sales actually continued through 1990 via the intercession of the U.S. Congress. In 1990, the owl was finally listed as threatened, and, in 1991, timber sales from federal lands were shut down by a second court order. Judge William Dwyer, who presided in that case, found "a deliberate and systematic refusal by the Forest Service and the Fish and Wildlife Service to comply with the laws protecting wildlife . . . , (demonstrating) a remarkable series of violations of the environmental laws."[20]

The fall in harvest levels left many vulnerable communities in the Pacific Northwest struggling and angry. With the owl providing a tangible symbol, debate between old-growth protection advocates and timber workers rose to a fevered pitch of competing sound bites and bumper stickers. However, by the time Bill Clinton campaigned in the Northwest in 1992, many parties were ready for a more civil discussion of the issues. If elected, Clinton promised to convene a summit within one hundred days of his inauguration to provide a forum for those involved and to begin development of a long-term solution to the problem.

Before the summit, many members of timber communities had accepted the fact that the allowable cut would not increase. The scientific evidence and the opinion of the American public supported old-growth protection, and no forest plan could pass through Judge Dwyer's court unless it complied with environmental laws. Therefore, many community representatives used the summit to expose the problems that their towns were facing—as an immediate consequence of the recession, not spotted owls—and to request economic assistance. A professor from the University of Washington observed, "We're moving into a process which looks an awful lot like what happened to the inner city. We're seeing the collapse of families, disintegration of families, disintegration of communities, loss of morale, homelessness, stranded elderly people, people whose lives are in disarray because of substance abuse."[21]

Many community members clearly recognized that their local problems were symptoms of a dramatically changing regional economy. They knew what they had to do to adjust, but they did not have the resources to do so. The mayor of one timber-dependent town explained: "We are working on tourism, and we're doing everything we can to diversify, but our biggest problem with diversification is that we have no industrial park. We have no warehouses. I don't know how many times we get inquiries for warehouse space. All we have to market is an empty log truck and a rusty spar pole. The industry in our county has been 85 percent timber, and it just has never been necessary to have the kinds of things you need to diversify."[22]

After the summit, an interagency governmental team evaluated ten policy options for forest management in the northern spotted owl region, which differed in the quantity and location of land placed in reserves, the activities permitted within the reserves, the delineation of land outside the reserves, and the activities allowed within the areas outside reserves. In their analysis, the team attempted to gauge the effects each option would have on the natural ecosystems and species, as well as its effects on timber-dependent communities.

In July 1993, the Clinton administration released "The Forest Plan for a Sustainable Economy and a Sustainable Environment." The Forest Plan, with minor modifications, was deemed adequate by Judge Dwyer for the protection of the spotted owl that was mandated by the Endangered Species Act. With Dwyer's approval, the remaining injunctions on federal timber sales were lifted.

Key elements of the ecological dimension of the Forest Plan included the use of watersheds as the fundamental building blocks, ten adaptive Management Areas for experimental forestry, protection of most old-growth in reserves, and authorization of some salvage and thinning within reserves. The plan allowed for annual timber harvests of 1.2 billion board feet in the spotted owl forests, later revised downward to 1.1 billion, which was far lower than the 1980 levels of over 5 billion. Finally, the Forest Plan also proposed an economic adjustment package that, while including the kind of retraining options that were offered to coal miners, reflected, at least in its conception, a broader regional development agenda.

JOB LOSS: PREDICTIONS AND OUTCOMES

In the political debate leading up to the timber summit, the forest-products industry in the Northwest armed itself with a nice round number: 102,000 jobs were at stake from spotted owl protection. In fact, predicting job losses from spotted owl protection became a popular (and reasonably lucrative) game among economists in the Pacific Northwest in the late 1980s and early 1990s. In rough form, here's how the first round was played:

1. Pick a "baseline" harvest level in the national forests. Your baseline will tell you what the harvest "would have been" in the year 2000 without any restriction. The harvest should be measured in millions of board feet. To illustrate, let's choose 5,000 million (5 billion) board feet.
2. Pick a "primary multiplier" that relates employment in the timber industry to the baseline harvest. For example, you might pick a number such as 6 workers employed per 1 million board feet cut.
3. Multiply the "baseline" harvest from (1) by the multiplier in (2). This gives you total employment supported by the baseline harvest. In this case, 5,000 million board feet × 6 workers per 1 million board feet = 30,000 jobs that are dependent on national forest timber under the "baseline."
4. Pick a harvest-reduction percentage due to spotted owl protection. Let's say 50 percent.
5. Multiply the "baseline" employment from (3) by the reduction in the harvest from (4). This gives the magic number. In this case, 30,000 jobs × 0.50 = 15,000 jobs lost as a consequence of the timber set asides.
6. Stuff the predicted layoff number from (5) into a thirty-page report, and then collect your consultant's paycheck.

At least six different groups of economists played the game by 1990, generating estimates of direct job loss in the timber industry. Four of these studies, roughly comparable in their overall modeling scenarios, employed harvest baseline levels close to the mid-1980s average. They predicted total job losses (direct and indirect) from the reduction of harvests on federal lands of between 21,000 and 87,000. The results differed depending on the primary multipliers and the harvest-reduction levels chosen. Not surprisingly, the high-end study was sponsored by the American Forest Resources Association (AFRA), a national trade group. The low-end estimates came from a study by the Wilderness Society, an environmental group.[23]

To confuse matters, not all of this projected job loss could be attributed to spotted owl protection. Because harvest levels in the late 1980s were not sustainable even from an industrial forestry point of view, the Forest Service had already been planning significant harvest reductions. Removing job declines from this source, and looking only at *direct* job losses in the timber industry, substantially closed the gap between the estimates; spotted owl protection by itself was estimated to generate direct timber-industry employment losses ranging from 8,500 to 18,200 by the year 2000.[24]

The AFRA-sponsored study got their big numbers (87,000 and 18,200) primarily by arguing in step (2) of the game that job categories directly threatened by harvest reductions should be broadened beyond a "narrow" definition of timber workers: loggers, saw mill and plywood workers, and secondary (e.g., kitchen cabinets and mobile homes) wood processors. AFRA also included employees of pulp and paper mills, Forest Service and other government employees, and a variety of secondary forest-related jobs.[25] The other studies stayed closer to the narrower view of jobs that were directly dependent on timber. In retrospect, this narrower perspective has proven justified. For example, pulp and paper employment in Oregon and Washington fell by only 400 from 1988 to 1996, while employment in lumber and wood products fell by 23,000.[26]

How well was the job-loss prediction game played? Harvests from national forests in Oregon and Washington States quickly declined from a "baseline" 1983 to 1988 average of 4,672 million board feet, to the 1,100 million level allotted by the Clinton Forest Plan. In fact, by 1994, harvests from national forests were at 800 million board feet and fell even lower over the next two years.[27] Thus, 1994 is the year that we should use to assess federal timber harvests close to the Clinton Forest Plan level. Figure 4.1 shows the employment losses in Oregon and Washington using the narrow definition of timber workers that was previously discussed. Average employment from 1983 to 1988 was about 105,000. By

1994, it had declined to 91,000, for a loss of 14,000 jobs. How much of this job loss was due to spotted owl protection?

Table 4.3 sorts this out in a crude way. The total decline in the federal harvest was about 3,800 million board feet. At the same time, however, and unrelated to the spotted owl, harvests on private and state land fell by 1,400 million board feet.[28] Thus, around 73 percent of the 14,000 jobs lost—10,230—can be ascribed to federal forest cutbacks. However, as noted earlier, not all of the harvest reductions in the national forests were in the service of owl habitat. Somewhere between 1,000 and 1,500 million board feet reflected the reduction that the Forest Service had planned *prior* to the inclusion of spotted owl in the Endangered Species List.[29] All of this means that protecting the habitat of the spotted owl took out of production only 2,300 to 2,800 million board feet of the federal total of 3,800. Thus, of the 10,230 lost job slots due to federal reductions, between 60 percent and 73 percent—6,190 to 7,540 jobs—were probably due to protecting the old-growth and its resident owl.

These figures may be a bit low. They do not include northern California, they are based on the narrow definition of timber workers, and, over time, industry is liable to adjust its production methods to the lower harvest levels, in the process becoming more efficient and laying off additional workers. However, the bulk of the job losses are certainly to be found in this sample of workers. It took only four years to achieve and then go well below the harvest restrictions envisioned in the studies, and yet job losses remain at the low end of the predicted levels.

It is worth digging a bit deeper into the details of these predictions. In step (4) of the game outlined earlier, the studies generally failed to anticipate harvest declines as sharp as were actually required by the Clinton Forest Plan. Rather than the 2,300 to 2,800 million board feet range,

TABLE 4.3. The employment impact of spotted owl habitat protection

Source of harvest reduction	Total harvest reduction (MBF)	Percentage of total harvest reduction	Job reduction
Federal[a]	3,800	73	10,230
Pre-spotted owl	1,000–1,500	26–40	2,690–4,040
Spotted owl	2,300–2,800	60–73	6,190–7,540
Private and state	1,400	26	3,770
TOTAL	5,200	100	14,000

[a] National forests only.
Source: Warren (1998).

most of the estimates assumed harvest declines of below 2,000 million board feet.[30] Holding everything else constant, this error should have led us to observe larger, not smaller, job losses than were predicted. However, step (5) in the game was also flawed, generating a bias in the opposite direction. All of the studies assumed that a drop in the harvest would lead to a proportional drop in employment, that is, a 10 percent reduction in the former leading to a 10 percent reduction in the latter. However, if we compare actual Oregon and Washington harvest levels against actual timber employment, a 10 percent decline in the former has led to only a 6 percent drop in the latter.[31]

Another way to put this is that productivity declined as harvests fell and the industry downsized. Over the period 1976 to 1982, it took 9.1 timber workers to harvest and process 1 million board feet; the average for the years 1982 to 1991 was 7.4 timber workers. However, this trend of increasing productivity abruptly reversed itself in the 1990s. Over the period 1992 to 1996, there were 10.1 timber workers employed for every 1 million board feet harvested. What happened?

First, by the late 1980s, opportunities for further mechanization began to dry up.[32] Second, as raw log exports dropped, employment began to shift from logging into the production of more labor-intensive secondary wood products.[33] Third, employment at some mills was sustained by increased imports of raw timber. And, finally, facing dramatic harvest declines, the industry may have been forced into logging and milling timber from less attractive, smaller, or more geographically segregated stands, thus requiring more workers. A similar phenomenon was observed after safety regulations were put in place in the underground coal-mining industry in the early 1970s: productivity declined and employment rose.[34]

Whatever the cause, if they continue, productivity declines will eventually render Northwest timber producers less competitive and will lead to long-run layoffs. In that case, over a decade or two, we may see larger employment declines as the timber industry adjusts to the new lower harvest levels. But it was the short-run, direct job losses of the 1990s that were of immediate concern to timber workers and timber-dependent communities. Unanticipated productivity declines have dramatically cushioned the short-term employment blow from federal harvest reductions in the service of protecting owl habitat. Direct timber-industry job losses will, in all probability, be less than 10,000—at the low end of the predictions—despite larger-than-expected logging cutbacks on federal lands.

What about indirect job losses? In round two of the job-loss prediction game, our friend from the eastern acid-rain debate—the "secondary multiplier"—crossed the country to play a pivotal role. Predictions of secondary multipliers ranged from a low of zero (the Wilderness Society) to a high of 1.31 nontimber jobs for every direct timber job lost (AFRA). The addition of these indirect impacts boosted the estimates for total (direct and indirect) job-slot loss due to spotted owl protection on federal land into a range from 8,500 (the Wilderness Society) to 42,000 (AFRA).

Now, 42,000 is a big number, but still a lot less than the timber industry's sound-bite figure of 102,000 jobs likely to be lost as a result protection of the spotted owl. Where did *that* prediction come from? The AFRA study tacked on another 60,000 (direct and indirect) jobs at risk if *private* landowners were forced to cut their harvest levels to protect old-growth habitat. While this was never a serious possibility, it nevertheless provided the padding for a suitably large job-loss estimate.

THE BASE MODEL STRIKES OUT AGAIN

In the previous section, we were able to hold up the direct job-loss predictions, in a rough and ready fashion, against the way things have actually turned out. We found that the low-end job-loss estimates were correct, though not for the right reasons. Unfortunately, there is no way of systematically checking on the predictions of secondary employment impacts, especially since the primary and secondary jobs are not necessarily geographically linked: logging cutbacks in rural Oregon might lead to layoffs by chain saw manufacturers in Seattle. But as we did for the coal country, we can evaluate the local, county-wide impact of declines in the timber "base" on employment in other sectors.

Table 4.4 undertakes such an exercise for the state of Oregon, showing all counties experiencing timber layoffs and in which lumber and wood products employment exceeded 5 percent of total nonagricultural employment. The table compares changes in timber, manufacturing, and total employment, this time over the period 1989 (the business-cycle peak) to 1994 (when harvest levels hit the Clinton Forest Plan target).

There is one noticeable difference in this table from the West Virginia data presented earlier. Counties in Oregon were more dependent on timber than West Virginia counties were on coal. In at least six Oregon counties, 15 percent or more jobs were directly timber-related; in tiny Grant County, which is located in the east-central part of Oregon, 24 percent, or 650 of its 2,700 total jobs, were in lumber and wood prod-

TABLE 4.4. Timber layoffs and total job growth in Oregon, 1989–1994

County	Timber's percentage of employment, 1989	Unemployment rate percentage, 1994	Change in timber employment, 1989–1994	Change in manufacturing[a] employment, 1989–1994	Change in "base" employment, 1989–1994	Change in total[b] employment, 1989–1994
Douglas	24	9.1	–1,820	300	–1,520	100
Grant	24	9.7	–140	–10	–150	130
Harney	22	10.1	–70	–30	–100	70
Klamath	18	8.7	–970	70	–900	110
Wallowa	17	7.3	–100	70	–30	90
Curry	16	7.7	–300	–40	–340	180
Union	14	6.4	–190	170	–20	520
Coos	13	8.6	–720	30	–690	940
Linn	13	7.0	–690	580	–110	2,780
Columbia	13	6.5	–440	180	–260	–590
Josephine	12	9.1	–710	–720	–1,430	1,060
Morrow	12	8.2	–80	20	–60	290
Deschutes	11	7.2	–660	500	–160	8,550
Jackson	11	6.7	–1,070	890	–180	7,690
Lane	10	5.5	–3,500	5,700	2,200	11,190
Baker	10	8.0	–10	40	30	420
Hood River	8	7.9	–50	150	100	890
Clatsop	6	6.4	–250	–490	–740	310
Benton	5	2.6	–370	2,100	1,730	4,170
TOTAL			–11,640	10,240	–1,400	38,900

[a] Excluding lumber and wood products manufacturing.
[b] Total nonfarm payroll.
Source: State of Oregon, Employment Department.

ucts. However, in spite of this fairly high timber dependence, predictions of regional disaster predicated on an economic base model of local economic development clearly did not materialize. From the information shown in table 4.4, in only one county (Columbia) is there any evidence for a persistent local secondary multiplier effect; that is, a loss of 260 base jobs and 590 total jobs suggests a secondary multiplier of a little over 1.

Consider, by contrast, Douglas County, Oregon. In 1989, it was 24 percent timber dependent and over the next five years it lost a whopping 1,820 lumber- and wood-product jobs. Nevertheless, the county still registered a small increase in total employment from 1989 to 1994. Notice as well that a couple of the counties that lost large numbers of timber jobs—Jackson, Lane, and Deschutes—saw substantial job growth over the same period. In contrast to northern West Virginia, the spotted owl country on the west side of Oregon experienced rapid economic growth in the early 1990s.

This is clear from the data presented on manufacturing employment. While West Virginia lost half as many manufacturing jobs as coal jobs from 1990 to 1996, Oregon manufacturing actually *grew* by almost the number of timber jobs lost from 1989 to 1994. Moreover, evidence for entrenched structural unemployment—1994 rates above 9 percent—is present in only four Oregon counties, compared to eight of the twelve West Virginia counties (with several of the coal counties registering rates greater than 12 percent).

Again, this is not to say that small towns within each of these counties saw no secondary layoffs from owl-induced declines in timber-industry employment. At the local level, multiplier effects could certainly be found. Instead, the point is that fears of widespread "ripple effects" on local jobs are not much in evidence when we move to the county level. This highlights once more the way in which a mechanical economic base model underestimates the resilience and flexibility of America's rural economies.

Beyond the county level, any regional secondary job impacts were simply swamped by the dynamics of robust growth in the economy of the Northwest. And it is very likely that the underlying health of the Northwest economy rests partially on forest habitat protection. In 1995, a group of sixty Northwest resource and environmental economists (myself included) endorsed a "consensus" report that maintained that if there was any base underlying growth in the region, it was not in natural resources, but rather in social and natural amenities.

> Anyone working with new residents and businesses coming into the Pacific Northwest is familiar with one factor that is driving the economy: The region is perceived as providing a superior, attractive environment in which to live, work and do business. . . . The natural environment appears to be especially important.
>
> The region retains a good part of its natural pristine character and is relatively uncrowded compared to other areas. These environmental features are not just aesthetic qualities that are nice but of little economic importance. They are also one source of the economic vitality of the region because of these two basic facts:

- Many people move to this region, and remain here, because they want to enjoy its high quality living environment.
- That growth in population stimulates the development of new businesses and the expansion of existing ones.

Of course, economic causality does not run one way, with migration stimulating job creation. Job creation also stimulates migration. A complex dynamic process has been triggered in the region. One part of that dynamic process seems to be clearly tied to the region's amenities.[35]

While forest protection may indeed be promoting the overall economic health of the region, it has cost some timber workers their jobs. What efforts did the Clinton Forest Plan make to assist timber workers and their communities as they faced the federal harvest reductions?

ADJUSTMENT ASSISTANCE AND THE FOREST PLAN

The Forest Plan had, at least in principle, a broader agenda than the aid package that was provided to coal miners. In addition to boosting funding for conventional JTPA services—training and job placement—the Forest Plan had two more innovative elements: assistance to rural communities and the Jobs in the Woods program. These elements made up the Northwest Economic Adjustment Initiative, which was dubbed simply "the Initiative" by its parents in the government bureaucracy.[36]

Community assistance under the Initiative took three main forms. First it guaranteed payments to local governments to replace timber tax revenues. These payments were based on the high harvest levels of the mid-1980s and were to be paid at a declining percentage over 10 years. Second, the Initiative promised increased funding for private economic-development projects (e.g., small business loans and business assistance), as well as the elimination of tax subsidies for the export of raw, unprocessed logs. (Raw log exports from federal lands were already illegal, however, the tax incentives continued to promote private exports.) Finally, the Initiative increased funding for public infrastructure investments.

In practice, little new money was allocated by Congress for the last items mentioned above, Instead, agencies were directed by President Clinton to focus discretionary funds on the affected region. In 1995 and 1996, total Initiative spending (including community assistance, JTPA, and Jobs in the Woods, but excluding the direct payments to counties) was around $215 million per year. While the majority of this was not "new" money for the region, the Initiative undoubtedly generated a significant increase in the inflow of federal dollars.

Table 4.5 illustrates the complex web of governmental agencies that were involved in the Initiative during 1996. To access funds from these

TABLE 4.5. Funding the Northwest economic adjustment initiative, 1996

Departmental program	Funds available	Funds spent in the region	Percentage of available dollars spent in the region
DEPARTMENT OF AGRICULTURE			
Forest Service (community assistance)	12,760,000	10,900,000	85
Forest Service (old-growth diversification)	3,000,000	2,890,000	96
Forest Service (watershed restoration/Jobs in the Woods)	13,510,000	13,510,000	100
Rural Development Administration (rural development)			
Rural business enterprise grants	4,100,000	4,420,000	108
Business and industry loan guarantees	50,000,000	26,680,000	53
Intermediary relending	8,000,000	8,320,000	104
Water and wastewater loans	34,080,000	39,840,000	117
Water and wastewater grants	13,400,000	29,303,000	217
Community facilities loans	24,700,000	21,570,000	87
Community facilities guaranteed loans	8,860,000	0	0
DEPARTMENT OF HOUSING AND URBAN DEVELOPMENT			
Community development block grants	1,900,000	17,750,000	934
DEPARTMENT OF LABOR			
Job Training Partnership Act (Secretary's reserve)	12,000,000	12,970,000	108

(continues)

TABLE 4.5 *(Continued)*

DEPARTMENT OF COMMERCE			
Economic Development Administration	5,000,000	9,930,000	199
DEPARTMENT OF THE INTERIOR			
Bureau of Land Management (watershed restoration/Jobs in the Woods)	7,700,000	7,580,000	98
Fish and Wildlife Service (watershed restoration/Jobs in the Woods)	2,370,000	2,100,000	89
Bureau of Indian Affairs (watershed restoration/Jobs in the Woods)	3,000,000	3,000,000	100
ENVIRONMENTAL PROTECTION AGENCY			
(Clean Water Act Section 319, research grants, nonpoint sources)	5,000,000	5,320,000	106
Total for the initiative	209,450,000	215,810,000	103
OTHER FEDERAL			
Small Business Administration loan guarantees	Target N/A	169,260,000	N/A

Source: Tuchmann et al. (1996).

agencies, each state in the region set up a committee that was composed of representatives of business; local, state and tribal governments; and the general public. These committees, called community economic revitalization teams (CERTs), then solicited and prioritized proposals from businesses and governments in the region.[37] The CERTs would then work with a lead government agency to obtain project funding, perhaps from a variety of agency sources. This "one-stop-shopping" process, while not completely free of bugs, nevertheless worked fairly well to eliminate red tape. It enabled local business and government officials to focus on developing project proposals and reduced delays in getting the dollars flowing.

This influx of federal dollars, which was fairly well targeted toward infrastructure and new business development in communities hit hardest by timber layoffs, helped stabilize overall employment and reduce any secondary job loss. For the timber workers themselves, the Initiative offered a standard JTPA package, as well as an innovative attempt at "conversion": the Jobs in the Woods Program.

Before evaluating these programs, however, it is worth taking a glance back at figure 4.2, which shows employment declines in the timber industry. The figure makes clear that by 1993, when President Clinton held the timber summit in Portland, the worst of the regional job losses had already been sustained. Employment dropped from 109,000 in 1988 to 90,000 during the year of the summit.

In fact, most of these layoffs could be immediately attributed to the recession, not old-growth protection. Federal timber sales had not been substantially reduced until 1990, and there was a backlog of federal timber available. Another way to see that the pre-1993 layoffs were mostly recession induced is to compare harvest reductions on federal land with those on private land, which were unaffected by spotted owl protection. During the early 1980s recession, private harvests fell by 24 percent, however, federal harvests fell by much more—49 percent. From 1988 to 1992, the figures were quite comparable: private harvests were down 27 percent and federal harvests were down 47 percent. These figures suggest that, by 1993, old-growth protection had had little impact on the timber market.

All this meant that the Initiative—through no fault of its own—arrived too late to help most timber workers. Indeed, the spotted-owl job-loss analyses that were discussed earlier were *not* framed as How many additional layoffs? in a recession-battered industry. Rather, as the timber industry recovered from recession, the question was, How many jobs would not return? When the Initiative got rolling in 1994, the bulk of the workers one might have thought it was intended to aid had lost their jobs four to five years earlier and had either moved on to new work or been forced into early retirement. Between 1994 and 1996, however, there were an additional 3,000 layoffs in the Oregon and Washington timber industries, which, again, were not all due to habitat protection. But it was primarily these workers who were served by the JTPA and Jobs in the Woods programs.

Unlike the West Virginia coal miners, these workers found themselves entering a generally robust regional economy, with little structural unemployment. This fact helps explain the reported success of the JTPA programs. By September 1995, some 2,700 workers had enrolled. Just over 1,000 had completed or left the program, with over 80 percent moving into new employment. Those of us who live in the area occasionally see media coverage of retraining success stories: former millworkers turned paralegal, truck driver, or small business owner. Based on the studies of dislocated workers elsewhere, however, paycuts were probably still the reality for most former timber workers. Wages in the Oregon wood-products industries averaged $12.65 per hour; in wholesale and retail trade, for example, the average was $9.83.[38] In addition to lower pay, some workers had to relocate to find jobs. And the loggers, of course, lost not only their jobs, but also a unique, outdoor way of life.

Keeping workers in the forests—full time and at decent pay—was the original promise of the Jobs in the Woods program. The idea was to train and employ former timber workers in "ecosystem management" (e.g., road removal, reforestation, and stream restoration for fish habitat). Margaret Hallock, an economist and director of a training institute in Oregon, put it this way:

> The fundamental goal seemed clear, if not simple; redesign forest and watershed work so that it provides good jobs that help sustain the community. In actuality, this goal represented a huge shift from the situation in 1993; a highly cost-competitive marketplace that produced high turnover, low-wage jobs which rarely drew from the community's labor pool, [instead relying on outside contractors].[39]

The challenge facing the Jobs in the Woods program was to try and transform what had traditionally been low-skill, low-productivity, low-wage work into a high-skill, high-productivity, high-wage industry. Better trained workers, it was argued, would be able to deliver a more cost-effective service because "the work that needs to be done in the woods is not a set of separate, unrelated tasks that can be prescribed by professionals and carried out by unskilled workers. Rather, ecosystem management is a complex and adaptive process requiring skilled workers who understand the ecosystem objectives and can analyze and solve problems in the field—workers who are more akin to 'applied ecologists' than tree-planters."[40]

Under Jobs in the Woods, there was an increase in federal funding for restoration work that was paid for by the Forest Service and Bureau of Land Management. About 600 full-time-equivalent positions were funded, which was not nearly enough to reemploy all laid off timber workers. These funds were to be the initial source of demand for high-skill restoration workers. Over the long term, the hope was that private landowners would shift their own demand for forest workers away from cheap contract crews to the high-skilled work teams. In short, program administrators who wanted Jobs in the Woods to be more than another temporary employment program hoped to foster a conversion, from a living-wage logging industry partially dependent on federal spending, to a living-wage restoration industry with a comparable structure.

The original promise of Jobs in the Woods quickly became hung up in a forest of snags. Under government rules, restoration contracts had to be put out for public bid, which often meant that local contractors lost the work to outsiders. Competitive bidding kept wages low. Short, seasonal jobs were inadequate for family support. Programs for training workers in the high-skill approach were set up—with support from private foundations—in only a handful of demonstration sites. These problems were recognized during the first year and were each addressed to varying degrees. Collectively, however, they led to the bulk of the federal restoration dollars being spent in the traditional fashion—on low-wage, part-time work, often using nonlocal crews.

And yet, on a modest scale, Jobs in the Woods succeeded. Over 150 workers completed the high-skill training program, which was imbedded in a curriculum based on fieldwork that paid decent wages and included benefits. Over a three-year period, high-skilled teams completed about $5 million in projects. In the process, the program demonstrated that the high-skill approach to restoration work was feasible and cost effective; that is, land management agencies could save money through reduced planning and supervision.

The really hard work facing Jobs in the Woods administrators was convincing employers—federal administrators and private landowners—that the new high-skill paradigm made economic sense. Most continued to stick with the traditional low-wage approach. As a consequence, many workers who went through the training programs were not able to get jobs upon graduation. On balance, Jobs in the Woods did succeed in creating a toehold in the restoration industry for skilled, living-wage jobs. Whether this new employment base will grow or not remains to be seen.

The Northwest Economic Adjustment Initiative, in summary, was a mix of infrastructure and development dollars for hard-hit communities, as well as traditional JTPA job search and training combined with a truly innovative conversion initiative for workers. Communities seem to have been fairly well served, and there are lessons to be learned from the Initiative about cutting red tape and effective targeting.

From the worker's perspective, however, both of the programs were deficient in major respects. JTPA training in the Northwest, as elsewhere, was funded at too low a level to make much difference in terms of improving a worker's earnings potential. And Jobs in the Woods—while providing an engaging glimpse at how conversion can work—received too few federal restoration contracts for the program to employ its graduates. Future efforts to promote conversion will need to have more serious commitments of government support on the demand side—commitments sufficiently long term to allow a new industry to develop.

SPOTTED OWLS REDUX

Entering the 1990s, a bitter jobs-versus-environment debate deeply polarized the Pacific Northwest. However, since the timber summit, tensions in the region have softened considerably. In 1994, the *New York Times* ran a front-page article whose headline summarized much of discussion: "Oregon, Foiling Forecasters, Thrives as It Protects Owls." Springfield, Oregon, a former logging center in Lane County, used some of the economic development money from the Initiative to help land a Sony CD plant. The town's mayor put it this way:

> Owls versus jobs was just plain false. What we've got here is quality of life. And as long as we don't screw that up, we'll always be able to attract people and business.[41]

The economy of the Pacific Northwest has left its dependence on natural resources behind. The robust growth in the region is now fueled by its high "quality of life," including easy access to relatively pristine mountains, forests, and oceans.

The spotted owl controversy needs to be understood in the late 1980s context of recession-induced layoffs in the timber industry, and high, regionwide cyclical unemployment. With 20,000 timber workers losing their jobs over the three-year stretch beginning in 1988, industry-sponsored predictions of 20,000 more—plus secondary job losses of comparable magnitude—seemed quite plausible. Widespread economic suffering from the cyclical workings of the economy sparked powerful worker resentment against protecting the old-growth forest.

In fact, since the Clinton Forest Plan went into effect, additional timber industry losses have numbered in the low thousands. The booming economy of the 1990s had no trouble absorbing this second round of layoffs, and under these favorable conditions, the job matching and training services available under JTPA—limited as they were—provided a number of workers with a boost toward finding new jobs. This was in stark contrast to the experience of coal miners in regions with high structural unemployment, where JTPA was simply not up to the task. But just as with the former coal miners, there is, nevertheless, little doubt that several thousand former timber workers paid a real price for environmental protection. While drops in income were not as dramatic as for coal miners, in spite of that, most laid-off timber workers are probably taking home a smaller paycheck than they did in 1988.

SLOPERS AND CARIBOU

There is one last jobs–environment conflict worth noting. For twenty years or so, the oil industry has been trying to obtain permission from Congress to drill for oil in the Arctic National Wildlife Refuge (ANWR) on Alaska's North Slope. ANWR, a 19-million-acre refuge that borders Canada and the Bering Sea, is also home to the Porcupine Caribou herd. Environmentalists have so far staved off attempts to drill in the refuge, arguing that the calving grounds of the herd will be disrupted.

ANWR clearly presents a local jobs–environment trade-off. If significant oil deposits were discovered in the refuge (an event the government views as unlikely), then several thousand new jobs would open up for "slopers"—mostly skilled oil-field and construction workers who spend month-long shifts working out of company barracks. Secondary employment in the oil-field supply industry, which is mostly in Anchorage, would also get a boost. Also, if tax revenues were high enough, the state government could also increase hiring.

The oil industry has tried to turn ANWR into a national jobs–environment debate, with claims that a significant find would yield 750,000 jobs nationwide. This number comes from a macromodeling exercise of the type discussed in chapter 2 and was done by a consulting firm formerly called Wharton Econometric Forecasting Associates (WEFA). In short, WEFA argues that ANWR oil drives down energy prices so much that U.S. economic growth accelerates significantly, leading to more jobs.

The first point to make here is that this argument won't fly as the economy approaches full employment. If lower energy prices did lead to faster growth, the Federal Reserve would then boost interest rates to head off inflation and thus slow growth back down again. However, even in a less than full-employment economy, when higher economic growth rates would be tolerated, the WEFA argument is highly implausible and rests on a number of dubious assumptions.[42] It does illustrate, however, the standard method for generating big jobs–environment trade-off allegations: first *assume* the economy is extremely sensitive to energy price changes and then *assert* that environmental protection will lead to big increases in energy costs. We examined this tactic in the NAM/DRI predictions of economic disaster from acid-rain control in chapter 2, and it is resurfacing now in attacks on global-warming control efforts—by both WEFA and DRI macromodelers, among others—as we shall see in chapter 6.

If this lower-gas-prices argument is fatuous, is there another case for a national jobs trade-off? Yes and no. The "yes" part of the story works only if the economy is at less than full employment. For example, an oil company consortium that borrows several billion to build and install pipelines and drilling rigs will help pump up aggregate demand. Assuming, generously, that all of the spending was a net addition, each billion would support about 14,000 jobs. According to industry sources, ANWR development would lead to spending of about $4.2 billion annually for five years—during a recession, these dollars might thus create about 60,000 net jobs nationwide.[43]

Recognize that these jobs are created because the companies are spending money developing a domestic resource instead of pumping out oil overseas. However, there are other ways to reduce oil imports and to keep that money for use in employing people at home. In chapter 2, we saw that investments in energy efficiency also fostered net job growth in recessions, precisely because the spending displaced oil imports. The Wilderness Society has argued that saving oil equivalent to ANWR's expected annual production through energy-efficiency measures would lead to an increase in net employment of more than the 750,000 figure offered by the oil industry.[44]

One need not accept this latter estimate uncritically to still recognize that cost-effective energy-efficiency investments will, during periods when there is cyclical joblessness, employ more people at home than will oil imports. If Congress were interested in boosting job growth by reducing oil dependency, they could do so in two ways: by opening up ANWR to development or by promoting energy-efficiency investments through regulation or (deficit-financed) subsidy. In this sense, there is no national jobs trade-off to be found on Alaska's North Slope. Domestic energy can be "produced" and national job growth encouraged (during periods of cyclical unemployment) as effectively through energy efficiency investments as through drilling in the refuge.

RESOURCES, JOB LOSSES, AND ADJUSTMENT ASSISTANCE

There are three themes to this chapter. The first is that significant local jobs–environment trade-offs emerge only when a large natural resource (e.g., high-sulfur coal, old-growth timber, ANWR oil) is placed off limits for development. Under these circumstances, job losses on a regional level can reach into the thousands. The low-end, direct job-loss predictions for coal and timber have been reasonably on target, if not always for the right reasons. Based on a review of the data, my estimate is that fewer than 10,000 jobs in each of the coal and timber industries disappeared over the 1990s as a result of environmental protection.

In both cases, fears of regulation-induced job loss were fanned by several years or more of widespread economic hardship and layoffs that resulted from recession and mechanization. It was simply bad luck that both debates occurred during the recession of the late 1980s and early 1990s, when cyclical unemployment—the beast that generates the worst hardships for workers and their families—was at a peak. Unfortunately, the emotional intensity captured in the media debate on the part of both workers and environmentalists has since framed a national perception of a widespread trade-off between employment and the preservation of a livable environment. This perception, as demonstrated earlier in this book, is simply false.

A second point of this chapter is that evidence for "secondary" job losses is quite hard to find at the most detailed level available—the county. Examining data from both Oregon and West Virginia, in only two counties were reductions in base employment (mining and manufacturing) accompanied by larger reductions in total employment, as a simple base model would predict. In spite of large declines in base jobs, the vast majority of counties registered net job growth. This suggests that while some retail and service industries certainly suffered from shutdowns and layoffs, the numbers were much smaller than had been feared. Environmental protection did not wreak secondary havoc even in small timber- and coal-dependent counties.

There are two lessons here. The first is that the economic base model is too simplistic to capture the flexible and resilient dynamics of economic development in America's rural counties. The second and related point is that predictions of secondary employment loss—usually as big or bigger than direct job losses—should generally be ignored. In part this is because secondary job-loss estimates are often derived from simplistic base models and are thus probably wrong. Moreover, they cannot be verified after the fact. More importantly, however, as the data in this chapter show, secondary job losses, to the extent that they do occur, are not locally concentrated the way direct layoffs are. When AT&T announced in 1996 that it was downsizing and laying off 40,000 people, news commentators did not mention that, based on the predictions of economic base models, another 40,000 people nationwide who sold products to the company and its employees might lose their jobs. This is in fact quite appropriate: it is the concentrated, direct layoffs that are of primary importance to the public in the local communities.

Given this, it is important to point out that even in these two "worst-case scenarios" of a local jobs–environment conflict, the direct job-loss numbers remain small—dwarfed even regionally by the impact of trade agreements, productivity improvements, capital flight, or corporate restructurings. In the mining case, regulation contributed to between one and 2,000 layoffs per year over five or six years across a multistate region. For spotted owls, the impact was even less direct: the majority of the timber workers ultimately affected by owl regulations were in fact initially laid off as a consequence of the recession in the late 1980s. This was several years before old-growth protection constrained the federal timber supply. They (or other workers) in the three-state region simply did not get timber jobs back in the mid-1990s when the lumber market picked up again.

The third and final theme of this chapter is the woeful inadequacy of the basic U.S. worker-adjustment program, the JTPA. For the workers who did lose their jobs in the woods or the mines, the experience has ranged from devastating to a manageable (and sometimes even positive) life transition. While the vast majority have found new work, most probably experienced pay cuts. For many coal miners and their families, income drops were precipitous. Timber workers, fortunate to land in a healthy regional economy, suffered less than miners. And, ironically, the adjustment package was probably more effective for the less needy group. The small boost available from JTPA job-search and training programs works best when there are employment choices actually available for workers. The underfunded JTPA is simply ineffective in areas with high structural unemployment, which is precisely where it is needed most.

In addition, no conversion effort such as Jobs in the Woods—limited as it was—was offered to coal miners. This was not for lack of restoration work to do. Miners could have been employed reclaiming abandoned strip mines or working to prevent acid-mine drainage. Finally, coal-mining communities—again, more in need than most timber towns on the West Coast—were also ignored in the adjustment package. No extra infrastructure investment or business assistance was offered to hard-hit communities.

Reviewing the elements of these adjustment packages is far from an academic exercise. The deals handed to miners and timber workers at the beginning of the 1990s will provide the springboard for congressional adjustment initiatives that will emerge in global-warming legislation over the next few years. From the workers perspective, a few extra dollars funneled through JTPA are not worth fighting for. Of more value would be income and health insurance support for long-term, rigorous retraining programs. In addition, older workers, who face the most difficult adjustment, deserve an income bridge to retirement. Beyond that, the Clinton Forest Plan has set interesting precedents in two areas: targeting community infrastructure and business development assistance to affected communities, as well as the small-scale conversion effort found in Jobs in the Woods.

But there is another dimension to this debate, and one to which I have so far only hinted. Up to this point I have laid out the facts that debunk the widespread myth of a national jobs–environment trade-off. Within the environmental community, however, there is an increasingly popular counter story: Instead of a trade-off, is it possible that there is a jobs–environment synergy? Can environmental protection form the basis of a national—or, barring that, at least local—strategy to create jobs and actually reduce unemployment?

NOTES

1. Author's calculations from the West Virginia Office of Labor and Economic Research, Bureau of Employment Programs.
2. Jacobson et al. (1993) and Kodrzycki (1996).
3. Energy Information Administration (1992).
4. National Acid Precipitation Program (1991).
5. Burtraw et al. (1997).
6. Dallas Burtraw (personal communication).
7. IAT Research (1990).
8. The EPA study was published by ICF (1989) and the U.S. Labor Department contracted with DRI (1989). The DRI numbers were higher than the ICF estimates. Kete (1991) discusses the EPA's adjusted estimates and provides the quote discussing secondary job loss.
9. Power (1996: 12).
10. IAT Research (1990: 16).
11. Power (1996: 60).
12. The last two paragraphs are drawn from Kete (1991).
13. IAT Research (1990).
14. The previous three paragraphs are drawn from LaLonde (1995); evidence for the effectiveness of training for displaced workers is in Jacobson et al. (1993).

15. Kodryzycki (1996: 22).
16. Forest Ecosystem Management Team (FEMAT) (1993: VII-13); Tuchmann et al. (1996). I am indebted to Holly Pettit for her research assistance and some of the writing in this chapter.
17. These productivity figures are calculated by the author from data in Warren (1998), and are based on employment in the lumber- and wood-product industries of Oregon and Washington.
18. Anderson and Olson (1991).
19. California employment data for 1990 is from Tuchmann et al. (1996: 148).
20. Tuchmann et al. (1996) provide a concise history; Dwyer quote is from *U.S. Newswire*, July 1, 1993.
21. FEMAT (1993: Appendix VII-A, 35).
22. FEMAT (1993: Appendix VII-A, 53).
23. In addition to AFRA [Beuter (1990)] and the Wilderness Society [Anderson and Olson (1991)], the other studies were done by the U.S. Department of Agriculture et al. (1990) and the so-called "Gang of Four," for the House Agricultural Committee [Johnston et al. (1991)]. The studies are reviewed and compared in Sample and LeMaster (1992). Gorte (1992) also reviews several of these studies, as well as two additional ones.
24. To obtain direct job-loss estimates for the "Critical Habitat Option"—closest to the Forest Plan reduction requirements—total job losses from Sample and LeMaster (1992: Table 11) were adjusted using the secondary multipliers found in Gorte (1992: Table 13).
25. Sample and LeMaster (1992: Table 10).
26. Calculated from data in Warren (1998). Gorte (1992) explains why paper and pulp production in the Northwest is largely independent of timber harvest levels.
27. Calculated from data in Warren (1998).
28. Again, from a 1983 to 1989 average; calculated from data in Warren (1998).
29. Sample and LeMaster (1992: Table 8); this is from the 4,672 million-board-feet baseline used earlier.
30. Sample and LeMaster (1992: Table 8).
31. Across the periods 1983 to 1991 and 1992 to 1996; calculated from data in Warren (1998). The use of a proportional relationship was recognized as a potential weakness in the studies by, among others, Gorte (1992).
32. Gorte (1992).
33. Tuchmann et al. (1996: 151).
34. Energy Information Administration (1992).
35. Power (1995: 6).
36. This discussion is drawn from Tuchmann et al. (1996).

37. State Community Economic Revitalization Teams (CERTs).
38. Tuchmann et al. (1996: 147).
39. Hallock (1998: 4); see also Brodsky and Hallock (1998). The high-wage approach was championed by the Ecosystem Workforce Project, which was a nongovernmental program housed at the Labor Education and Research Center at the University of Oregon.
40. Hallock (1998: 7).
41. *New York Times*, October, 11 1994.
42. In a truly extraordinary feat of macroeconomic modeling, WEFA (1990), writing for the American Petroleum Institute, manages to predict a net employment gain of 750,000 jobs *via* ANWR development in a "high-resource" case (deemed only a 5 percent probability by the U.S. Geological Survey). This translates into roughly 178,000 jobs for every $1 billion in expenditures, as against the economy-wide average of 14,000.

In a critique of the report, Breslow et al. (1992) find that the alleged employment effect is not being driven by an increase in aggregate demand discussed in the previous text, but rather is flowing from ANWR's "expected" impact on world oil prices. The idea behind the WEFA study can be summarized as follows:

1. ANWR-supplied oil will drive down world oil prices significantly.
2. As a result, U.S. GNP will be larger in the long run.
3. Finally, WEFA assumes that higher long-run GNP levels will generate lower unemployment levels.

Step (1) is the weakest point in the argument. First, the WEFA number of 750,000 net jobs is based on a hypothetical oil strike deemed highly unlikely by government scientists. The more likely mean ANWR oil field is an even tinier portion of world and national reserves. Second, in the WEFA study, a 0.9 percent increase in world oil supply from ANWR (the field's theoretical maximum) translated into a 4.5 percent decrease in world oil prices. This is an implied demand elasticity of 0.2 percent, which is less than one-third the value of generally accepted estimates. Third, WEFA assumes that OPEC will not react to an increase in U.S. production, and subsequent price decrease, by curtailing its own. Finally, the report adopts unreasonably high price forecasts for oil.

Step (2) of the argument is also quite problematic. If ANWR oil is so important for the health of the U.S. macroeconomy, one must also wonder what happens beyond the forecast period, when ANWR supplies are exhausted. If the United States is then forced to quickly and dramatically boost reliance on expensive imports, the negative macroeconomic consequences and job losses would presumably be dramatic.

Finally, step (3) holds only for an economy with less than full employ-ment, as noted in the text.

43. WEFA (1990). The spending figures are in 1996 dollars.
44. Breslow et al. (1992).

Chapter 5

A Jobs–Environment Synergy?

Back in 1979—the era before the megabookstore—I wandered into a small local shop and picked up a slim book that was already becoming highly influential in the environmental movement. Called *Soft Energy Paths: Towards a Durable Peace*, it was written by an American physicist named Amory Lovins.[1] Lovins viewed the United States as being at a crossroads, from which two paths diverged. The first was the road then being followed of a society based on the promotion and production of electricity via an increased reliance on coal, oil, and nuclear power. He termed this the "hard" path. In contrast, the "soft" path involved a conscious governmental effort to redirect the economy toward efficient use of energy and the promotion of renewable energy technologies, especially solar power.

What was truly innovative about Lovins's analysis was his claim that the soft path was the cheaper of the two. From his perspective, a variety of relatively small marketplace barriers stood in the way of dramatic improvements in energy efficiency and renewable energy production that would cut our reliance on imported fossil fuels and, at the same time, lead to a cleaner environment. Because the soft path was both profitable and fostered greater reliance on locally available resources, it promised many social benefits: "A soft path simultaneously offers jobs for the unemployed, capital for business people, environmental protection for conservationists, enhanced national security for the military,

[and] opportunities for small business to innovate and for big business to recycle itself. . . .[2]

Lovins—who went on to found a research organization called the Rocky Mountain Institute—likes to characterize his approach as a form of intellectual jujitsu, in which the opponent's argument is turned back on itself. And, indeed, *Soft Energy Paths* helped reframe perceptions not only about the profitability of energy efficiency and renewable investments, but also about the fundamental existence of a jobs–environment trade-off. Instead of layoffs, the path to a cleaner environment promised "jobs for the unemployed."

Another person who read Lovins's book in the late 1970s was a young congressman from middle Tennessee. Just prior to becoming vice president of the United States beginning in 1992, Al Gore wrote his own book, called *Earth in the Balance*. Gore also saw a positive synergy between jobs and the environment, but in a somewhat different light. In his vision, environmental concerns could lay the foundation for effective U.S. industrial policy within the context of a "Global Marshall Plan":

> The fundamental purpose of the Strategic Environment Initiative is to enable us to make dramatic progress in the effort to heal the global environment; in my opinion, that goal will eventually become so compelling that America will demand the kind of inspired leadership that made the Apollo program so productive and inspiring. The new program could reinvigorate our ability to excel at applied as well as basic research, spur gains in productivity, lead to innovations, breakthroughs and spin-offs in other fields of inquiry, and reestablish the United States as the world's leader in applied technology.[3]

Are Lovins and Gore onto something? Can we, as a side benefit of environmental protection, create more jobs in the economy by not sticking with a business-as-usual approach? This chapter looks critically at these questions.

Before beginning, however, we need to recognize the macroeconomic limits that any "job-creation" strategy faces. Successful investments that create jobs at the microlevel, whether based on environmental technology or other foundations, nevertheless still occur in an economy where national unemployment rates are largely determined by business-cycle forces. This means that, on the one hand, shifting invest-ment from "dirty" to "clean" technologies will generally have little impact on unemployment rates if the economy is tanking and heading into a recession. (Although, as discussed in chapter 2 and later in this chapter, if environmental regulation increases overall investment during a slump, this will help.)

By the same token, in boom times, job-creation efforts will ultimately run up against the strong hand of the U.S. Federal Reserve. Also, as dis-cussed in chapter 2, the Fed simply will not tolerate national unemploy-ment rates too far below 4.5 percent for fear of inflation. Put another way, we need to recognize at the outset that a green-jobs strategy will have little impact on cyclical unemployment. Having said this, the envi-ronmental perspective that Lovins and Gore sketched out may still have validity for individual regions in developed countries (or for developing nations) that are facing persistent structural unemployment.

There are seven potential avenues by which investment in clean tech-nologies or environmentally conscious production might reduce unem-ployment at the local level. These are listed in table 5.1.

These changes in production might increase net employment in one of two ways. The first is to redeploy existing resources in the economy so that the same pool of income now supports more workers. The first three measures listed in the table, labor intensive technology, import substitu-tion, and job sharing, fall into this category. Lovins's soft-energy path envisioned job growth that would arise primarily by substituting domes-tic resources for imports.

The second way that environmental spending might increase employment would be by boosting economic growth. Measures 4 and 5

TABLE 5.1. Potential sources of net job growth

Net job growth based on existing resources
 (1) Shifting to more labor intensive technology
 (2) Import substitution, especially for oil
 (3) Shifting to job sharing and a shorter work week

Net job growth through "green growth"?
 (4) Dynamic spillovers from environmental technology
 (5) Export promotion
 (6) Amenity-based growth
 (7) Boosting government and private sector investment
     spending during recessions

in the table, dynamic spillovers from new environmental technologies and the attendant boost in exports, form the heart of Gore's thesis. A third possibility arises when environmental protection enhances the livability of a region, thereby attracting talented workers and new businesses. This process is known as "amenity-based growth." Finally, government and government-mandated environmental investment spending, as discussed in chapter 2, can help boost job growth when the economy is in a slump. Measures 4 through 7 in the category net growth through "green growth" all have the potential to undercut their environmental advantage *if* the higher growth leads to accelerated environmental degradation.

INCREASED EMPLOYMENT FROM EXISTING RESOURCES

This section critically evaluates the opportunities for increasing employment without relying on economic growth. Any such strategy requires a shift to what can be called a "clean technology."[4] A clean technology has three main attributes: it provides a service of comparable quality to existing technology; it does so at a long-run, private cost that is comparable to that of existing technology; and it does so in a "cleaner," less environmentally damaging fashion than existing technology.

Many advocates of clean technologies have focused on only the third attribute—environmental superiority. However, the first two are equally vital. If potential clean technologies do not provide a comparable service at a comparable market price (including taxes and imbedded regulatory expenses), consumers and businesses are unlikely to adopt them regardless of their environmental benefit. Moreover, if clean technologies raise costs significantly, they have the potential to reduce the competitiveness of U.S. firms and thus promote capital flight. This notion of cost-competitive clean technologies was the key insight Lovins provided in his argument for the soft-energy path.

Examples of potential or current clean technologies include: energy- and water-efficiency technologies, solar-electric (photovoltaic [PV] and solar-thermal) power, wind-powered electricity, electric and hybrid vehicles, high-speed rail for intercity transport, waste-reduction and reuse technologies in manufacturing and agriculture, certain types of recycling, and mass transit in certain locations.

In addition, a simple shift in our approach to production qualifies as a clean technology: a 35-hour workweek with 35-hour pay. This is clearly a cost-effective change in production methods, but in what way does it improve the environment? The flip side of overconsumption in developed countries is overwork. If workers chose to "downshift" and ease off on the rat race a bit, then, the theory goes, lower incomes would mean less consumption. Less consumption, in turn, would mean reduced pressure on the environment. An environmentally beneficial reduction in the workweek to increase employment would only be feasible, however, if workers were broadly interested in voluntarily accepting greater leisure and time for family and community in exchange for less consumption.

Because clean technologies simply replace existing "dirty" technologies in a cost-effective manner, they do not lay the foundation for additional economic growth per se. However, they nevertheless have the potential for increasing employment in one of three ways: increased labor intensity, greater domestic content, or directly via job sharing.

LABOR-INTENSIVE PRODUCTION

The first way to increase employment using current resources is to shift to clean technologies that are more labor intensive. Since clean technologies are, by definition, cost competitive, a firm (or household or nation) that adopts them will find little change in their income. With the same income, more jobs are supported by labor-intensive technologies for two reasons. First, when firms use labor-intensive rather than capital-intensive technologies, they typically pay lower wages. For example, consider a switch from coal-fired electricity to energy efficiency, which would reduce employment in the fossil-fuel sector and increase it in construction (for retrofits) and manufacturing (for insulation and other energy efficient products). In 1990, $1 million of spending on coal supported seven jobs (direct and indirect), while comparable spending on construction supported twenty jobs and in manufactured goods about twenty as well. Average wages in the coal industry were $16.71, in construction $13.77, and in manufacturing $10.83.[5]

Part of the reason for the wage gap is the higher unionization rate in coal. But there is a market-driven reason as well: since more workers are being employed to achieve the same output, their productivity is lower. Lower productivity tends to correlate with lower wages. Note that "lower" doesn't mean "low": construction and manufacturing still pay relatively well. Nevertheless, this is an obvious drawback of labor-intensive production. But the good news is that lower wages are not the primary reason for the increased employment that accompanies a switch to labor-intensive production.

Labor-intensive jobs also require less capital. With less capital in use, the share of income paid out as profit falls, while the wage share rises.[6] This means that by holding the wage constant, more workers can be supported for a given level of firm (or household or national) income.

Tufts University economist Frank Ackerman, a recycling expert, puts it this way:

> Money spent on recycling creates more jobs than the same amount spent on garbage disposal. Recycling is a labor-intensive activity, involving sorting and processing of waste materials. Disposal, in contrast, involves heavy equipment, large tracts of land, and very little labor. In the simplest terms, most of the money spent on recycling goes to workers in the form of wages rather than to owners of holes in the ground.

Ackerman goes on to warn that for there to be a job benefit, recycling must be cost-competitive:

> There is a crucial limitation, however, to the power of recycling to boost employment. Recycling is sure to create more jobs *if* it costs the same amount as disposal. If it costs more than disposal, then the outcome is less certain. For instance, suppose a recycling program costs $1,200,000 and reduces spending on garbage disposal by $1,000,000. The increased cost will probably be paid, one way or another, by the households of the community. They will therefore have to reduce consumption of something else by $200,000; a likely candidate is consumer spending at retail outlets.[7]

Ackerman also points out that if recycling is more expensive, than extra jobs created locally in recycling have to be compared with jobs lost locally in retailing. He concludes: "expensive recycling is worse for employment than cheap disposal."[8]

To demonstrate a regional or local jobs benefit, all job gains and losses from a switch to a clean technology must be evaluated. This means that both the direct and indirect employment has to be tracked for both the dirty and clean technologies. Recall from chapter 2 that indirect jobs are the "upstream" employment opportunities created by final consumer, government, or business spending. Indirect jobs from recycling, for example, would include jobs in the manufacture of recycling trucks; jobs for workers who made the steel, rubber, textiles, and vinyl that went into the auto-recycling trucks; jobs for workers who mined the ore and produced the electricity and the machine tools that went into the steel, rubber textiles, and vinyl; and so on, ad infinitum. Again, economists use input–output models to track the complex direct and indirect job impacts of a switch in final demand from, for example, incineration of garbage to recycling.

A raft of input–output studies have examined proposed shifts in investment spending to energy-efficient technologies, solar energy, and solid-waste recycling. These studies have concluded that such technologies boost employment through increased labor intensity. The impact can be relatively small—an estimated net increase of 400 jobs in New York City from a switch to recycling—or relatively large. One study conducted by the American Council for Energy Efficiency looked at cost-effective energy-efficiency investments as a way to battle greenhouse gas emissions. The study found that a large-scale, but still cost-neutral, shift in investment out of capital-intensive oil, gas, and electricity sectors and into more labor-intensive manufacturing and installation of energy-efficient technologies would increase U.S. employment on net by just over one million jobs by the year 2010.[9]

It is possible to break this estimated increase of one million jobs down into proximate "causes": a shift into somewhat lower wage sectors; a higher share of national income being paid out as wages instead of profit; and the substitution of domestic production of energy-efficient technologies for imported oil. (Import substitution is discussed further in the next section.) Almost half of the increased employment comes from the increase in the wage share of GDP; another 25 percent comes from a shift to lower-wage employment sectors; and the final 25 percent comes from an increase in national income resulting from the replacement of oil imports with domestically produced energy-efficient technologies. The point here is that a shift to labor-intensive production boosts employment not simply, or even primarily, by lowering wages. In fact, most of the predicted increase in employment in this study is financed by a reduction in the profit share of GDP.[10]

At this point, it is worth pausing to recall that predicted job gains from the adoption of clean technology—whether 400 or 1,000,000—are simply estimates from a particular type of model and should not be taken as more than that. As noted in chapter 2, input–output studies are limited by their assumption of a costless readjustment of resources, particularly in terms of trained workers. If oil workers are laid off in Texas and energy-efficiency jobs are created in Nebraska, the presumption is that there are workers in Nebraska who both need the jobs and who are trained to do them. Given this, nationwide input–output models of large-scale job shifts should be taken with a grain or two of salt. Having stated that, the input–output studies of energy-efficiency investments do all point in the same direction: more jobs are likely, largely due to greater labor intensity.

One way to promote more labor-intensive production is to shift to more labor-intensive, clean technologies, such as energy efficiency, solar electricity, or solid-waste recycling. A second possibility would be to change the composition of government spending. For example, suppose the government were to support a large-scale reforestation program. This is a highly labor-intensive (and relatively low-wage) process. To finance such a program, cuts might be made in weapons production, which is a highly capital-intensive process. The result would be net job gains. Again, these gains would occur not only because of lower wages in the forestry sector, but also because a smaller percentage of national income would be paid out as profit on capital investment—in this case to investors in weapons companies.

Yet a third way to promote more labor-intensive production, particularly in manufacturing, is to shift some of the production cost burden from labor taxes to pollution taxes (e.g., taxes on carbon-dioxide emissions that cause global warming). How would this work? As one example, fixed costs associated with employer-provided health care reduce employment in manufacturing in the United States, as firms opt instead to pay overtime. If health-care costs were financed out of general (e.g., energy) tax revenues under a single-payer system, this disincentive for hiring workers would disappear.[11]

In summary, one way to increase net employment without relying on economic growth is to shift toward more labor-intensive production. This, however, has one drawback. Labor-intensive jobs are generally lower (though, again, not necessarily low) wage jobs. The lower wages are, indeed, one way in which increased employment is financed. However, another and more important effect of increased labor intensity is the increase in wage share of GDP. There is, therefore, no one-to-one trade-off between more jobs and lower wages.

Another potential drawback of a shift to labor-intensive production is a possible loss of competitiveness and a shift in production out of the country. However, we have ruled out this problem by defining a clean-technology as one that is both environmentally superior *and* cost effective. In essence, lower labor productivity is compensated for by an increase in the efficiency of other resource use. Thus, the adoption of clean technologies will not raise the costs of host country products vis-à-vis competitors.

IMPORT SUBSTITUTION

Beyond increased labor intensity, reducing reliance on imported goods in a cost-effective manner provides another way to increase domestic employment. Technically, such a move will increase domestic GDP and, thus, domestic growth, however, it will have an offsetting effect on the exporting country. Therefore, there will be no increase in overall global output and possibly little impact on global employment. In effect, reducing imports is a way to reshuffle jobs from the exporting to the importing country.

That being the case, cost-effective reductions in imports remain a good idea from an environmental point of view. Long-distance trade in goods and services generates important environmental costs. International trade accounts for around one-eighth of world oil consumption; fossil fuels are associated with a variety of environmental problems that range from oil spills to urban air pollution, acid rain, and global warming. In addition, energy production is heavily subsidized, to the tune of $28 billion per year in the United States, not including military expenditures to protect Persian Gulf oil fields and shipping lanes. Developing countries also engage in massive energy subsidies, with electricity prices averaging half of the industrialized countries. Trade, when based on subsidized and highly polluting energy use, is truly a waste of global resources.[12]

Moreover, import substitution can be a critical local development tool. Material, energy, and water wastes are important, underutilized resources for many communities. The idea of "industrial ecology"—in which the waste products from one industry become the feedstock for another—has great appeal from an environmental perspective. Such closed-loop production, mimicking natural systems where "all waste is food," can reduce pollution problems.

In addition, when industrial waste streams are transformed into raw materials, they also form a local basis for job growth. Comparable gains can be made at the residential and commercial levels when households and businesses "plug the leaks" created by inefficient use of water and energy. Reducing imports of these resources can free up community capital for investment in other areas. Working out of Lovins's Rocky Mountain Institute, Michael Kinsley has been both advocating and fostering this approach to economic development for well over a decade. He can point to dozens of success stories, including the following:

- The University of Northern Iowa spent $7,000 in 1994 to install efficient showerheads and is now saving $67,000 each year on water heating.
- Osage, Iowa (population 3,800), plowed $7.8 million back into its local economy between 1974 and 1991, thanks to a series of weatherization and energy-efficiency projects that continue today through the efforts of local utility and service groups. As a result of efficiency, 1995 electric rates were 50 percent lower than the state average. Much of the saved money is respent locally.
- A study by students and faculty of Hendrix College in Fox, Arkansas, revealed that the college was buying most of its food from distant suppliers, even though the majority of those food items were, or could be, produced locally. In 1987, the college changed its purchasing policy and is now committed to buying locally, and area farmers have learned how to produce for the college's specific food needs.[13]

Of course, we need to recognize that these job gains are initially local: reduced imports or increased exports mean that job gains at home are at least partially coming at the expense of job losses elsewhere. However, over the long term, economic growth that is induced by import substitution may provide economy-wide net employment growth opportunities.

In summary, cost-effective import substitution can provide an important foundation for job growth. While some of this job growth comes at the expense of exporters, import substitution provides an important tool to help spark economic growth, particularly at the local level. It may, therefore, lay the foundation for more positive sum job gains over the long term. Moreover, import substitution has clear environmental benefits.

JOB SHARING

The final way to increase employment without relying on growth in production is to move toward policies that promote sharing existing work and income (i.e., a 35-hour workweek at 35-hour pay). This option has been widely discussed in Europe. One of the large German unions has already won a 35-hour work week for its members, and the French government has proposed reducing the workweek. In Asia, Korean unions have recently proposed job sharing as an alternative to layoffs under the International Monetary Fund (IMF) bailout plan.

In her book, *The Overworked American*, Harvard economist Juliet Schor suggests that Americans are "overworked" in the sense that many of us would trade future increases in income for reduced work hours. If this were to happen, higher levels of future consumption, as well as its associated pollution, would be traded for more time spent with family or in the community. At the same time, the existing work, and income, would be shared out in the form of more part-time jobs.

Paradoxically, however, Schor finds that the workweek in the United States has been rising over the last several decades, though not in Europe. Her argument is that Americans get trapped in a "work-and-spend" cycle. Employers demand long hours to increase the output from salaried workers and to avoid paying benefits to new workers. Overwork then gets translated into overconsumption, as workers try to make the best of a bad bargain. High unemployment and the declining power of unions have meant there has been little resistance to this trend.[14]

In the early 1990s, both the French and Canadian governments commissioned macromodeling analyses of the impact of job sharing on employment rates. French researchers concluded that, as a result of productivity gains, labor time could be reduced up to 15 percent without creating new jobs. But beyond this point, reductions in labor time would lead to employment gains; for example, over a 5-year period, a 35-hour workweek might generate 1.5 million new jobs on net.[15]

The Canadian model is based on a 10 percent reduction in work time, coupled with an assumed 5 percent productivity increase. Over a 10-year period, the study predicts a substantial decline in the unemployment rate, from a baseline of 10 percent to around 6 percent. In addition, disposable income and GDP would also decline, the former by about 0.3 percent, as leisure time increases. With less income and less production, the policy was thus predicted to yield environmental benefits.[16]

Both of these studies suggest large potential employment increases as a result of major shifts to a shorter workweek and job sharing. However, realizing these gains requires that the high unemployment experienced in these countries be structural and not cyclical. In part, because of greater labor-market protections for workers (e.g., higher minimum wages and better unemployment benefits), inflationary pressures build more quickly in Europe and Canada as unemployment rates fall than is the case in the

United States. Canadian and European central bankers—like their counterparts at the U.S. Federal Reserve—might not tolerate large drops in unemployment for fear of increasing inflation. Stated bluntly—from the perspective of central bankers, high Canadian and French unemployment rates may in fact be required to keep workers from successfully pressing for "excessive" wage increases. And via their power to raise interest rates, central bankers could cut off any job gains won by reducing the work week if the gains were viewed as inflationary.

There are also some drawbacks to a shorter workweek. Part-time work can and does meet the needs of some workers seeking more flexibility. However, it can also be an avenue for discriminating against workers in terms of pay, promotion opportunities, and fringe benefits. These issues must be dealt with before a more general move to a shorter workweek will be feasible. In countries without universal health coverage, the provision or at least prorated provision of health benefits to part-time workers is needed to promote job sharing. Beyond this, Schor suggests other policies, including increased vacation- and family-leave time, legislating work hours for salaried employees, and replacing overtime with comp time.[17]

This section has considered job growth policies that rely on reallocating resources while maintaining a constant level of production. I now turn to the possibility of boosting net job growth through increases in output.

INCREASED EMPLOYMENT FROM "GREEN GROWTH"?

Many authors have argued that the term "green growth" is an oxymoron. For example, former World Bank economist Herman Daly maintains that the North should "stabilize its resource consumption" and assist the southern countries via transfers to promote global sustainable development. The logic behind this argument is straightforward: more consumption means more production, which means more resource degradation. Daly argues that in the United States (though not in developing countries), the negative effects on social well-being and quality of life resulting from economic growth currently outweigh the positive contributions from increased material consumption.[18]

Even if this view were widely accepted, it is highly unlikely that northern countries would halt their growth in the near term. Therefore, growing in as green a fashion as possible—by investing increasing shares of national output into environmental clean up and less natural-resource-intensive technology—may present the feasible road to a potentially sustainable future. In the section that follows, I consider two related paths to net employment growth that also depend on growth in production.

DYNAMIC SPILLOVERS

The most ambitious claims for job growth from environmental investment are based on "dynamic spillovers"—a situation in which fundamentally new environmental technologies launch an extended period of economic growth. The quote at the beginning of this chapter from Vice President Gore's book gives the flavor of this argument. The following is a comparable view from a recent government report titled *Promoting Growth and Job Creation Through Emerging Environmental Technologies:*

> These (environmental technology) markets have steep learning curves, they have dramatically lower per-unit costs as the scale of production increases, they provide benefits that are broadly distributed and difficult for individual firms to capture—in short they pose a major dilemma. Individual firms will have significant disincentives to enter these markets without outside support or regulation because of high start-up costs. Yet the firm (or country) that pursues innovation in environmental technologies can gain a competitive foothold that may provide an advantage for years to come. Start down the learning curve or pursue economies of scale and you may be ahead of the competition in a huge, expanding market. . . . The environmental technology market is vast and expanding, the social benefits of the industry extend well beyond what the individual firms can capture, and early entrants can stay ahead in the future. . . .[19]

Here is the Lovins argument once again: potentially profitable, environmentally superior industries, but ones facing barriers to marketplace development. In this case, the barrier is a variation on one that is well known to economists. New environmental technologies, such as PV solar cells, windpower, or electric and fuel cell or hybrid vehicles, are "infant industries"—ones that are caught, to mix metaphors, in a "chicken-and-egg" dilemma.

In the case of PVs, if this industry were producing in large quantities, it could capture economies of scale to surpass, or at least match, the competition—coal- and natural-gas-fired power plants—on price. If PV could do this, it would generate tremendous environmental benefits, including vastly reduced levels of urban air pollution and greenhouse gas emissions. And the worldwide market would indeed be tremendous. However, at its current small-scale ("infant") production levels, PV production is not profitable, and thus no private firm will make the investment needed to grow the industry to make it competitive.

The infant-industry argument has been used in the past to justify temporary trade protection, for example, as when a developing country is attempting to build up a textile, steel, or automobile industry. In this case, however, it is powerful and entrenched domestic competitors—of gasoline-powered vehicles and fossil-fuel-fired electricity—against whom new environmental technologies must struggle. How to break out of this catch-22? The answer is government regulatory or subsidy policy. On the regulatory front, for example, the CAA amendments of 1990 included a provision that 10 percent of all cars sold in California must be "zero-emission" vehicles by 2003. The goal was to attack persistent problems of urban air pollution. Because California's market is so big, the regulation has sparked significant research and development (R&D) spending on low-emission, electric, fuel-cell, and hybrid vehicles by the major car companies.

We also have good evidence that subsidy policy can be the catalyst for launching cost-effective clean technologies.[20] During the mid-1970s, in the face of the OPEC oil-price hikes, the U.S. Congress became concerned about energy security. They took three principal measures. First, Congress funded substantial R&D in renewable technologies; second, they instituted a 15 percent tax credit for energy investments; and, third, they required public utilities to purchase any power produced by qualifying independent facilities at the utility's "avoided" or marginal cost of production.

Of all the states, California took the most aggressive stance toward developing alternative energy sources by instituting their own 25 percent energy-investment tax credit and a property-tax exemption for solar facilities, as well as by requiring utilities to provide ten-year, avoided-cost contracts to independent power producers. These contracts were based on the high energy prices of the early 1980s. At the time, they appeared to shield ratepayers from further fuel increases. In retrospect, they protected alternative energy producers from the dramatic decline in oil prices.

This attractive environment fueled a rush of investors, many of whom were looking only for lucrative tax shelters. In fact, at the height of California's efforts to promote alternative energy, investors were guaranteed a return on their investment through the tax benefits alone. The federal credit required only that the project be in service (even limited service) for five years, while the California tax credits could not be recovered by the government if the project failed to generate any power after its first year.

Into this environment, a variety of technology and design options were introduced, most of which were of dubious value and failed. Many of the better ideas, however, were based on work that had begun under the federal R&D programs. Eventually, two success stories emerged: wind and solar-thermal electricity. Figure 5.1 illustrates the dramatic progress that has been made in reducing costs for wind power over the last fifteen years. Wind power is now below $0.05 per kilowatt hour. Combined with an ongoing federal subsidy of one and one-half cents per kilowatt hour, wind power is now competitive with coal and near competitive with natural gas, and it has become the new generation technology of choice in many regions of the country.

There is little doubt that, without aggressive governmental action in the early 1980s, wind today would not be a commercial option for producing power. The industry is highly concentrated in California, which in the early 1990s was producing about 80 percent of the world's wind power. The state today has more than enough wind capacity to meet the power needs of the city of San Francisco. Also, California's largest utility has announced that it will rely solely on wind power and energy efficiency to meet increased demand into the twenty-first century.

The optimistic moral of this story is that government policy can be effective in promoting clean technology. The pessimistic moral is that the

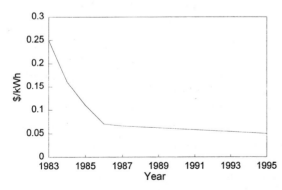

FIGURE 5.1. Costs of wind. *Sources:* Based on Robert H. Williams (1990). "Low-Cost Strategies for Coping with CO_2 Emission Limits," *The Energy Journal* 11(4): 35–59; and David Milborrow (1999). "Wind Has Plenty in Reserve in Competetive Cost Stakes," *Windpower Monthly,* February.

government can spend much more money than is necessary to do so. The R&D and tax-credit policies of the mid-to-late 1970s were untargeted and poorly designed. Spurred on by fears of $40-a-barrel oil, as well as unrealistic promises from the supporters of renewable energy, the government programs soon set out to secure new sources of energy at any price. As a result, a lot of money went toward uneconomic demonstration projects and into the hands of tax farmers rather than wind farmers. That being the case, government subsidy policy in retrospect has turned out to be wildly successful. For a couple of hundred million dollars in taxpayer money (the equivalent of a few miles of interstate highway) we have at hand a critical and cost-effective new tool for addressing the problem of global warming.

LONG WAVES AND ECONOMIC GROWTH

Can wind power achieve more than this? Will investment in clean technologies such as wind spark a dramatic and sustained period of growth for the U.S. economy? Fundamental technological breakthroughs have for some time been argued to form the backbone of so-called "long waves" of growth in capitalist economies. One economic historian found that the post–World War II boom in America was preceded and driven by a remarkable burst of major product innovation. He lists twenty-three radical product innovations in the period 1930 to 1950, as against only five from 1950 to 1970.[21]

In the environmental arena, technologies such as PV solar energy and hydrogen fuel cells are viewed as the latest in a series of truly revolutionary innovations, along the lines of the automobile or the microchip. Such technologies help provide the foundation for what economist Edward Nell has called "transformational growth—growth that transforms the economy, changes its structure—meaning the relative sizes of its sectors (agriculture, manufacturing, services)—and, as a result and then as an interacting cause, the distribution of income and the urban–rural relationship, together with the nature of work, of household life, and so on."[22]

Such overarching change unleashes a tremendous and expansionary demand for new products and services. In the case of automobiles, the demand was for the manufacturing, sale, and repair of cars. Through ensuing suburbanization, however, snowballing demand for new highways, shopping malls, spacious home construction, home furnishings, and lawn care, to name a few products, was spawned.

It is difficult to predict the impact of a new technology and, in particular, to assess the new patterns of production and demand it might generate. However, along with biotechnology, fiber optics, and microchips, PV energy and fuel cells may lie at the core of a cluster of radical innovations on which a new long wave of economic growth might be based.

There is, however, a caveat. As the globalization of production proceeds, it is not clear whether episodes of transformational growth can still generate high levels of domestic employment. The microchip, for example, has had very mixed impacts on employment in developed countries. By revolutionizing communication technologies, the microchip has contributed to the offshoring of production facilities. This is perhaps most evident in the production of the microchips and computer components themselves. While deindustrialization in the United States cannot be blamed primarily on the microchip, the increased demand that has been spawned by information-age transformations has not solved structural unemployment problems. Indeed, as technology itself becomes more mobile, it is possible that economic development that is based on technological leadership may have become an obsolete strategy.[23]

Given this, the strongest employment argument from dynamic spillovers is a defensive one—some share of the good jobs in the early twenty-first century will be tied to leadership in PVs and fuel cells. A sensible industrial policy should seek to enlarge that share.

EXPORT PROMOTION

Export promotion is the flip side of import substitution, and as such we should be cautious of embracing it as a "green" policy. Increased exports often require the displacement of local production in the area of importation. Greek economist J. N. Lekakais, for example, argues that substantial job loss may arise in his country as pollution-control equipment must be imported from other countries in the European economic community.[24] Moreover, increased exports will surely generate transportation-related environmental costs, the reduction of which make import substitution attractive.

That being the case, even opponents of growth in rich countries view technology transfer from the North to the South as being an essential component of sustainable global development. One could envision, for example, a program of tied foreign aid in which solar panels that are manufactured in the United States are "sold" to Brazil through the use aid dollars. In this way, exports can provide jobs in developed countries without increasing consumption in the United States, since U.S. workers' incomes from the panel production are offset by increased taxes (society-wide) to fund the aid purchases. Brazil, meanwhile, receives a low pollution-energy source (with free fuel) to further its own development agenda.

Green export growth can come from three sectors: (1) environmental clean-up equipment and services (e.g., scrubbers or hazardous waste clean up); (2) the export of clean technology (e.g., electric cars or solar cells); and (3) the growth of industries based on sustainable use of raw materials or currently untapped waste flows. Regarding the first potential source, several studies have suggested that markets for clean-up technology and services are, relatively speaking, likely to remain rather small. In 1990, the United States exported about $1.3 billion in pollution-control equipment. Exports in this sector were a bit larger than in sporting goods and a little smaller than in machine tools. Analysts argue that in spite of the increasing need for waste management technology in the developing world, commercial demand has been and will be slow to develop.[25]

Given this, the export of leading edge, clean technologies have more potential for boosting domestic employment. This returns us to the discussion of dynamic spillovers in the previous section. If environmental technology lays the foundation for transformative growth, one side effect would almost certainly be an improvement in the balance of payment via an increase in exports. And, assuming this did not lead to excessive job growth from the point of view of the Fed, the short-run result would mean more U.S. jobs.

Export growth of clean technology is dependent, at the policy level, on changes emanating from Washington, such as greater R&D and development funding for cutting-edge environmental technology. In contrast, at the local level, businesses and "green"-development non-governmental organizations (NGOs) have been experimenting with a different kind of export promotion to lay a foundation for more sustainable economic development.

Hundreds of such efforts are under way around the country. In recent years, two interesting initiatives have been launched my home town of Portland, Oregon. In both instances, NGOs have been working with the private sector to foster new production based on local resources. The organizations differ somewhat in their focus. One has concentrated primarily on industrial ecology and the other on the promotion of industry based on a sustainable—and even restorative—use of natural resources.

Bob Doppelt is an environmental entrepreneur. In his mid-30s, he had already founded and brought to national prominence the Pacific

Rivers Council (PRC), an environmental organization. PRC was focused on watershed protection and, in particular, the defense and restoration of salmon habitat in the Northwest. The organization succeeded by marrying strong science and economics with good, innovative policy initiatives and an active legal strategy.

However, in 1995, Doppelt was ready to move on. While PRC had accomplished a lot with its focus on habitat protection and restoration, Doppelt was increasingly convinced that this kind of focus on the "back end" of the materials cycle was too limited; at best it could only slow a steady tide of environmental degradation. Instead, big environmental gains would only come when there were fundamental changes in the "front end" of the economic system: "product designs, material feedstocks, manufacturing processes, distribution systems, or even the missions of entire firms."

Doppelt went on to found another environmental NGO, this one called the Center for Watershed and Community Health (CWCH or "Sea-witch"). The CWCH has an ambitious agenda: turning Oregon into a national leader in the effort to promote sustainable economic development. Weary of the spotted-owl, jobs-versus-environment debates through which he had guided the PRC, Doppelt was looking for a positive alternative in which green production could form the basis for local job growth. In addition, having played legal hardball with industry in our adversarial regulatory system, Doppelt became intrigued with the Dutch model of a more cooperative regulatory regime. In the Netherlands, the government and business actually negotiate targets for pollution reduction on a sector-by-sector basis.

This kind of constructive engagement with the business sector, while no replacement for government regulation, must be an important complement to it in both making regulation work better and transcending its limits. The CWCH is working at several levels—from statewide policy initiatives, to microlevel business development—to try and promote this approach. In terms of job creation, Doppelt and his team have worked since 1997 with the Institute for Local Self-Reliance to survey waste-based manufacturing opportunities in several Oregon watersheds. The project has identified dozens of opportunities ranging from wood-pallet recycling to the manufacture of plastic furniture. Two of these projects have moved to the advanced development stage: a $13-million pulping facility in the Columbia River gorge will use recycled paper as feedstock and a futon manufacturing plant in central Oregon will use old mattresses and waste wood for its raw materials.

While the CWCH's approach to economic development has capital-
ized on waste-based manufactures, another innovative Oregon group has
focused on sustainable, natural-resource-based rural development.
Ecotrust, a Portland-based NGO, was founded with the intent of protecting the "rain forests of home"—the once vast swath of forest ecosystem that stretches from northern California up to southeast Alaska.
Another restless Northwest environmentalist, Spencer Beebe, had earlier
headed up the D.C.-based Conservation International, whose mission is
to protect habitat in developing countries. His experience there shaped
the vision behind Ecotrust: protecting the rain forests required strength-
ening their human communities. Racked by the decline of fishing and
timber, coastal towns found their only salvation in lower paying, and
equally seasonal, tourism industries. Poverty rates were high, as was the
out-migration of young people. The critical connection between communities and the land was being severed.

In 1992, Ecotrust began conversations with a nontraditional commercial bank in Chicago called Shorebank Corporation, which for many
years has been a leader in pioneering lending to small businesses and
homeowners in low-income communities. Out of these discussions,
ShoreBank Pacific was launched. Chartered in Washington State, Shore-
Bank Pacific lends at commercial rates. Its mission is to promote the
growth of businesses that use sustainably harvested materials, that need
funds to invest in ecoefficiency measures, or that are renovating existing
properties rather than pursing greenfield development.

Preceding this commercial operation, Ecotrust and Shorebank Corporation set up a nonprofit business development organization with a
revolving loan fund called Shorebank Enterprise Pacific (SEP). SEP has
provided high-risk credit to rural businesses that are committed to sustainable operations in the depressed fishing and logging communities of
coastal Washington and Oregon. SEP success stories include support to
a guitar-top manufacturer who employs nine times more workers per
cubic meter of wood used than conventional lumber manufacturers; a fish
buyer who commands premium prices for salmon caught by selective
methods that protect dwindling or endangered fish stocks; and oyster
producers whose business success makes them vigilant protectors of the
water quality in a West Coast bay.[26]

ShoreBank Pacific, the commercial bank, has found a market niche
in entrepreneurial-style banking by working with its customers to find
and finance profitable environmental improvements. Conventional commercial banks won't do this simply because they are not interested

enough (or lack the expertise) to make money in this way. In contrast, SEP is functioning more like a traditional community development organization. First-time creditors and small businesses with good ideas but little collateral often find banks reluctant to lend. Community development agencies have stepped in nationwide by providing both credit and business-development training in an effort to jump start fledgling new firms.

What is new about SEP is its commitment to lending based on sustainable approaches. In the past, high-wage jobs in rural areas have often been based on the mining of raw materials from streams, forests, and mineral deposits. Today, these resources when utilized more sustainably can still support high value-added jobs. The key is developing the capital, both physical and human, to make this happen.

ShoreBank Pacific and CWCH are in the business of economic development by trying to bring new jobs to areas whose traditional employment base has been withering, leaving behind punishing structural unemployment. The guiding principle for both institutions is to create jobs on the back of green product exports. While this is not the only way to pursue economic development, it is a good way and for two reasons. First, in all instances the new jobs come with a reduction in direct environmental impact, clean up, or even restoration of damaged ecosystems. Second, both organizations have uncovered sources of local economic vitality that have often been ignored in the past. Waste-based manufacturing or adding value to natural-resource products will not be the answers to all local development problems. But they do provide a solid starting point.

AMENITY-BASED GROWTH

Environmental protection lends a final source of economic vitality to a community in a straightforward way. Communities with clean water and air, as well as easy access to undegraded sites for fishing, camping, boating, skiing, and hiking, are nice places to live. These kinds of "environmental amenities" attract in-migration. People who can afford to choose where they will live often have either high skill levels or else independent sources of income (e.g., retirement or veterans benefits). These immigrants thus bring with them both the human and monetary capital needed to undergird robust economic growth.[27]

Because there is a larger than normal supply of talented workers (the human capital side), firms that are located in the area can pay somewhat lower wages than in other regions. I know this from personal experience, having taken a significant pay cut in order to relocate to Portland, Oregon, from a job in the Northeast. When I was interviewing for the position, the president of the college pointed out the window of his office at the glorious view of snowcapped Mount Hood rising above the city and said, not jokingly, "that's why we pay less than they do back East."

A stable supply of talented workers, lower average wages, a consumer base with a steady inflow of nonlabor income, and the quality-of-life appeal for business owners—all of these factors attract "footloose" new industry to areas that, by virtue of their amenities, are attracting in-migration of people. Amenities include not only environmental assets, but also more traditional public goods, such as quality schools, low crime rates, and nice weather. Indeed, sunny southern California is the classic example of a region that has prospered from amenity-based growth.

The Los Angeles basin also illustrates how the process can be self-limiting. As people flood into an area in search of amenities, it becomes congested, and without good planning, many of the amenities become degraded. Schools get overcrowded; crime, traffic congestion, and pollution all rise; and once-pristine natural environments become overcrowded. This is the same dynamic that underlies urban sprawl, and the attendant, ever-expanding rings of suburbs that surround many urban areas.

In the 1990s, amenity-based growth has been evident in much of the mountain West and the Pacific Northwest. In chapter 4, I noted that robust growth in the latter region—due in some measure to the existence of forest protection itself—has made the transition out of wood products much easier for timber workers than has been the case for coal miners laid off in the East. Indeed, a strong argument can be made that, in the future, more forest protection rather than more timber extraction will be the best economic use of forests in the Northwest.[28]

This is true in part because of the environmental damage that is inflicted by logging—damage that generates a direct "jobs–jobs" conflict. For example, as clear-cutting reduces salmon runs, employment in both commercial and recreational fishing industries suffer. But the point of this section is that there is a much more significant economic benefit to forest preservation: recreational opportunities offered by intact public forests (and other ecosystems) are one of the important amenities driving modern regional growth. This is likely to become even more of a truism as population and income growth generate an even greater scarcity of such resources.

As with import substitution and export promotion, the jobs created by amenity-based growth are not, at least immediately, net jobs. Since the process is driven by in-migration of workers and retirees, some other part of the country (or world) must be experiencing a comparable out-migration of both talent and nonlabor income. From a local development perspective, however, forests, deserts, rivers, and streams will clearly play less of their traditional role as sources of raw materials and more of a role in attracting the footloose skills and businesses that are the hallmark of our increasingly globalized economy.

JOBS IN AN ECOLOGICAL ECONOMY

In his engaging book *The Ecology of Commerce*, Paul Hawken argues that a truly sustainable global economy must ultimately mimic the globe's natural ecology. This in turn will require the business system to be organized around (at least) two central principles: that all waste is food and that the solar energy ultimately powering the system must be utilized efficiently.[29] One technology that captures this idea is the so-called "living machine." A living machine is comprised of a series of pools that supports a complex artificial wetland that digests human waste, turning raw sewage into fresh drinking water, while at the same time generating agricultural commodities (e.g., fish and plant material) as by-products. Here the idea of waste as food is a literal one; moreover, the plants in a living machine also directly convert sunlight into energy.

As (or if) our economy moves toward a system based on industrial ecology and renewable energy resources, opportunities for job growth over and above a business-as-usual approach may emerge. For example, if living machines do indeed replace chemical sewage plants, net jobs will be gained at the local level if:

- production is more labor intensive;
- production is more domestic-content intensive;
- weekly work hours are reduced;
- the new technology helps spawn an era of rapid growth;
- exports are promoted; and/or
- the cleaned-up environment attracts skilled workers or new businesses.

Given these requirements, a region that is transitioning to a more ecological economy is by no means guaranteed higher than average levels of job growth. However, a significant number of new environmentally sensitive technologies and production methods do hold out the promise of jobs–environment synergies at the local level.

This chapter has laid out in a systematic fashion different theoretical arguments for why such a synergy might exist. Capitalizing on several of these opportunities would entail policy shifts at the national level toward greater energy efficiency and reliance on renewables; shorter workweeks; and higher levels of governmental support for environmental technology. More local green businesses and NGOs have been fostering economic development through a mix of import substitution (e.g., energy and water efficiency and buying locally) and export promotion, both of which are based on environmental technology, industrial ecology, and sustainably managed natural resources.

To this point, the general thesis of this book has been that the job losses and gains that have resulted from environmental regulation are small, gradual, and tend to balance each other out. This chapter reinforces that message. While jobs–environment synergies are real, they are not, at the economy-wide level, large. Nevertheless, fostering greener production can be an important element in a local economic-development strategy. From this discussion of local synergies it is now time to head back to economy-wide trade-offs and, specifically, to what some would have us believe will be the mother of all jobs–environment trade-offs. If we do begin to reduce greenhouse gas emissions over the first decade of the new millenium, what will be the impact on American workers?

NOTES

1. Lovins acknowledges his debt to another author, E. F. Schumacher, whose equally influential book *Small Is Beautiful: Economics as if People Mattered* was published in 1973. Lovins, however, redirected the debate away from a philosophical commitment to issues of scale toward questions of economic transition.
2. Lovins (1979: 23).
3. Gore (1992: 337).
4. Goodstein (1998b).
5. Multipliers are from Geller et al. (1992), and wage rates are from the *Statistical Abstract of the United States*.
6. Note this does not mean that the profit rate falls. A reduction in the profit share will not trigger capital flight.
7. Kinsley (1997).
8. Ackerman (1997: 81).

9. Laitner et al. (1999), Geller et al. (1992), Colt (1989), Muller et al. (1992), and Breslow et al. (1992).
10. Goodstein (1996).
11. Ehrenberg and Smith (1994: 135–144) and Repetto et al. (1992).
12. The trade share of energy use is from Daly and Goodland (1994); subsidies are from Koplow (1993); OECD energy use is from Daly (1993).
13. Kinsley (1997).
14. Schor (1991).
15. Przeworski (1995).
16. Human Resources Development Canada (1993).
17. See also Callaghan and Hartmann (1991).
18. Daly and Goodland (1994), Daly and Cobb (1989).
19. Hoerner et al. (1995).
20. The wind example is discussed in Goodstein (1998b: chapter 20).
21. Long-wave theory began with Kondratieff (1935) and Schumpeter (1939). On innovations, see Klienknecht (1987: 66).
22. Nell (1987).
23. Nelson and Wright (1992).
24. Lekakis (1991).
25. U.S. EPA (1993) and Elkington and Shopley (1989).
26. Grossman (1998) and conversations with Ted Wolf, communications director at Ecotrust.
27. Power (1996) presents this theory in detail.
28. Power (1995).
29. Hawken (1993: 12). There is actually a third principle, diversity of size and function, but it is less relevant to this discussion.

Chapter 6

Global Warming
and American Jobs

I get my greenhouse updates via the Internet. Some thoughtful soul has taken the time to put me on a mailing list announcing the U.S. Global Change Research Program Seminar Series. Every month, top greenhouse researchers present their results to policy makers on Capitol Hill. Unfortunately, it is a long commute from Portland, Oregon, to Washington, D.C., so I have to make do with the lengthy abstracts that accompany the announcements. Here are three observations from a late 1998 seminar:

- By using modern statistical techniques to match the widespread instrumental record of the 20th century to natural archives or "proxy" climate indicators such as tree-ring, coral, and ice-core records, combined with the suite of long historical climate records, global patterns of annual temperature have been reconstructed several centuries back in time, with relatively small uncertainties. . . . The evidence suggests that the decade of the 1990s, especially the years 1990, 1993, and 1997, are almost certainly the warmest back to A.D. 1400 for the Northern Hemisphere as a whole. The El Niño phenomenon also appears to have increased in intensity in recent decades relative to its pre-20th century behavior.

- The results of this analysis suggest that the significant temperature variations in past centuries likely have their origins in natural climate forcing—variations in the brightness of the Sun in particular. . . . [In contrast,] the recent warming shows a sharply emerging significant correlation with increasing greenhouse gases during the past couple of decades. In this sense, the human-enhanced greenhouse warming signal now appears to be detectable above the background of natural climate variability.
- Grinnell Glacier, one of the larger glaciers in Glacier National Park, decreased in area from 2.2 to 1.0 square kilometers (0.9–0.4 square miles) from 1900 to 1981, and calculations indicate that it will be gone in 50 to 70 years, and with it virtually all the glaciers in this National Park.[1]

Week after week evidence such as this dribbles in, and almost all of it points in the direction of a warming climate, with greenhouse gasses being the likely culprit. The bottom line here is that there is broad agreement in the scientific community that global warming is real and is with us now. In spite of industry efforts to greenwash, most people recognize this.

What is perhaps more surprising is that there is also fairly widespread agreement among economists who have actually studied the greenhouse issue that reducing greenhouse emissions is a good idea from an economic point of view. The economic consensus is not as strong as the scientific one, and it tends to break down along ideological lines—liberals and moderates versus conservatives and libertarians. Yet over 2,500 economists, including eight Nobel Prize winners, signed a statement that urged the United States to take a leadership role during the Kyoto Summit. The statement read, in part: "There are many potential policies to reduce greenhouse gas emissions for which the total benefits exceed the total costs."[2] Signatories also included people such as Yale University's William Nordhaus and MIT's Dale Jorgenson, both of whom have done groundbreaking work on estimating the costs and benefits of greenhouse gas control.

Undoubtedly, some of those costs will be borne by U.S. workers. In principle, layoffs from complying with the Kyoto agreement could arise in four different ways:

- direct employment losses in fossil-fuel-related sectors;
- direct layoffs in energy-intensive industries that are facing competition from developing countries with lower energy prices;
- regional downturns if "secondary" job losses generate a snowball effect; and
- an increase in economy-wide, cyclical unemployment if climate change policy throws the nation into a recession.

Is the employment impact likely to be small and localized, or big and national?

Up to this point in the book, I have evaluated other people's job loss predictions against actual outcomes. This exercise has illustrated two clear lessons. First, past forecasts of widespread job loss arising from environmental regulation, whether national macroeconomic disaster or regional recession, have simply failed to materialize. Second, direct, industry-specific job-loss estimates for timber workers and coal miners have tended to be roughly on target, if a bit high. However, the actual job-loss numbers in these worse-case scenarios have been, even by regional standards, quite modest—in each case, fewer than 10,000 jobs lost, with layoffs stretching over multiyear periods.

In this chapter I am going to make some (general) forecasts of my own. As has held true in our past experience with environmental regulation, I argue that both the macroeconomic and regional employment implications of greenhouse gas control are liable to be quite small; at the same time, groups of workers in particular industries will indeed face layoffs. The real challenge will thus be to craft a much better adjustment package than we have delivered in the past to help these workers and their communities, particularly in depressed areas such as the eastern coal country.

In 1997, the President's Council of Economic Advisors released their initial evaluation of the economic effect of achieving the Kyoto targets. Janet Yellen, chair of the council, summed it up this way: "if we do it dumb, [climate change policy] could cost a lot, but if we do it smart, it will cost much less and indeed could produce net benefits in the long run."[3] In part, this chapter explores what Yellen meant by "doing it smart." More significantly, I argue here that in our highly flexible market economy, "doing it dumb" is, in fact, a very unlikely outcome.

THE ROAD FROM KYOTO

In December 1997, the major industrial countries, including the United States, signed an agreement in Kyoto, Japan, committing themselves to a reduction in greenhouse gas emissions to average 5.2 percent below 1990 levels, with the target to be achieved between 2008 and 2012. The United States, by far the biggest greenhouse polluter, accepted a higher emission-reduction target than the average—around 7 percent below 1990 levels.

Developing countries were not signatories to the agreement. The reasoning here was twofold. First, the rich countries clearly bore the lion's share of responsibility for the build up of carbon dioxide in the atmosphere. Asking them to take the first steps toward solving the problem seemed only fair. And second, faced with pressing problems of economic underdevelopment, poor countries simply could not afford immediate action to control greenhouse gas emissions. This aspect of the Kyoto accord followed the precedent set by the successful 1986 Montreal Protocol to protect the ozone layer, in which developing countries were granted a ten-year grace period before they were expected to reduce production of ozone-destroying CFCs.

However, in a ninety-five-to-zero nonbinding resolution, the U.S. Senate announced to President Clinton in mid-1997 that it would not even consider ratifying the Kyoto Protocol unless developing countries also made commitments to future greenhouse gas reductions. The politics behind this senatorial consensus were, at first blush, easy to understand. Conservatives were simply opposed to the treaty; liberals were expressing concern that American workers would be disadvantaged by a treaty that exempted developing nations.

However, the most stunning aspect of the vote was the complete absence of environmental leadership in the Senate. In spite of their significant "inside-the-beltway" lobbying presence in Washington, environmentalists could not deliver a single vote in support of the Kyoto process. In chapter 1, I argued that the vote reflected the decline of genuine liberalism in the Senate, which in turn is a function of the weakening power of American labor unions. The 1996 version of Senate liberals, few in number, facing an organized and ideologically committed opposition, and without strong leadership of their own, took the easy way out. Whatever the politics might have been, by the spring of 1999, no broad agreement with developing countries had been reached, and President Clinton made it clear that he would not be bringing the treaty to the Senate for debate that year.[4]

What exactly would the Kyoto agreement require? In 1990, the United States emitted about 1,340 million metric tons of carbon into the atmosphere. Depending on assumptions about technological improvement (in the absence of required reductions), these emissions are expected to grow to about 1,800 million metric tons by the year 2010. Achieving a target of 7 percent below 1990 levels—1,246 million metric tons—would thus mean a reduction of carbon emissions of around 30 percent.[5]

This reduction could be achieved in a number of different ways. In heat and power generation, one would expect a shift away from high-carbon coal toward low-carbon natural gas (both are likely in any event), as well as a shift away from fossil fuels to renewables (e.g., wind- and solar-power production) combined with large savings from energy-efficiency investments. In transport, the biggest reductions would come, in the short term, from increased fuel efficiency. Larger gains can be made over the medium term from the adoption of hybrid-electric or fuel-cell vehicles. Reductions in emissions from power and transport could be supplemented by efforts as simple as tree planting.

Another important component of U.S. "reductions" is expected to come from abroad. In Kyoto, U.S. negotiators successfully pushed a concept called "joint implementation" (JI). The theory underlying JI is based on the fact that the geographic source of greenhouse gas emissions is irrelevant; a pound of carbon dioxide released from Toledo is just as dangerous as a pound emitted from Jakarta. Moreover, because industrial processes in developing countries tend to be much less efficient than in the developed world, the cost of carbon reduction in poor countries is typically much less than in rich countries.

Under JI, developed nations can get credit for carbon-emission reductions by helping developing nations reduce their emissions. For example, if a U.S. electric utility finances replacement of an inefficient Chinese coal plant with a cleaner, modern design, the carbon reductions will be allocated to that firm and count as part of the U.S. commitment. There will also be opportunities for country-to-country trading among developed regions, including the former Soviet Union and Eastern Europe, where a lot of low-cost carbon reduction can be achieved. Provided it can be adequately monitored and enforced, JI will be an important component of cost-effective greenhouse-emission reduction. Moreover, when done right, it presents a win–win scenario: rich countries get carbon reduction at a reduced price, and poor countries get access to cleaner technology. Given this background on Kyoto mechanics, what will be the employment impact of compliance with the treaty?

MODELING GREENHOUSE CONTROL IMPACTS: COSTS VERSUS JOBS

Global warming has already created a number of jobs, a generous portion of which seem to have been allocated to the economics profession. If predicting job losses from protecting spotted owls was something of a cottage industry in the Northwest in the late 1980s, forecasting the costs of reducing greenhouse gas emissions is now a full-blown, global big business. From industry-sponsored studies done by consulting firms, to in-house studies performed by environmental groups, to modeling efforts by both partisan and nonpartisan think tanks, to reports emanating from government agencies, to more scholarly papers produced by academics— the stack of cost estimates is impressive and, even for an economist such as myself, intimidating.

However, once you plunge in, you find that the water is not really so bad. To begin with, an important distinction needs to be made between "costs" and "jobs." The vast majority of studies have examined the possible long-run impact on GDP of carbon reductions. If forecasted GDP, after compliance with Kyoto, is lower than predicted GDP under a baseline scenario, then the treaty imposes costs on society. On the other hand, if GDP rises relative to the baseline case, as it sometimes does, then net benefits are forecast.

Because they focus on the long run, most of these studies have nothing to say about jobs. In the long run, lower GDP does not mean more unemployment; it just means a lower "material" standard of living that is exchanged for a more stable climate. Similarly, in the long run, higher GDP does not mean more jobs for the unemployed; it means a higher level of material consumption per person. The long-run focus of these studies means that they ignore business cycles and any cyclical unemployment generated by climate-change policy. Put another way, they explicitly assume full employment.

Having said this, it is useful to delve a bit into this extensive cost literature, because the predictions from employment models we will look at in the next section essentially hinge on the same issues. If, in the short run, reducing greenhouse gas emissions is quite costly, then it is likely to trigger a period of slower growth or even a recession. It is through this macroeconomic channel—high short-run costs, a near-term slowdown in growth, and an increase in cyclical unemployment—that forecasters can generate big, negative job impacts from climate-change policy.

In 1997, economists Robert Repetto and Duncan Austin of the World Resources Institute performed a very useful service by writing a pamphlet called *The Costs of Climate Protection: A Guide for the Perplexed.*

Repetto and Austin looked at sixteen of the most well-known models of the cost of climate-change control, compared their approaches, and then boiled down their differences. The authors began with 162 different predictions based on different assumptions that were plugged into the various models. Impacts on long-run GDP clustered around zero and, with a few exceptions, ranged from mildly positive to mildly negative for emission reductions up to the Kyoto range of 40 percent below the baseline. For deeper reductions, most of the GDP estimates were negative. (Again, most of these studies generally assumed full employment and, therefore, said nothing about job impacts.)

Looking deeper, however, Repetto and Austin concluded that the different predictions depended much less on differences between the models than they did on the underlying assumptions used by the models. The authors identified eight key assumptions that, along with the required reduction in carbon emissions, explained 80 percent of the difference in cost estimates. They concluded:

> This is good news. People don't have to be Ph.D. economists to understand the debate over the economic impacts of climate policy. Rather, people can use their own judgment and common sense to decide which of these basic assumptions are more realistic.[6]

More good news is that Repetto and Austin's eight assumptions can be reduced to four by answering for each model the following questions:

1. How flexible and innovative is the American economy?
2. Will some emission reduction be achieved through JI?
3. What happens to revenues the government obtains through pollution taxes or permit sales?
4. What direct and indirect *benefits* are achieved from climate protection?

The first question reflects an amusing twist to the climate-change policy debate. The conservative, high-cost view is rooted in a vision of the American economy as a rigid dinosaur, unresponsive, almost Soviet-like. In contrast, the progressive, low-cost perspective assumes a highly flexible and innovative economy. The irony is that it is progressives, not conservatives, who are championing the virtue of the free market. In concrete terms, high-cost models assume: (1) the scope for interfuel and interproduct substitution is minimal; (2) there is little room for cost-effective improvements in energy efficiency, and the rate of energy-efficiency innovations will not increase if climate-change policies are put in place; (3) energy sources other than fossil fuels will not become cost competitive. Are these assumptions of an inflexible economy valid? Some of the evidence on these points will be evaluated later in this chapter.

The second assumption listed earlier relates to joint implementation. As explained earlier, JI is expected to significantly lower the costs of reducing emissions. One way to raise cost forecasts is to eliminate any possibility of international trading and to simply assume all U.S. reductions must be domestic.

The third assumption has to do with revenues collected by the government. Most models assume that the government will discourage fossil-fuel use in one of two ways. The first would be to impose a tax on the carbon content of fuels. Taxes ranging anywhere from $20 per ton of carbon to over $200 per ton have been discussed. Under this scenario, the price of the "dirtiest" fossil fuel (coal) would rise the most, and the "cleanest" (natural gas) would rise the least. In 1997, the White House predicted that a $100-per-ton tax would raise gasoline prices by about 25 percent and electricity prices by about $0.02 per kilowatt hour.[7]

A second and related approach would be to auction off "tradeable permits" to firms. The idea here is that in order to emit a ton of carbon each day for a year, a firm must have a permit to do so. These permits would be bought from the government at annual auctions, and once purchased, they could be resold. This "tradability" of permits increases flexibility for industry as companies explore different approaches to complying with carbon-reduction requirements. Increased flexibility in turn lowers costs. However, costs do remain: for a given level of pollution reduction, permit systems generate about the same energy cost increases as do pollution taxes.

Yet another variation on this idea is to simply give permits away and then allow firms to buy and sell them. This was the approach taken in the highly successful sulfur-dioxide emission-reduction program, which was discussed in chapter 2 and which attacked acid rain under the CAA amendments. While retaining the desirable flexibility for industry, however, a permit giveaway does raise substantially the costs to society more than would a tax system or a permit auction. This is because permit giveaways provide a new, free-of-charge form of wealth to firms. In the case of carbon permit giveaways, energy prices go up, because permits are in short supply. Costs, however, do not. Therefore, firms get "windfall profits." For the acid-rain permit-giveaway program, the best estimate is that U.S. electric utilities will see their profits rise by a whopping $10 to $20 billion.[8]

Taxes and permit auctions are much less costly to the economy as a whole, because the government can use the revenues to offset the impact of higher energy prices. There are several ways to do this. Revenues might be invested in R&D of renewable energy sources or in subsidizing energy-efficiency measures. Funds could also be rebated directly back to workers in the form of payroll tax cuts, thereby stimulating work and consumption. The bottom line is that there are "smart" and "dumb" ways of reducing fossil-fuel use. The dumb ways—permit giveaways or, if money is raised, the wrong types of spending policies or tax cuts—raise costs.

Finally, the fourth assumption addresses the issue of climate-stabilization benefits. Recall that cost studies compare predicted GDP with carbon reductions against baseline GDP that assume no reductions. The baseline, of course, should include subtractions from (or additions to) GDP due to global warming, such as changes in agricultural output (negative or positive); losses due to increased incidence of severe weather; increased air-conditioning costs; reduced heating costs, and the like. In addition, reducing fossil-fuel use will mean significantly lower rates of conventional air pollutants, such as particulates, smog, and acid-rain precursors. These benefits should also be factored in. Studies forecasting high costs assume away these benefits of climate-control policy, arguing that they tend to be small.

In short, predictions of low costs—or actual net GDP benefits—from reducing greenhouse gas emissions assume: (1) a flexible and innovative economy; (2) some U.S. emission reductions come from joint implementation; (3) intelligent use of revenues from fossil-fuel taxes or permit sales; and (4) significant benefits from climate stabilization. To get high costs, regardless of the model employed, simply assume the opposite. Achieving significant reductions through trading and using permit or tax revenues intelligently is what CEA chair Yellen meant by "doing it smart." Neglecting trading opportunities and squandering revenues would be "doing it dumb."

My own belief that greenhouse gas emissions reductions will come at relatively low cost revolves around the assumption of a flexible and innovative economy. The economic system of the United States is not without its problems. However, the one thing at which U.S. capitalism clearly excels is innovation. Given a specific target—produce commodity x emitting y percent less carbon—I have little doubt that U.S. business firms will figure out how to do it at less than half the cost that economists think possible today.

My optimism is supported by research. In 1997, a coauthor and I examined all the cases we could find of cost forecasts for environmental regulations for which actual compliance cost estimates later became available. In every case but one, the actual costs were less than half the predicted costs. In the best known of recent cases, the sulfur-dioxide trading program, actual costs have been two to four times lower than the EPA expected, as well as four to eight times below industry estimates. Based on this record, I think that the private sector is very unlikely to "do it dumb" and that the economy will adjust with minimal disruption to the phasing in of carbon restrictions.

Repetto and Austin, in their review of the different cost models, agree:

> Predictions that a carbon tax . . . would seriously harm the economy are unrealistic. They stem from worst-case assumptions. Under more reasonable assumptions and preferable policy approaches, a carbon tax is a cost effective way of reducing the risks of climate change and would do no damage to the economy. . . . The real issues that need resolution are how to cushion the impacts on those few industries, regions, and communities that would be adversely affected. . . .

GREENHOUSE POLICY AND THE NEXT RECESSION: WHAT THE MODELS SAY

Janet Yellen, Robert Repetto, and I all agree that reducing greenhouse gas emissions will not cause a significant, short-run slowdown in growth. However, not everyone shares this perspective. This section will look at a few of the models that have been used to predict the short-run—five-to-ten-year—employment impacts of climate-change policy. As with long-run cost estimates, the model results are driven more by underlying assumptions than by fundamental differences in modeling technique. Optimistic assumptions generate actual job gains over a baseline, while pessimistic assumptions throw the economy into a recession and generate widespread job loss.

Nicely underlining this point is the fact that the same macromodel we discussed in chapter 2—the one owned by DRI—has produced widely divergent sets of predictions regarding the costs of controlling greenhouse gas emissions. The government hired DRI to do its short-run macroeconomic analysis, which was completed in July 1997. It found only modest impacts on growth and formed part of the basis for CEA chair Yellen's optimistic remarks quoted at the beginning of this chapter. However, by September of that year, the UMWA (along with the Bituminous Coal Operators Association) had commissioned and released a second DRI study, which reported a major growth slowdown and significant job loss.

The government's study was conducted by an interagency task force (IAT).[9] The IAT actually used several different models, however, they relied on DRI for their short-run analysis. The IAT report gave concrete job-loss forecasts for only a single "starting point" scenario, with no joint implementation and without creative use of revenues from carbon taxes. Under this scenario, GDP growth slowed down a bit and predicted unemployment increased by 0.4 percent—about 500,000 jobs nationwide.

There are a few things to note about this figure. First, it does not mean 500,000 layoffs. While the model predicts some direct job loss due to climate policy, most of the increased unemployment reflects slower growth of new jobs than under the baseline. In a normal growth year, the U.S. economy typically adds between one and two million jobs. If job growth slowed by half a million, this would mean that the unemployed, as well as new entrants into the labor market, would have a somewhat harder time finding work.

Moreover, as indicated in figure 6.1, month-to-month fluctuations in U.S. employment average 100,000 to 200,000 jobs and are sometimes

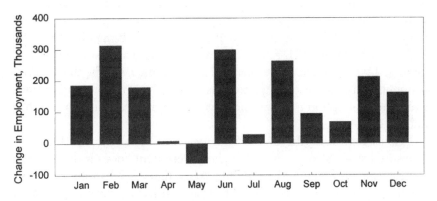

FIGURE 6.1. Month-to-month employment changes, 1995.
Source: Council of Economic Advisors (1996: Table B-42).

larger. Between April and May of 1995, for example, the economy lost over 60,000 jobs, but gained 300,000 the next month. Thus, while the 500,000 fewer jobs predicted by the DRI model is, in some ways, a big number, it is also just a bit larger than what we are accustomed to as our economy adjusts to everyday shifts in supply and demand.

Indeed, the IAT found that relying on international emissions trading and assuming a slightly faster rate of energy-efficiency improvement quickly brought short-run GDP losses down to essentially zero. With no significant growth slowdown predicted by the model, there would be no consequent increase in cyclical unemployment. From this modeling exercise, as well as other data, Yellen has concluded: "Although there may be job gains in some sectors and losses in others, we do not anticipate any significant aggregate employment effect if we achieve the conditions we have discussed."

Under the IAT's set of "smarter" assumptions, the DRI model predicts little slowdown in growth and thus no noticeable impact economy-wide on unemployment rates. In contrast, later that year, the UMWA released another DRI analysis. This time, however, the model was predicting a serious slowdown in GDP growth that bordered on recession. Forecasted job losses in the trough of the slowdown ranged from 1.6 million up to 2.7 million. These are big numbers even by the model's standards. Well above background fluctuations, they would reflect not just job growth slowdowns, but widespread layoffs.

Economist Rob Scott wrote up the DRI analysis for the UMWA.[10] According to Scott, there were two major differences between the UMWA and IAT assumptions. First, IAT assumed a higher rate of technological change, and, second, IAT assumed that consumers and firms would more rapidly find substitute products as energy prices rose. This reduced demand, in turn, means that prices would ultimately not rise as high. The UMWA/DRI, report, for example, predicts gasoline prices to increase by 50 percent more than the IAT. In other words, the UMWA maintained that the economy was substantially less "flexible and innovative" (the assumption number one discussed in the previous section) than did the IAT.

Consistent with the IAT's "starting-point" analysis, the UMWA-sponsored study also assumes that the government "does it dumb" with respect to tax revenues. The highest job loss figure—2.7 million—occurs when the government gives permits away and has no revenues to offset the impact of higher energy prices.[11] Finally, UMWA/DRI, like the original "starting-point" IAT estimates, assumed no joint implementation. In other words, all of the carbon-emission reductions had to come from the United States.

The UMWA/DRI study is much more temperate in its analysis than was the NAM/DRI report on proposed acid-rain legislation back in the late 1980s, which was discussed in chapter 2. Recall that the conclusion from the NAM/DRI study warned that initiatives such as acid-rain control would "achieve only the dubious distinction of moving the United States towards the status of a second-class industrial power by the end of the century." In contrast, Scott does a good job of highlighting the different assumptions that drive the UMWA/DRI model predictions of near-term recession. He even acknowledges in his conclusion that, "in the past, such modeling exercises [such as DRI's] have produced estimates that have proved, in retrospect, to significantly overestimate the costs of new pollution controls."

The UMWA/DRI model generates predictions comparable to those from other industry-sponsored macromodeling exercises. In April 1998, a Republican-controlled House subcommittee held hearings with the wonderfully loaded title: "Kyoto Protocol: Is the Clinton–Gore Administration Selling Out Americans?" Lined up to take on CEA chair Yellen were senior associates and presidents from the big three private macromodeling firms: WEFA (formerly Wharton Econometric Forecasting Associates), Charles River Associates (CRA), and DRI. WEFA's work on climate change has been financed by the American Petroleum Institute, who, along with the American Association of Automobile Manufacturers also helped bankroll CRA's modeling efforts.

WEFA—who we last saw in chapter 4 forecasting wildly large job gains from developing North Slope oil—won the award for the biggest greenhouse job-loss forecasts: 2.5 million. The reasons are familiar. As one example, in the WEFA model, the economy adopts renewable energy at a snail's pace. Between 2000 and 2010, the WEFA model predicts that for every 1 percent increase in fossil-fuel prices, renewable energy use will increase by 1.2 percent. During the energy crisis of the 1970s, however, renewables grew at a rate 40 percent faster than that in response to higher oil prices. The energy crisis, of course, was a surprise event. Facing Kyoto limits to be phased in over the course of a decade, one would expect to see more rather than less progress in adopting alternate technologies. But WEFA, along with the other for-hire macromodelers, assume otherwise.[12] These gloomy, industry-sponsored forecasts are all basically consistent with Yellen's message that if we do it dumb, it will cost a lot.

DOING IT SMART

A more optimistic set of assumptions, not surprisingly, generates fore-casts of employment gains. The starting point for this kind of model is a belief that today substantial opportunities exist for *profitable* investment in energy-efficiency technologies. A variety of market barriers, however, prevent firms from seizing these opportunities. Changes in government policy, combined with market incentives in the form of carbon taxes or a cap-and-trade system of marketable permits, can quickly induce firms to adopt these energy-saving measures. Savings on fuel costs would soon exceed the initial investment, and the economy would wind up with slightly higher GDP growth.

However, it is not faster growth that boosts short-run employment in this analysis. Instead, harking back to the discussions in chapters 2 and 5 of input–output models, consumer and business spending becomes both more "domestic content" and labor intensive. Oil imports fall, which leads to a lower trade deficit, and expenditures shift from capital-inten-sive fossil-fuel production to labor-intensive energy-efficiency invest-ment.

EPA analyst Skip Laitner and coauthors have made this argument. They maintain that a package of "smart" government policies could help promote dramatic energy reductions. The policies include:

- an advanced vehicles initiative that promotes highly fuel-efficient cars;
- tax credits for investments in energy efficiency;
- increased government spending on R&D for renewables and effi-ciency technologies;
- direct promotion of low-carbon technologies through information sharing, technology demonstrations, and government procurement policies; and
- energy standards for appliances and buildings.

Laitner and his coauthors argue that a combination of these measures would lead to cost-effective reductions in carbon emissions sufficient to achieve a carbon reduction of 10 percent below 1990 levels by 2010. Doing so, they estimate, would lead to an increase in economy-wide employment of 773,000 jobs.[13] (Again, given the imprecision of econ-omy-wide models, this should not be considered a large increase.)

The critical optimistic assumption here is the widespread existence of profitable energy-efficiency investments. If there is indeed money to be made by becoming more energy efficient, why aren't firms already doing so? A favorite analogy in this debate involves $100 bills lying on the sidewalk. They aren't often there, critics argue, because if they were, some-body would have already picked them up. In response, Laitner and oth-ers—most notably Amory Lovins, whose book *Soft Energy Paths* was dis-cussed in chapter 5—have maintained that a variety of market barriers, such as poor information, capital rationing, and variance between private and social risk, prevent firms from seizing otherwise profitable efficiency opportunities. Lovins argues that we can, in fact, get over half of the needed carbon reductions from already competitive energy-efficiency investments. It is the job of government policy to remove the barriers to realizing these opportunities.[14]

Successful policy initiatives such as the EPA's "Energy Star" rating program have proven the existence of substantial, cost-effective energy-saving potential in the economy. The EPA has worked with appliance manufacturers to create more energy-efficient units. If you own an energy-efficient computer, you may notice the Energy Star label on your monitor when the machine boots up. Analysts at the national Lawrence Berkeley Laboratory have estimated that if everyone adopted Energy Star products, the nation would save $100 billion on electricity over the next fifteen years. While some Energy Star products are more expensive than their energy-intensive counterparts, many are not; therefore, the net savings to the economy would still be quite large.[15]

Optimists such as Laitner and Lovins can also point to a battery of engineering studies that have identified, at least on paper, a host of cost-effective energy-saving investments. One of the most recent, the so-called "five-lab study" from the Department of Energy, basically concurs with Lovins. This study found that a combination of already existing energy-efficiency and renewable-energy technologies could achieve cost-effective reductions of up to 390 million metric tons of carbon, assuming relatively low energy price hikes. This is well over half of the reductions needed to achieve the Kyoto target.[16]

Beyond this key assumption about technology options, the predic-tion made by Laitner and others of three-quarter million new jobs is based on a simple input–output model. As such, it does not take into account the macroeconomic consequences of higher fossil-fuel prices the way the DRI model does—possible reductions in aggregate demand and increases in inflation or interest rates. In short, the model rules out by assumption the possibility that climate-change policy might induce an economic slowdown. This is justified, in the context of the model, by the assumption of so many low-cost compliance options.

And, indeed, when these assumptions are fed back into the DRI model—along with significant levels of international JI—the macro-economic consequences are small. This point was established by the IAT researchers. Laitner and his coauthors in fact recognize that macroeconomic impacts complicate the analysis. Ultimately, the use-fulness of the optimistic input–output model is that it reminds us of an employment impact that is not captured in the macromodeling efforts used by DRI. If climate policy encourages substantial increases in energy efficiency—domestically produced and more labor-intensive sources of energy than fossil fuels—this will tend to offset negative employment impacts if any growth slowdown in fact results from higher energy prices.

Given that climate-change policy is unlikely to induce a recession, we can now turn to direct sectoral impacts. These may be relatively con-tained and focussed on fossil-fuel-dependent jobs, such as coal mining and coal shipping and oil and utility work. Alternatively—and this is the fear expressed in the Senate resolution opposing the Kyoto Treaty as negotiated—U.S. manufacturing as a whole could take a beating from developing countries. Under the Kyoto Treaty, poor countries will not immediately face carbon restrictions and ensuing energy-cost increases. Will manufacturing capital relocate to take advantage of lower energy prices?

WHAT ABOUT TRADE? POLLUTION HAVENS ONCE AGAIN

Here is a taste of the scary rhetoric surrounding the issue from the Kentucky Coal Marketing and Export Council:

> After several months of attempting to hide the informa-tion from the public, the U.S. Department of Energy (DOE) was forced to admit that its own Argonne National Laboratory had completed a study which examined the economic impacts of the proposed United Nations emissions reduction treaty on U.S. industries. The study found that six energy-intensive strategic industries (steel, aluminum, pulp and paper, chemicals, cement, and petroleum refining) would experience dev-astating consequences under the current Kyoto scenario. In completing the study, Argonne relied upon input from experts from within each of the industrial sectors, not guesses and forecasts from government bureaucrats. Some of the study's findings include:

- 20–30 percent of our nation's basic chemical industry would move to developing countries.
- All primary aluminum plants in [the United States] would close by 2010.
- U.S. steel shipments would be cut by about 30 percent, and about 100,000 jobs would be lost in that industrial sector.
- In each case, these strategic industries suffer economic impacts that would have a profound effect on the nation's economy.
- [The] DOE has tried to distance itself from this study. The fact remains—experts from within these industrial sectors are convinced that a Kyoto treaty that results in driving up energy costs in the [United States] will have a dramatically negative impact on the key industries that drive the U.S. economy.[17]

After reading about this coming apocalypse, it is worth turning back to 1990 and recalling a similar quote that appeared in chapter 3. The quote comes from an industry-sponsored report that predicted dire, swift, and certain impacts from the CAA amendments: ". . . this study leaves little doubt that a *minimum* of 200,000 (plus) jobs will be quickly lost, with plants closing in dozens of states. This number could easily exceed one million jobs—and even two million jobs—at the more extreme assumptions about residual risk" (emphasis in the original). As you may recall, since the CAA amendments passed in 1990, the future has in fact turned out to be quite a bit rosier than was forecast in the industry-sponsored report. Fewer than 8,000 workers nationwide have applied for adjustment assistance because they were laid off as a consequence of the CAA legislation. There was no apocalypse then, and there will be none now.

The DOE report predicting widespread havoc from greenhouse gas control has received a lot of attention. It was featured repeatedly during the Senate floor debate over the 1997 resolution demanding that developing countries participate at Kyoto, and shows up prominently in the conservative Heritage Foundation's briefing paper on the costs of global warming.[18] But rather than an objective bit of analysis, the study instead was a forum for industry perspectives. The job-loss estimate for chemicals, for example, came from a background paper that was written by an employee of the chemical giant Monsanto. Some of the panels of "industry experts" had token representation from environmental or energy efficiency groups, however, all were dominated by industry, labor, and government officials, with many of the last coming from the industry-friendly side of government—the Department of Commerce and the International Trade Administration. Ronald Sutherland, the report's lead author, left Argonne soon after the publication of the study to work for the American Petroleum Institute.[19]

Underlying some of the industry gloom and doom were sizable energy price increases from a $100-per-ton carbon tax: 50 percent for electricity, 100 percent for coal, and 70 to 80 percent for fuel oil and natural gas. (Indicative of the simplistic flavor of the report, no offsetting policies, such as tax-revenue rebates to help affected industries, were even considered. The money collected in taxes just disappeared.) The report, in fact, was called "The Impact of High Energy Price Scenarios on Energy-Intensive Sectors: Perspectives from Industry Workshops." The extent of plant shutdowns and layoffs, if any, from higher energy prices will clearly depend on how high prices actually rise when carbon emissions are restricted.

Energy prices would rise under a carbon tax because fossil fuels are carbon intensive. Carbon taxes would encourage firms and consumers to: (1) switch from dirty (carbon-intensive) fossil fuels such as coal to cleaner ones such as natural gas; (2) switch from fossil fuels to renewables; and (3) reduce energy usage by investing in efficiency. However, in the United States, we are unlikely to use a direct carbon tax to meet the Kyoto targets. Instead we are apt to see a "cap-and-trade" policy such as the one we have successfully employed to reduce sulfur-dioxide emissions.

Under a cap-and-trade system, the government can either auction off permits to emit carbon or give them away for free under a "grandfathering" system in which all carbon emitters would be entitled to a share of the permits based on their past emissions. With either a tax or auction, it is easy to see why fossil-fuel prices would rise—firms will pass on some of the tax or the cost of the permits to consumers. It turns out, somewhat surprisingly, that grandfathering has the same effect. This is because firms will have fewer permits than they need, and therefore they will either have to buy them from other firms or spend money reducing carbon emissions. These expenses then get passed on to businesses and consumers as higher energy prices.

Are U.S. firms dependent for their profitable operation on low energy prices? Dramatic differences in energy prices already exist across countries, and yet they seem to have little influence on industry competitiveness or location decisions. Again, quoting CEA chair Yellen's congressional testimony: "In 1996, premium gasoline cost $1.28 per gallon in the United States, but only $0.08 per gallon in Venezuela. Similarly, gas prices were $3.71 per gallon in Switzerland, and $4.41 per gallon in France. Electricity prices also vary significantly; in the United States, for industry they were 5 cents per kilowatt hour in 1995, a fraction of prices in Switzerland of 13 cents per kilowatt hour. Yet U.S. industry is not moving en masse to Venezuela, nor is Swiss industry moving to the United States."[20]

This debate is reminiscent of the pollution-haven argument evaluated, and largely discredited, in chapter 3. Few U.S. industries will flee overseas in search of marginally lower energy prices, for the same reasons that few relocate to escape pollution regulations in developed countries. First, energy prices, such as pollution-compliance costs, are a small fraction of total business costs. More than 90 percent of U.S. workers in the tradeable-goods sector work in industries where energy costs are less than 3 percent of sales.

Moreover, even for more energy-intensive industries, the traditional factors that drive location decisions—proximity to markets, low-wage (and/or high-productivity) labor forces, solid transportation, communication and financial infrastructures, and proximity to raw materials—will remain determinate. Robert Repetto at the World Resources Institute, for example, looked at U.S. investment abroad in two energy-intensive sectors, chemicals and primary metals, that together account for over one-third of the energy used in U.S. manufacturing. In 1996, more than 80 percent of investment abroad by U.S. companies was in other industrialized nations. Repetto also notes that in recent years the major developing countries have been, unilaterally, cutting subsidies for energy, and have thus seen rising energy prices.[21]

Given this background, it is evident that it would take both a large energy-price increase and, at the same time, no medium-term prospect for rising energy prices in developing countries for shutdowns and relocations to poor nations of energy-intensive industry to become significant. So, how high will energy prices rise in the United States if the Kyoto target of a 7 percent reduction below 1990 levels by the deadline of 2008 to 2012 is met?

Economic models of climate-change policy all report a "price of carbon," which is either the carbon tax level or an estimate of what the price of a tradeable carbon permit will turn out to be. As I wrote this chapter (winter of 1998), the Clinton administration seemed to be settling in around a carbon price estimate of between $25 and $50 per ton. Government analysts argue that, given this price range, we can get half or more of our emission reductions at home through known, cost-effective technologies, such as fuel switching, increased use of renewables, and, most importantly, investments in energy efficiency. The other half of U.S. emission reductions would come from unforeseen technological improvements, changes in agricultural and forestry practices, the reduction of non-CO_2 greenhouse gasses (methane, nitrous oxide, and CFCs), and the purchasing of carbon-reduction credits from abroad. At a $25 per ton carbon price, energy-price increases will be quite trivial: natural gas prices will rise 5 percent, and gas and electricity prices will go up 4 percent. These changes barely rise above the background noise of year-to-year price fluctuations. Add to this the fact that the price increases would be phased in over a ten-year period and that electricity prices for industrial users will drop anyway due to deregulation, and you get the conclusion that most American consumers simply won't notice.[22]

If prices don't rise much, how will we achieve big carbon savings at home? The beauty of the cap-and-trade system is that it is forward looking. Businesses will know the carbon targets they will need to meet several years in advance if they are to stay within their permitted levels and reduce their exposure to the external permit market. This will initiate private investment in energy efficiency and fuel switching. In addition, business and government partnerships will emerge that will promote research development and diffusion for new and existing carbon-reducing technologies, energy-use standards for new products, and education and outreach efforts. By the time that the carbon caps begin to bite in 2008, the need for purchase of permits from abroad will be greatly reduced. With lower demand for permits, carbon prices, and thus energy prices, will not rise greatly. (There is one interesting possible side-effect of large-scale investment in efficiency. Because U.S. demand is a big part of world demand for oil and natural gas, a significant decline in U.S. demand might actually lead oil and gas prices to drop. One government study concludes that this is in fact likely under a high-efficiency scenario, though electricity prices do still rise modestly in the model. Overall energy use does not rise with the declining prices because the economy has become so energy efficient.[23])

In this "smart" scenario, the cap-and-trade system is viewed as a powerful market signal, as well as one that has the attractive feature of avoiding large price increases. Instead, it is argued, a cap-and-trade policy will focus corporate and government attention on a host of already existing low-cost energy-efficiency and renewable technologies. A decade of phased-in investment of this kind will prevent the need for a price shock to achieve carbon reductions.

In contrast, relying on higher energy prices alone to reduce emissions (i.e., no proactive business–government partnerships; no government policy promoting alternatives; no international trading) would be more costly. The U.S. government's initial 1997 assessment was that a $100-per-ton carbon tax would be required to freeze emissions at 1990 levels. This would translate into roughly a 25 percent increase in both gasoline and electricity prices. If the economy were made less "flexible and innovative," carbon prices would begin to shoot up. The UMWA/DRI report estimates prices of between $180 and $270 per ton by 2010, while WEFA again takes the top prize with their predicted value of $360 per ton by 2020.

So how high will energy prices go? My own assessment is, in the short run, not very much. The reason is that we, as a nation, will try to "do it smart" by aggressively promoting low-cost energy-efficiency measures at home and by exploiting low-cost purchases of carbon-emission reduction from abroad. There is simply no constituency out there for large energy-price increases. Industry is obviously opposed, and people on the environmental side seem convinced that the Kyoto goals can be met without relying too heavily on price incentives. Put another way, no policy will be seriously contemplated that leads to a 30 percent decline in U.S. chemical industry employment, the shutdown of all aluminum plants by 2010, or the lose of 100,000 jobs in the steel industry. And nor is one necessary.

The Clinton administration may be wrong. Carbon prices on the world market may rise higher than $25–$50 per ton, indicating that there were fewer easy emission-reduction targets than were thought, and that energy-efficiency measures may be more costly than analysts anticipated. But regardless, it will take time to figure this out. And if we try this approach and fail, black helicopters from the United Nations will not descend across the countryside, carting the U.S. population off to jail. All it will mean is that, in 2005, or whenever, serious energy-price increases will be back on the table for Congress to consider.

Given that large energy-price increases are not on the horizon, significant capital flight due to dramatically higher energy prices is highly unlikely. Also, few U.S. manufacturing plants will shut down because they are being undercut by firms from developing countries with lower energy prices. This is not to say, however, that it will never happen. Some plants will undoubtedly shut down. But, consistent with our 30-year experience of the impact of environmental regulation on manufacturing employment, the numbers are likely to be small in both relative and absolute terms.

If, contrary to this expectation, carbon-permit prices do rise above the $100-per-ton level, energy-inefficient plants in highly energy-intensive industries may need temporary trade protection as they adjust to the new conditions and invest in more energy-efficient production processes. One possibility that has been discussed is a border tax to be levied on the energy or carbon content of imports.[24]

This chapter has so far ruled out (1) increases in cyclical unemployment due to a climate-policy-induced recession, and (2) significant increases in structural unemployment arising from large-scale shutdowns in energy-intensive industries. This leaves the primary greenhouse jobs burden on the shoulders of workers in fossil-fuel-related industries: coal miners, oil-field workers, coal- and oil-shipping employees, and coal- and oil-fired electric-utility workers.

SECTOR-SPECIFIC IMPACTS

Given the uncertainty surrounding how the United States would meet the Kyoto targets, one cannot put a precise number on overall potential job losses in the fossil-fuel industries. However, history does provide some guidance here. The Kyoto Treaty requires that we reduce carbon emissions by 2010 to a level some 30 to 40 percent below what they would be, assuming no controls. The United States has achieved quite comparable reductions in conventional air pollutants over a similar time frame. As a consequence of the clean-air regulations that were enacted in the mid-1970s, by 1988, relative to where we would have been with no controls, particulate concentrations in the air were down well over 70 percent; lead over 95 percent; sulfur dioxide over 42 percent; and carbon monoxide over 57 percent. Between 1990 and 1994, concentrations of all of these pollutants fell at least another 10 percent.[25] And all of this was achieved with minimal job loss. As documented in chapter 3, total regulation-induced layoffs have varied from 1,000 to 3,000 nationwide over the last couple of decades. And not all of these job losses were due to air-quality regulation.

Are job losses from climate policy likely to be this low? They may be somewhat higher, but will still probably be of a comparable magnitude. I have argued in this chapter that greenhouse gas control is unlikely to generate many direct layoffs outside of fossil-fuel-related sectors. One can get a feel for possible impacts in these industries by looking at forecasts for the coal industry. The UMWA/DRI study discussed earlier predicts that, even in the absence of greenhouse gas controls, coal-industry employment will fall by 36,000 workers between 1995 and 2020. If carbon emissions are restricted, the analysis projects a further decline of an additional 36,000 job slots, or about 1,500 per year.

This industry-sponsored estimate is in rough agreement with the more optimistic analysis by Laitner and his coauthors at the EPA, which, in contrast to the UMWA/DRI report, predicted overall job gains from meeting the Kyoto targets. For the coal industry in particular, the Laitner study forecasted job slot losses of about 1,200 per year between 2000 and 2010.[26] Given these estimates for coal, and recognizing that the biggest layoff impacts are certain to be in this industry, it seems likely that total annual job losses in the fossil-fuels sector from greenhouse gas policy are likely to number in the low thousands. And this figure is quite comparable in magnitude to the regulation-induced layoffs we have observed over the last twenty-five years.

What will be new about climate policy is the cumulative, negative impact on coal communities. While annual coal job losses are likely to be comparable to those experienced as a consequence of the CAA amendments in the early to mid-1990s, the difference will be that these thousand-plus layoffs will be sustained year after year, over a twenty-year period. Total losses of coal jobs due to greenhouse gas control are estimated to be triple to quadruple those from the acid-rain program. At the same time, as noted earlier, the industry is forecasting about a 25 percent decline in jobs over the next twenty years, even without global warming regulations. Given this, and with only a few exceptions, eastern coal counties are likely to see high unemployment rates from 2000 to 2020, which will dramatically compound the hardship faced by laid off workers in these areas.

ADJUSTMENT ASSISTANCE OPTIONS

Under these circumstances, what kind of adjustment assistance program should we be talking about? In chapter 4, I discussed the adjustment programs that were made available to coal miners under the CAA amendments of 1990 for retraining, and to timber workers under Clinton's 1993 Forest Plan for retraining, conversion, and community assistance. Box 6.1 lists the main findings from that survey. Based on this information, it is useful to think about adjustment programs for two different groups of workers: those who are living in areas of high structural unemployment (e.g., many coal miners) and those who are not.

Box 6.1. Adjustment lessons from the CAA amendments
and the Forest Plan

RETRAINING

- Job counseling and search programs provided under the Job
  Training and Partnership Act (JTPA) can help; these services are
  most effective when the unemployment rate is low.
- Short-term JTPA training has no impact on raising workers'
  incomes.
- Good, long-term retraining can raise wages a few thousand dollars per year.
- Dislocated workers typically find new jobs that pay 10–25 percent less than their old ones. Many coal miners probably saw cuts
  in pay closer to 50 percent.
- Lack of income support and health insurance often prohibit
  workers from pursuing long-term retraining options available
  under JTPA.
- In areas of high structural unemployment, skills obtained under
  retraining may not match available jobs.
- Retraining makes less economic sense for older workers, who
  also have the hardest time adjusting to job loss.

CONVERSION

- The Jobs in the Woods Program succeeded in demonstrating
  that a high-skills/high-wage approach to ecosystem management
  was feasible.
- Conversion or other direct job creation efforts need long-term
  commitments of support from government if they are to succeed.

COMMUNITY ASSISTANCE AND DEVELOPMENT

- The one-stop-shopping policy in the Forest Plan helped reduce
  red tape and funnel federal dollars to communities hit by mill
  shutdowns.

Source: Summary of chapter 4.

The group of workers who are not living in areas of high structural unemployment will face the immediate problems of all dislocated workers: the trauma of unemployment and, without quality retraining, a likely drop in income of 10 percent to 25 percent. The primary obstacle with which these workers have to deal is how to maintain a family and pay the bills over the time needed for meaningful retraining. At a minimum, two years of UI benefits and access to low-cost health insurance will be needed to allow workers to pursue the kind of serious retraining necessary to make a difference in their lives. The basic JTPA package, for practical purposes, can only serve workers for the six or so months that they have access to UI. Some JTPA programs, such as the trade adjustment program and the program set up under the CAA amendments, do provide extended UI. The system, however, is very complex. A significant number of coal miners, for example, got tied up in red tape and were unable to access the extended benefits to which they were entitled. And many dislocated workers are unsure of the category into which they fall.

The wrong thing to do here is to create yet another set of JTPA eligibility rules for regulation-induced layoffs resulting from greenhouse gas control. Instead, climate-change legislation presents an opportunity for environmentalists and labor to work together to simplify and restructure the whole JTPA program. Given that short-term training is known to be of very limited value, all workers who are eligible for training programs—regardless of the cause of the layoff—should be able to tap into two years of UI benefits. In addition, laid off workers should be given an opportunity to buy into a low-cost health-insurance program.[27]

For workers who live in areas of high structural unemployment, good, long-term, supported training is also necessary, but will, in and of itself, be insufficient. Under these conditions, retrained workers may well find that their new skills fail to bring them any employment advantage. In such a case, community infrastructure and development assistance can provide temporary jobs, as well as begin to lay a foundation for longer-term growth. Another option to support direct reemployment in the coal country might be a spin-off of the Jobs in the Woods program. In the East, the government could provide funds to train and employ workers in strip-mine restoration and in the clean up of acid-mine drainage.

For practical purposes, "workers living in areas of high structural unemployment" will most often mean coal miners. Yet another issue that coal miners face that further sets them apart from most dislocated workers is that no other group will experience such significant cuts in income. As noted in box 6.1, most dislocated workers do experience drops in pay, typically on the order of 10 to 25 percent. In contrast, an average miner in Monongalia County, West Virginia, would take a 50 percent annual pay cut—a loss of $23,000—if he took a job that paid the county-wide average wage. Thus, it is no exaggeration to say that many coal-mining families will be sacrificing well over $100,000 in income as a consequence of global-warming controls. No other group will bear costs even close to this magnitude.

Should adjustment policy acknowledge this sacrifice? Some would argue that coal miners should not complain. After all, they had the good-paying jobs as long as they lasted. However, it seems only fair for society to recognize that if some pay more than others for a cooler climate, coal miners will clearly pay the most. Add to this the fact that older workers face the hardest adjustment path, especially in areas of high structural unemployment, and a strong case can be made for a buyout of coal miners with substantial seniority.

Senator Byrd of West Virginia proposed a buyout policy in the debates leading up to the 1990 acid-rain-control legislation. Under his plan, the final version of which failed in the Senate by a single vote, coal miners who lost their jobs as a result of the CAA amendments would have been paid by the government a declining fraction of their base salary for four years—80 percent the first year, declining to 50 percent in the final year.[28] This would have been in lieu of unemployment benefits and included other traditional adjustment assistance options, such as job training. Senator Byrd's approach might be modified today to include only miners above a certain age (e.g., 45) with a certain number of years on the job (e.g., 10 or more). While such payments would be far from restoring most miner's foregone income, they would serve to acknowledge the sacrifices made, as well as provide a critical income bridge to retirement for older miners.

Ultimately, even the best adjustment program will not make workers and their communities "whole." Coal miners and coal-dependent towns will lose out as a result of climate policy. And in an era when corporate CEOs are guaranteed golden parachutes before being shown the door, it seems only just to supply average American workers with parachutes of their own. Moreover, if not gold, at least they need to be made of material that is sturdy enough to keep laid-off workers from breaking their legs when they hit the ground.

WINNERS, LOSERS, AND GLOBAL WARMING

One of the principal tenets of economic theory is that if the benefits of an action exceed the costs, then a "win–win" outcome is always conceivable. Out of the bigger pie, the story goes, the winners could compensate the losers, leaving everybody better off. In practice, of course, this seldom happens. Most changes in the economy, even if beneficial on net, create both winners and losers. But it does present a just ideal toward which progress can be made.

Reducing greenhouse gas emissions, many economists believe, is one of those cases. As noted earlier, over 2,000 economists, including a large number who have done research in the area, signed off on a statement that read in part, "There are many potential policies to reduce greenhouse gas emissions for which the total benefits exceed the total costs." Across the globe, literally billions of people will profit from greater climate stability, fewer droughts and tropical storms, lower sea-level rise, and fewer extinctions of natural species. Adjustment assistance is the mechanism by which this large group of winners can compensate some of the losers from climate policy—if not fully, at least partially.

How many workers will lose? In this chapter, I have argued that, in fact, the future is liable to look a lot like the past. Just as over the 1980s and 1990s, when new environmental regulations were proposed, we are today seeing industry-sponsored predictions of a macroeconomic slow-down coupled with massive capital flight to less-developed countries. Millions of jobs, it is alleged, will soon be lost. And just as in the past, it is likely that these predictions will fail, and fail miserably.

Smart climate policy will not push the U.S. economy into a recession because businesses will respond creatively and flexibly to carbon restrictions. Known, low-cost energy-efficiency and renewable technologies can bring us half way to the Kyoto targets. Ten more years of technological innovation, combined with the policies like tree planting and the purchase of carbon permits from abroad, mean that energy prices will stay relatively low. Without large increases in energy costs, business firms will not close their doors and flee to low-priced energy havens. This is especially true since energy prices, even for energy-intensive businesses, are seldom the determinate factor in location decisions. Add in the fact that investments in energy efficiency are both more labor and domestic-content intensive than is fossil-fuel production, and negative, economy-wide job impacts become even less probable.

All of this leads to the conclusion that finally, as in the past, the number of regulation-induced layoffs is likely to be small in both absolute and relative terms—on the order of a few thousand per year nationwide. Weighed against industry-sponsored, macromodel estimates of job losses in the millions, this layoff prediction may seem impossibly small. To that I can only respond that we have been at this same decision point, evaluating predictions of devastating job–environment trade-offs, many times before. And history is clearly on my side.

NOTES

1. Mann and Meier (1998).
2. "Economic Scene," *New York Times*, February 13, 1997, p. C2.
3. Yellen (1997). Regarding employment impacts, Yellen (1998) does not "anticipate any significant aggregate employment effect," again, if it is done "smart."
4. In December 1998, Argentina and Kazakhstan agreed in principle to a cap-and-trade system.
5. U.S. Department of Energy (1997).
6. Repetto and Austin (1997: 14).
7. "White House Predicts Lower Costs for Controlling Emissions," *New York Times*, July 16, 1997, p. A10.
8. Burtraw (1998).
9. IAT (1997).
10. Scott (1997). Scott works at the Economic Policy Institute (EPI), which published the report. I am also involved with EPI as a research associate. EPI, as part of its mission, tries to bridge environmental and labor concerns. EPI originally sponsored much of the research that went into this book, and has been very supportive of my work and that of others demonstrating the myth of a widespread jobs–environment trade-off. Life at the "red–green" crossroad sometimes generates tensions.
11. The DRI model likes options that increase savings in the long run, because in the model, increased savings lead automatically to increased investment in the United States. Thus DRI actually favors permit giveaways in the long run—which increase corporate profits—over reducing income taxes. See Scott (1997) and Burtraw (1998) for a critique of this perspective.
12. For a critical analysis of the WEFA model, see Barrett (1998). Since I wrote this chapter, DRI (on behalf of the coal operators) has come out with an even gloomier forecast than WEFA's.
13. Laitner (1998); see also Koomey et al. (1998) for a generally comparable analysis.
14. I provide an overview of this debate in Goodstein (1998b); see also Lovins and Lovins (1997).
15. Webber and Brown (1998). The $100 billion is the present value of savings in 1995 dollars, discounted at a 4 percent real rate.
16. Interlaboratory Working Group (1997). These reductions assume price incentives from a $50-per-ton carbon tax. Koomey et al. (1998) foresee cost-

effective reductions equal to about half of the Kyoto target with a $23-per-ton tax.

17. Kentucky Coal Marketing and Export Council Website (www.coaleducation.org). The report is Sutherland et al. (1997).

18. Antonelli and Schafer (1997).

19. The methodology of the report was to assume we do it very dumb: a $100-per-ton carbon tax; no tax rebates for the affected industries; and no carbon restrictions in the developing world down the road. Then they commissioned a background paper for each industrial sector in which the author provided back-of-the-envelope, personal estimates of potential job losses from these large, unmitigated energy-price increases. They then had industry experts discuss (and generally ratify) the background papers.

But even given this context—very crude job-loss predictions from a single source; a panel stacked with industry-friendly representatives; big energy-price increases with no offsetting policies such as tax rebates to help industry adjust; and developing countries facing no medium-term energy-price increases—most of the background papers themselves make much less scary reading than the executive summary cited in note 17. For example, take the chemical-industry report. The author, Dan Steinmeyer from Monsanto, argued that "The history of the chemical industry does not show many clear examples of plants that have been shut down purely because of energy costs. However, when plants are shut down for whatever reason, the choice of location for the replacement plant carries a heavy input from projected energy costs at alternate sites. . . ." Steinmeyer foresaw a gradual shift—over a twenty-five-year period—in new investment in the energy-intensive portion of the chemical industry toward the Middle East and China, again assuming that these countries never faced their own carbon restrictions or energy-price increases. At the end of this period, he argued, the United States would have lost between 5 and 10 percent of the value added, and about 10 percent of the jobs in the industry—around 100,000 in total. Somehow—in a fashion not clear to at least one of the panel participants with whom I spoke—this guesstimate then got translated in the executive summary of the report as the claim that "20–30 percent of our of our nation's basic chemical industry would move to developing countries."

For a comparable critique of the aluminum projections, see Barrett (1998).

20. Yellen (1998).

21. Repetto and Maurer (1997).

22. Yellen (1998); Koomey et al. (1998).

23. Koomey et al. (1998).

24. Scott (1997).
25. Goodstein (1998b: Table 14.1).
26. Scott (1997) and Laitner et al. (1998).
27. See Young (1998) for a labor perspective on this issue.
28. Kete (1992).

Chapter 7

FICTIONS, FACTS, AND THE FUTURE

In the fall of 1998, I had the opportunity to attend a panel discussion on global warming. The first three speakers were nationally prominent scientists. Each, from a different disciplinary perspective, presented the mounting evidence that the globe was indeed getting hotter and that greenhouse gas emissions were the likely cause. The fourth speaker, who was from the Competitiveness Policy Institute, a corporate-backed, free-market advocacy group in Washington, was invited to provide some "balance." A full-time and well-paid opponent of the Kyoto Treaty, he presented a superficial but persuasive attack on the accord, arguing that it would be both ineffective and, of course, have a devastating impact on U.S. jobs. He relied heavily on the macromodeling exercises from DRI and WEFA, which were discussed in chapter 6, to make his case.

After the presentations, students in the audience stood up to express clear frustration. On the one hand, the scientists were telling them that global warming was real and serious and, on the other hand, they were being told that action to stop it was both very costly and ultimately futile. The panel organizers must have assumed that the three scientists would respond and argue for the Kyoto Treaty. The scientists, however, refused to get involved in a messy political discussion, perhaps because they felt it was out of their area of expertise, or because they feared losing their impartial status as scientists. So, oddly, there was no balance. The only voice that was raised on the panel was a very sophisticated call for inaction. For the students, it was a deeply disempowering experience, which was exactly, I suspect, what the corporate funders of the anti-Kyoto movement would have desired.

The evening could not have provided a clearer demonstration of the source of a jobs–environment trade-off myth: in this case, a hired-gun out of D.C. who relied on industry-sponsored studies done by consulting firms in New York and Boston. A couple of hundred members of the audience, including half a dozen reporters, took in his well-packaged story about the high costs of environmental regulation and the predictions of widespread job loss. And though the audience that night may have been skeptical of the source, the tale has been repeated often enough that for most Americans it has, unfortunately, started to ring true.

This book has tried to set the record straight. In the United States, we have over twenty-five years of experience with stringent national environmental regulation, ranging from the Clean Air Act of 1972, to the Clinton Forest Plan of 1993. In each regulatory debate, claims about a jobs–environment trade-off have loomed large. Back in 1972, no one knew for certain what the jobs impacts of environmental protection would turn out to be. But from what we have learned in the last quarter century, here are the fictions, as well as facts, about jobs and the environment:

Fiction 1: Environmental regulation has created economy-wide, cyclical unemployment either by deepening recessions or preventing the economy from achieving full employment.

Fact 1: Regulation has neither caused nor deepened recessions. Before macromodeling became politicized in the mid-1980s, scholarly uses of the tool provided consistent evidence that regulation had no significant negative impact on short-term growth. If anything, government-mandated investment spending has probably boosted employment during recessions. Environmental regulation has not prevented the economy from achieving full employment. In fact, during the mid-1990s—when an unprecedented $160 billion per year was spent on environmental clean up—unemployment rates were nevertheless as low as they had been since the 1960s. Indeed, in 1995, job growth was *too fast* for the Federal Reserve Board. Fearing inflation, the Fed raised interest rates to slow down job growth.

Fiction 2: Even if it has had no economy-wide impact, regulation has nevertheless led to widespread plant shutdowns and layoffs, aggravating structural unemployment at the regional level.

Fact 2: Layoffs from plants that shut down due to environmental regulation have averaged between 1,000 and 3,000 annually nationwide since federal regulations were instituted in the 1970s. This number is clearly small compared to even a single corporate restructuring. In an economy in which over two million workers are laid off each year, this number is very, very small. In an average year, environmental regulation accounts for less than one-tenth of 1 percent of all layoffs. Even in the extremely high profile cases of northwestern timber workers and eastern coal miners, total job-slot losses have been in each case less than 10,000, spread out over several years and over multistate regions.

Fiction 3: Even if there are no economy-wide impacts, and even if plants don't often shut down, environmental regulation has nevertheless encouraged most new investment in pollution-intensive industries to relocate to poor countries that do not have strict regulations. Since this new investment would have occurred in traditional manufacturing areas of the United States, such capital flight to "pollution havens" has made structural unemployment worse.

Fact 3: There is a kernel of truth to fiction 3, but not much more than that. While it is possible to point to individual plants for which this is true, they can be counted on the fingers of a couple of hands. Since the 1970s, economists have looked hard for pollution havens, and they just are not there in any significant number. And for what reasons? Environmental regulatory costs are a small portion of total business costs; costs are only one factor in relocation decisions; and in modern production facilities, pollution-control devices are often embedded in the technology to begin with.

Fiction 4: Granted that there are no economy-wide job losses, firms seldom shut down, and new investment is not fleeing to pollution havens. Nevertheless, environmental regulation has still accelerated the shift out of manufacturing jobs and into service jobs.

Fact 4: On net, environmental regulation supports more jobs than average in traditional blue-collar sectors of the economy—31 percent of employment supported by environmental spending is in construction and manufacturing, compared to 20 percent for the economy as a whole. This is because environmental clean up is fundamentally an industrial business, requiring the manufacture of pollution-control devices, equipment for hazardous waste clean up, and the construction of sewage treatment facilities.

Fiction 5: In rural counties, the ripple effect on secondary employment arising from job losses in base industries (e.g., mining and logging) is often bigger than the primary job loss.

Fact 5: There is simply no evidence supporting these kinds of predictions from crude "base models." In fact, rural economies are either so poorly developed that they lack much secondary employment supported by the base industry, or they are sufficiently developed so that they are resilient to shutdowns in mining and lumbering. This is not to say that there are no secondary impacts, especially in very small towns. Rather, the point is that in very small towns, there are few secondary jobs.

Fiction 6: Government retraining programs provide adequately for the needs of workers who were laid off due to environmental regulation (or other more prevalent causes).

Fact 6: The typical dislocated worker will see a drop in earnings from 10 to 25 percent. The figure is higher for many eastern coal miners. Short-term JTPA training has *no* impact on raising the incomes of laid off workers, but because extended UI and health benefits are often not available, workers cannot take advantage of the longer-term retraining that could make a difference. In addition, retraining does little to help older workers, who have a harder time funding new work and need a bridge to retirement.

Fiction 7: An economy-wide shift to clean technology would significantly reduce unemployment at the national level.

Fact 7: Just as environmental regulations don't create cyclical unemployment, neither can they cure it. Nationwide unemployment rates are determined by business-cycle forces and government-fiscal and interest-rate policy, not the composition of investment spending on the factory floor. However, at the local or regional level, adoption of ecologically sound production technologies can often provide a basis for employment growth.

These seven facts are the fruits of our more than two decades of experience with large-scale, national environmental regulation. The next major round of environmental legislation—if and when it comes—will focus on reducing greenhouse gas emissions. There are, of course, no facts yet available about the employment impact of such legislation; however, that has not prevented dozens of predictions by everyone from industry to environmentalists.

FROM FACTS TO THE FUTURE

Most forecasts of the job impacts of climate policy have come from fancy and expensive macromodeling exercises. Those sponsored by industry argue that climate-change legislation would bring on a minirecession, leading to short-term job losses on the order of 2.5 million. Comparable exercises done by the government—in some cases using the same consulting firm's model—find negligible impacts on short-term employment and growth. These dueling exercises have proven useful primarily for confirming that the differing predictions of high or low short-term costs, and high or negligible employment impacts, are in fact assumption and not model driven.

If one believes that as the price of fossil fuels rises, people will not find existing substitutes for fossil fuels; if one argues that technological progress on fossil-fuel substitutes will progress only slowly and will not be accelerated by the climate-change policy itself; if one assumes that there will be little international trading of carbon rights, so the United States will have to achieve all of its mandated reductions at home; and if one believes that revenues from permit sales will be squandered—in short, if one assumes we were to "do it dumb," then one can indeed tell a story about how meeting the Kyoto targets will have high short-term costs, meaning a recession and substantial job loss. Reverse those assumptions, or "do it smart," and the economic costs of Kyoto are small—no recession and only localized job impacts.

Over the last thirty years, we as a people have instituted a whole series of major environmental laws. Each time that a new regulation is put in place we have been able to gather more evidence to support a reasonable judgment about potential jobs–environment trade-offs. And our experience to date shows unambiguously that the negative job impacts from environmental regulation have been small and gradual and have tended to be balanced by gains from the same legislation. For example, in spite of apocalyptic predictions from industry-sponsored macromodels about the consequences of acid-rain control, not even a smidgen of economic slowdown has emerged from this successful clean-up program. I see no reason to think that the global warming case will be dramatically different. Based on the record, and after looking closely at the industries most likely to suffer localized impacts, a reasonable prediction for greenhouse gas control includes layoffs averaging a few thousand annually nationwide.

FICTIONS, FACTS, AND ECONOMIC INSECURITY

This book has traced the technical roots of the fiction of a major jobs–environment trade-off back through twenty-five years of industry-sponsored, and deeply flawed, economic studies, accompanied always by dire and universally unrealized predictions. However, even after exposing the source of the myth, it is easy to understand why a belief in a jobs–environment trade-off finds fertile ground among workers in today's economy.

In spite of the fact that the 1990s has been a "good" decade for the United States economy as a whole, it has not been so kind to working people. It was not until 1998, for example, that the median family saw its income recover to the level it had been during the last business-cycle peak of almost a decade earlier. Job stability also continued to decline. Between 1985 and 1996, the average number of years on the job for males greater than thirty-four declined by around a year. And the most disturbing trend of the 1980s—a rise in childhood poverty—was not reversed. In 1996, 23.2 percent of children under the age of six were growing up in poor families, a percentage point *higher* than at a comparable phase of the business cycle in the late 1980s.[1] If economic conditions for the majority of people were, at best, stagnant, what was happening to all the new wealth generated over eight years of economic expansion? The rich got richer. Virtually all of the income growth in recent years has been concentrated in the top 20 percent of the wealthiest households.

In chapter 1, we looked at some of the factors that have been promoting these trends toward both inequality and insecurity. The same information technologies that are driving the globalization of trade and finance, and throwing U.S. workers into competition with workers overseas, are also creating centralization and concentration in domestic industry. With each round of mergers of course have come more layoffs. At the same time, an anti-union climate has led to the decline of the primary institution on which working people have historically relied to protect themselves from the downside of rapid economic change.

The point here is that even in good times, most working people in the United States are living from paycheck to paycheck, aware that the next buyout or restructuring could mean economic disaster. As the economy moves into recession, these fears will in fact be realized for millions more Americans. And in this kind of climate, environmental regulation can become an easy scapegoat. Northwest timber workers and eastern coal miners—with their jobs under siege by both technological innovation and the late 1980s recession—found in spotted owls and clean-air regulations tangible symbols on which to focus their anger and frustration.

TAKING LABOR SERIOUSLY

The twin pillars undergirding the myth of a jobs–environment trade-off are, on the one hand, major corporate-backed public-relations campaigns, and, on the other hand, an audience who, given their precarious economic situation, are receptive to the message. But that message is wrong. And it is worth stressing that there is not much that is dramatically new or even controversial in pointing this out. Among economists, the idea that full employment and environmental protection are fully compatible is the consensus view. Likewise, we have known for over a decade that layoffs arising from environmental regulation total annually between 1,000 and 3,000 nationwide. And, finally, economists' failure to find evidence of any significant capital flight to pollution havens is a widely accepted fact in the profession.

Clearly, however, the professional consensus on these issues has not derailed well-financed disinformation campaigns that claim the contrary. Ultimately, the way to take away the power of the trade-off myth is to address the underlying economic insecurity in which it is able to take root. By way of example we can look to many western European countries, where the jobs–environment issue is not so bitterly polarized. Nowhere in western Europe, for example, is there the kind of powerful organized opposition to greenhouse gas regulations that we see in the United States. This is in spite of the fact that unemployment in Europe is generally much higher than in the United States. What explains the difference?

Europe has been buffeted by the same forces of globalization that are impacting the United States. One difference is that, in the face of these pressures, much stronger labor unions have protected, and in some cases even strengthened, the social safety net. Laid off workers in Europe may have a hard time finding a new job, but they have much less fear that a spell of unemployment will lead to economic catastrophe. With more social services, better adjustment assistance programs, and, most importantly, universal health care, workers can free themselves from a desperate fear of layoffs.

Under these conditions, the perceived tensions between employment and environmental protection have been dramatically reduced. The real job trade-offs and opportunities can be identified, evaluated, and addressed, and in this political climate, the foundation for progress toward a sustainable world can emerge. In stark contrast to the United States, where environmentalists and workers seldom make common cause, with the election of the Social Democrats in Germany this year, we have seen the formation of the first self-declared "red–green" (labor–environmentalist) national government in history.

Of course the mere formation of a government explicitly committed to the twin goals of social justice and ecological restoration does not mean that either will be achieved overnight. But it is clearly a historic step. Here in the United States these twin battles must also be fought together if either is to be won. This book has focused a lot of attention on the obstacles that the myth of a jobs–environment trade-off is throwing in the way of ratifying the Kyoto global warming treaty. But even if the Senate is convinced by the people of the United States to ratify the Kyoto Treaty, that will be only a first step. Once the treaty is ratified, there will be a struggle stretching over a decade or more to implement the laws needed to redirect the U.S. economy onto a more sustainable path.

The larger point here is that on a planet whose population is set to roughly double over the next fifty years, ecological issues *should* increasingly dominate the policy agenda of government. However, if our economic system continues to fail us in terms of providing a reasonable level of income security, then each and every legislative effort to build a sustainable future will be politically vulnerable to jobs–environment blackmail, regardless of the facts of the matter.

Any ecologically sustainable society must build in basic economic security as an integral component. In that world, it will be easier to recognize that the principal impact of environmental protection is a gradual shift in jobs from one sector to another. Regulation has created no economy-wide trade-offs, very small local impacts, and no significant capital flight to pollution havens. There are also a variety of jobs–environment synergies. In communities around the country, ecologically sound production techniques are forming the basis for a new kind of economic development.

Where I live, in the Pacific Northwest, protection of forests has attracted high-tech manufacturing plants seeking "quality of life" for their employees, while, simultaneously, it has accelerated the ongoing decline of the timber economy. But even here, in the highest profile jobs–environment conflict ever experienced in the United States, the numbers of jobs ultimately lost were fewer than those resulting from a medium-sized corporate merger. And in the long run, clearly the trade-off involved in new environmental protection measures has not been jobs versus the environment, but rather jobs versus jobs. Protecting—or not protecting—the environment shapes not only the world our children will live in but also the work they will do.

NOTE

1. Mishel et al. (1998).

REFERENCES

Ackerman, Frank (1997). *Why Do We Recycle? Markets, Values, and Public Policy* (Washington, D.C.: Island Press).

Anderson, H. Michael, and Jeffrey T. Olson (1991). *Federal Forests and the Economic Base of the Pacific Northwest* (Washington, D.C.: Wilderness Society).

Antonelli, Angela, and Brett Schafer (1997). *The Road to Kyoto: How The Global Climate Treaty Fosters Economic Impoverishment and Endangers U.S. Security* (Washington, D.C.: Heritage Foundation).

Barrett, James P. (1998). *Global Warming: The High Cost of the WEFA Model* (Washington, D.C.: Economic Policy Institute).

Batt, Rosemary, and Paul Osterman (1993). *A National Policy For Workplace Training* (Washington, D.C.: Economic Policy Institute).

Becker, Randy, and Vernon Henderson (1997). "Effects of Air Quality Regulations on Polluting Industries." Presented at the American Economic Association Meetings, Chicago, January 3–5, 1998.

Berman, Eli, and Linda Bui (1997). *Clearing the Air: The Impact of Air Quality on Jobs* (Washington, D.C.: Economic Policy Institute).

Beuter, John (1990). *Social and Economic Impacts of Spotted Owl Conservation Strategy* (Washington, D.C.: American Forest Resource Alliance).

Bezdek, Roger H. (1993). "Environment and Economy: What's the Bottom Line?" *Environment* 35(7): 7–32.

Bezdek, Roger H., Robert M. Wendling, and Jonathan D. Jones (1989). "The Economic and Employment Effects of Investments in Pollution Abatement and Control Technologies." *Ambio* 18(5): 274–279.

Birdsall, Nancy, and David Wheeler (1993). "Trade Policy and Industrial Pollution in Latin America: Where Are the Pollution Havens?" *Journal of Environment and Development* 2(1): 137–149.

Breslow, Marc, John Stutz, and Frank Ackerman (1993). *Creating Jobs for the 90s: A Report to the Wilderness Society* (Boston: Tellus Institute).

Breslow, Marc, John Stutz, Paul Lignon, Frank Ackerman, Nancy Ilgenfritz, and Peter Murad (1992). *Socioeconomic Impacts of Solid Waste Scenarios for New York City: A Report to the New York City Department of Sanitation* (Boston: Tellus Institute).

Brodsky, Jerry, and Margaret Hallock (1998). *The High Skill Approach to Ecosystem Management: Combining Economic, Ecological, and Social Objectives* (Eugene, OR: Labor Education and Research Center).

Bronfennbrenner, Kate (1994). "Employer Behavior in Certification Elections and First Contract Campaigns: Implications for Labor Law Reform." In Sheldon Friedman, Richard Hurd, Rudolph Oswald, and Ronald Seeber (eds.) *Restoring the Promise of American Labor Law Reform* (Ithaca, NY: ILR).

Burtraw, Dallas (1998). "Cost Savings, Market Performance, and Economic Benefits of the U.S. Acid Rain Program." Discussion Paper 98-28 REV (Washington, D.C.: Resources for the Future).

————— (1996). "Trading Emissions to Clean the Air: Exchanges Few But Savings Many." *Resources* 122: 3–6.

Burtraw, Dallas, Alan Krupnick, Erin Manusr, David Austin, and Dierdre Farrel (1998). "Reducing Air Pollution and Acid Rain." *Contemporary Economic Policy* 16(4): 379–400.

Callaghan, Polly, and Heidi Hartmann (1991). *Contingent Work: A Chart Book on Part-time and Temporary Employment* (Washington, D.C.: Economic Policy Institute).

Carlin, Alan (1990). *Environmental Investments: The Cost of a Clean Environment, Summary* (Washington, D.C.: U.S. Environmental Protection Agency).

Chapman, Duane (1991). "Environmental Standards and International Trade in Automobiles and Copper: The Case for a Social Tariff." *Natural Resources Journal* 31(3): 449–462.

Cohen-Rosenthal, Ed (1998). *Labor, Climate Change, and the Environment* (Ithaca, NY: Cornell Center for the Environment).

Colt, Steve (1989). "Income and Employment Impacts of Alaska's Low Income Weatherization Program." ISER Working Paper No. 89-2. (Anchorage: University of Alaska).

Cook, Elizabeth, and Alan Miller (1996). "Framing Policies to Reduce Greenhouse Gas Emissions and Promote Technological Innovation." Paper presented at the Climate Change Analysis Workshop, Springfield, Virginia, June 6–7.

Council of Economic Advisors (1996). *Economic Report of the President* (Washington, D.C.: U.S. Government Printing Office).

Daly, Herman (1993). "The Perils of Free Trade." *Scientific American* 269(5): 50.

Daly, Herman, and John Cobb (1989). *For the Common Good* (New York: Beacon Press).

Daly, Herman, and Robert Goodland (1994). "An Ecological-Economic Assessment of Deregulation of International Commerce under GATT." *Ecological Economics* 9: 13–22.

Data Resources, Inc. (1989). "Employment Effects: Administration Acid Rain Control Options." (Washington, D.C.: U.S. Department of Labor, Office of Policy).

——— (1981). *The Macroeconomic Impacts of Federal Pollution Control Programs: 1981 Assessment* (Washington, D.C.: U.S. Environmental Protection Agency).

——— (1979). *The Macroeconomic Impacts of Federal Pollution Control Programs: 1978 Assessment* (Washington, D.C.: U.S. Environmental Protection Agency).

Dean, Judith (1992). "Trade and the Environment: A Survey of the Literature." *Policy Research Working Paper WPS966* (Washington, D.C.: World Bank).

Duffy-Deno, Kevin T. (1992). "Pollution Abatement Expenditures and Regional Manufacturing Activity." *Journal of Regional Science* 32(4): 419–436.

Ehrenberg, Ronald, and Robert Smith (1994). *Modern Labor Economics* (New York: HarperCollins).

Elkington, John, and Jonathan Shopley (1989). *Cleaning Up: U.S. Waste Management Technology and the Third World.* (Washington, D.C.: World Resources Institute).

Energy Information Administration (1992). *Coal Industry Annual* (Washington, D.C.: Department of Energy).

Forest Ecosystem Management Assessment Team (1993). *Forest Ecosystem Management: An Ecological, Economic, and Social Assessment.* (Washington, D.C.: U.S. Forest Service).

Friedman, Sheldon, Richard Hurd, Rudolph Oswald, and Ronald Seeber, eds. (1994). *Restoring the Promise of American Labor Law Reform* (Ithaca, NY: ILR).

Geller, Howard, John DeCicco, and Skip Laitner (1992). *Energy Efficiency and Job Creation: The Employment and Income Benefits from Investing in Energy Conserving Technologies* (Washington, D.C.: American Council for an Energy Efficient Economy).

Goodstein, Eban (1998a). "Malthus Redux? Globalization, Sustainability, and Policy." In Dean Baker, Gerald Epstein, and Robert Pollin (eds.) *Globaliza-*

tion and Progressive Economic Policy (Cambridge, England: Cambridge University Press).

———— (1998b). *Economics and the Environment* (Englewood Cliffs, NJ: Prentice-Hall).

———— (1997). "A New Look at Environmental Regulation and Competitiveness." EPI Briefing Paper No. 70 (Washington, D.C.: Economic Policy Institute).

———— (1996). "Jobs and the Environment: An Overview." *Environmental Management* 20(3): 313–321.

———— (1994). *Jobs and the Environment: The Myth of a National Trade-Off* (Washington, D.C.: Economic Policy Institute).

Goodstein, Eban, and Hart Hodges (1997). "Polluted Data: Overestimating the Costs of Environmental Regulation." *The American Prospect* 35 (November–December): 64–69.

Gore, Albert (1992). *Earth in the Balance: Ecology and the Human Spirit* (New York: Houghton-Mifflin).

Gorte, Ross W. (1992). *Economic Impacts of Protecting Spotted Owls: A Comparison and Analysis of Existing Studies*, CRS Report for Congress 92-922 ENR (Washington, D.C.: Congressional Research Service).

Gray, Wayne B. (1997). "Comment on 'State Regulatory Policy and Economic Development,'" *New England Economic Review* (March–April): 99–104.

————. (1987). "The Cost of Regulation: OSHA, EPA, and the Productivity Slowdown." *The American Economic Review* 7: 998–1006.

Gray, Wayne B., and Mary E. Deily (1991). "Enforcement of Pollution Regulations in a Declining Industry." Clark University Working Paper 89-8. (Worcester, MA: Department of Economics, Clark University).

Gray, Wayne B., and Ronald J. Shadbegian (1998). "Do Firms Avoid Regulation by Shifting Production?" Paper presented at the American Economic Association Meetings, Chicago, January 3–5, 1998.

Grossman, Elizabeth (1998). "Banking on a Healthy Environment." *Orion Afield* 2(4): 18–22.

Grossman, Gene M., and Alan B. Krueger (1991). "Environmental Impacts of a North American Free Trade Agreement." Working Paper 3914 (Cambridge, MA: National Bureau of Economic Research).

Hahn, Margaret (1998). *Improving Jobs, Community, and the Environment: Lessons from the Ecosystem Workforce Project* (Eugene, OR: Labor Education and Research Center).

Hahn, Robert, and Wilbur Steger (1990). *An Analysis of Jobs at Risk and Job Losses from the Proposed Clean Air Act Amendments* (Pittsburgh: CONSAD Research Corporation).

Harrington, Winston, Richard Morgenstern, and Peter Nelson (1999). *On the Accuracy of Regulatory Cost Estimates*, Discussion Paper 99-18 (Washington, D.C.: Resources for the Future).

Hawken, Paul (1993). *The Ecology of Commerce* (New York: HarperCollins).

Hazilla, Michael, and Raymond J. Kopp (1991). "Social Cost of Environmental Regulations: A General Equilibrium Analysis." *Journal of Political Economy* 98(4).

Henderson, J. Vernon (1996). "Effects of Air Quality Regulation." *American Economic Review* 86(4): 789–813.

Hettige, Hemamala, Robert E. B. Lucas, and David Wheeler (1992). "The Toxic Intensity of Industrial Production: Global Patterns, Trends, and Trade Policy." *The American Economic Review* 82(2): 478–481.

Hodges, Hart (1997). "Falling Prices: Cost of Complying with Environmental Regulation Almost Always Less than Advertised." *EPI Briefing Paper* No. 69 (Washington, D.C.: Economic Policy Institute).

Hoerner, J. Andrew, Alan Miller, and Frank Müller (1995). *Promoting Growth and Job Creation Through Emerging Environmental Technologies* (Washington, D.C.: National Commission for Employment Policy).

Hollenbeck, Kevin (1978) "The Employment and Earnings Impacts of the Regulation of Stationary Source Air Pollution." *Journal of Environmental Economics and Management* 6(2): 208–221.

Hopkins, Thomas D. (1992). *Regulation and Jobs—Sorting Out the Consequences* (Washington, D.C.: American Petroleum Institute).

House Democratic Policy Committee (1996). *Downsizing the American Dream.* Staff Report (Washington, D.C.: House Democratic Policy Committee).

Human Resources Development Canada (1993). *Report of the Advisory Group on Working Time and the Distribution of Work* (Hull, Quebec: Minister of Supply and Services).

ICF (1989). "Economic Analysis of Title V (Acid Rain Provisions) of the Administration's Proposed Clean Air Act Amendments." (Washington, D.C.: U.S. EPA).

Institute for Advanced Technology Research (1990). "Mitigation of Clean Air Act Impacts on Employment in Coal Field Communities." (Washington, D.C.: U.S. Environmental Protection Agency, Office of Policy Planning and Evaluation).

Interagency Analytic Team (1997). "Economic Effects of Global Climate Change Policies," draft of May 30, as released to the House Commerce Subcommittee on Energy and Power. Washington, D.C.: Climate Change Taskforce.

Intergovernmental Panel on Climate Change (1996). *Climate Change 1995: The Science of Climate Change* (Oxford, England: Cambridge University Press).

Interlaboratory Working Group (1997). *Scenarios of U.S. Carbon Reductions: Potential Impacts of Energy Efficient and Low Carbon Technologies by 2010 and Beyond* (Oak Ridge, TN: Oak Ridge and Lawrence Berkeley National Laboratories).

Jacobson, Louis S., Robert J. LaLonde, and Daniel G. Sullivan (1993a). "Earnings Losses of Displaced Workers." *American Economic Review* 83(4): 685–709.

——— (1993b). "The Returns from Classroom Training for Displaced Workers." Federal Reserve Bank of Chicago, Working Paper 94-27. (Chicago: Federal Reserve Bank of Chicago).

Jaffe, Adam B., Steven R. Peterson, Paul R. Portney, and Robert N. Stavins (1995). "Environmental Regulation and the Competitiveness of U.S. Manufacturing: What Does the Evidence Tell Us?" *Journal of Economic Literature* 33(1): 132–163.

Johnson, Norman, Jerry Franklin, Jack Ward Thomas, and John Gordon (1991). *Alternatives for Management of Late-Successional Forests of the Pacific Northwest.* Report to the Agriculture and Merchant Marine and Fisheries Committees of the U.S. House of Representatives, October 8.

Jorgenson, Dale W., and Peter J. Wilcoxen (1990). "Environmental Regulation and U.S. Economic Growth." *Rand Journal of Economics* 21(2): 314–340.

Jorgensen, Helene (1998). *Report on Workers Dismissed During Organizing Campaigns.* (Washington, D.C.: AFL-CIO Public Policy Department).

Kahn, Matthew (1998). "The Silver Lining of Rust Belt Manufacturing Decline." Harvard Institute of Economic Research Discussion Paper No. 1828 (Cambridge, MA: Harvard University).

——— (1997). "Particulate Pollution Trends in the United States." *Regional Science and Urban Economics* 27: 87–107.

Kalt, Joseph (1988). "The Impact of Domestic Regulatory Policies on U.S. International Competitiveness." In A. Michael Spence and Heather Hazard (eds.) *International Competitiveness* (Cambridge, MA: Harper and Row).

Karliner, Joshua (1998). "Earth Predators." *Dollars and Sense* 218 (July–August): 7.

—— (1997). *The Corporate Planet: Ecology and Politics in the Age of Globalization* (San Francisco: Sierra Club).

Kete, Nancy (1991). *The Politics of Markets: The Acid Rain Control Policy in the 1990 Clean Air Act Amendments* (Baltimore: University of Maryland).

Kieschnick, Michael (1978). *Environmental Protection and Economic Development* (Washington, D.C.: U.S. Department of Commerce, Economic Development Administration).

Kinsley, Michael (1997). *The Economic Renewal Guide*, 3rd edition (Snowmass, CO: Rocky Mountain Institute).

Kleinknecht, A. (1987). *Innovation Patterns in Crisis and Prosperity* (New York: St. Martin's).

Kodryzycki, Yolanda (1996). "Laid-Off Workers in a Time of Structural Change." *New England Economic Review* (July–August): 3–26.

Koechlin, Timothy (1992). "Determinants of the Location of U.S.A. Foreign Investment." *International Review of Applied Economics* 6(2): 203–216.

Kontdratieff, Nikolai (1935). "The Long Waves in Economic Life." *Review of Economic Statistics* 17(6): 105–115.

Koomey, John, R. Cooper Richey, Skip Laitner, Alan Sanstad, Robert Markel, and Chris Murray (1998). *Technology and Greenhouse Gas Emissions: An Integrated Scenario Analysis Using the LBNL-NEMS Model*. LBNL-42054 (Berkeley, CA: Lawrence Berkeley National Laboratory, Environmental Energy Technologies Division, Energy Analysis Program).

Koplow, Douglas (1993). *Federal Energy Subsidies: Energy, Environmental, and Fiscal Impacts*. (Washington, D.C.: Alliance to Save Energy).

Krosnick, Jon, and Penny Visser (1998). "The Impact of the Fall 1997 Debate About Global Warming on Public Opinion." *Weathervane* (Washington, D.C.: Resources for the Future).

Laitner, Skip, Stephen Bernow, and John DeCicco (1998). "Employment and Other Macroeconomic Benefits of an Innovation-Led Climate Strategy for the United States." *Energy Policy* 26(5): 425–432.

LaLonde, Robert J. (1995). "The Promise of Public Sector-Sponsored Training Programs." *Journal of Economic Perspectives* 9(2): 149–168.

Lekakis, J. N. (1991). "Employment Effects of Environmental Policies in Greece." *Environment and Planning* 23: 1627–1637.

Leonard, H. Jeffrey (1984). *Are Environmental Regulations Driving U.S. Industry Overseas?* (Washington, D.C.: The Conservation Foundation).

Lovins, Amory (1979). *Soft Energy Paths: Towards a Durable Peace* (New York: Harper and Row).

Lovins, Amory, and Hunter Lovins (1997). *Climate: Making Sense and Making Money* (Snowmass, CO: Rocky Mountain Institute).

Lucas, Robert E. B., David Wheeler, and Hemamala Hettige (1992). *Economic Development, Environmental Regulation, and the International Migration of Toxic Industrial Pollution 1960–1988.* (Washington, D.C.: World Bank).

Mann, Michael E., and Mark Meier (1998). "Reconstruction of the Earth's Temperature Record for the Last Six Centuries: Are the Earth's Glaciers Responding to Climate Change?" Paper presented at the U.S. Global Change Research Program Seminar Series, July 20, Washington, D.C.

Markusen, Ann, and Catherine Hill (1992). *Converting the Cold War Economy* (Washington, D.C.: Economic Policy Institute).

Mason, Keith (1991). "The Economic Impact." *EPA Journal* (January–February).

Meyer, Stephen (1993). *Environmentalism and Prosperity: An Update.* (Cambridge, MA: MIT Project on Environmental Politics and Policy).

——— (1992). *Environmentalism and Prosperity: Testing the Environmental Impact Hypothesis.* (Cambridge, MA: MIT Project on Environmental Politics and Policy).

Mishel, Lawrence, Jared Bernstien, and John Schmitt (1998). *The State of Working America, 1988–1999* (Ithaca, NY: Cornell University Press).

Moberg, David (1998). "Organizing to Win?" *In These Times* 22(18): 11–133.

Morgenstern, Richard D., William Pizer, and Jhih-Shyang Shih (1998a). "Jobs Versus the Environment: Is There a Trade-Off?" Discussion Paper No. 99-01 (Washington, D.C.: Resources for the Future).

——— (1998b). "The Costs of Environmental Protection." (Washington, D.C.: Resources for the Future).

Müller, Frank G. (1981). "The Employment Effects of Environmental Policy: An International Comparison, Germany and the USA." *Journal of Environmental Systems* 1(2): 119–137.

Müller, Frank, Skip Laitner, and Lyuba Zarsky (1992). "Jobs Benefits of Expanding Investment in Solar Energy." *Solar Industry Journal* (Fourth Quarter): 17–25.

National Acid Precipitation Program (1991). *National Acid Precipitation Program, 1990 Integrated Assessment Report* (Washington, D.C.: National Acid Precipitation Program).

National Association of Manufacturers (1987). *Acid Rain Legislation and the Econ-*

omy: Executive Summary (Washington, D.C.: National Association of Manufacturers).

Neimi, E., E. Whitelaw, and A. Johnson (1999). *The Sky Did NOT Fall: The Pacific Northwest's Response to Logging Reductions* (Eugene, OR: ECONorthwest).

Nell, Edward (1987). *Prosperity and Public Spending* (Boston: Unwin Hyman).

Nelson, Richard R., and Gavin Wright (1992). "The Rise and Fall of American Technological Leadership." *Journal of Economic Literature* 30(4): 1931–1964.

New York Times (1994). "Oregon, Foiling Forecasters, Thrives as it Protects Owls." *New York Times*, October 11, A1.

Organization for Economic Cooperation Development (1995). "The Employment Potential of Environmental Policies." *OECD Letter*, January–February 4(1).

——— (1991). *OECD Economic Surveys: United States* (Paris: Organization for Economic Cooperation and Development).

——— (1984). *Environment and Economics* (Paris: Organization for Economic Cooperation and Development).

——— (1978). *Employment and Environment* (Paris: Organization for Economic Cooperation and Development).

Palmer, Karen, Wallace Oates, and Paul Portney (1995). "Tightening Environmental Standards: The Benefit-Cost or the No-Cost Paradigm?" *Journal of Economic Perspectives* 9(4): 119–132.

Porter, Michael, and Claas van der Linde (1995). "Toward a New Conception of the Environment-Competitiveness Relationship." *Journal of Economic Perspectives* 9(4): 97–118.

Power, Thomas (1995). *Lost Landscapes and Failed Economies: The Search for a Value of Place* (Washington, D.C.: Island Press).

——— (ed.) (1996). *Economic Well-Being and Environmental Protection in the Northwest: A Consensus Report by Pacific Northwest Economists* (Armonk, NY: M. E. Sharpe).

Przeworski, A. (1995) "Less is More: In France, the Future of Unemployment Lies in Leisure." *Dollars and Sense* 200 (July–August).

Rauscher, Michael (1997). "Environmental Regulation and International Capital Allocation." In Carlo Carrarro and Domenico Siniscalco (eds.) *New Directions in the Economic Theory of the Environment* (Cambridge, England: Cambridge University Press).

Repetto, Robert, and Duncan Austin (1997). *The Costs of Climate Protection: A Guide for the Perplexed* (Washington, D.C.: World Resources Institute).

Repetto, Robert, and Cresencia Maurer (1997). *U.S. Competitiveness Is Not at Risk in the Climate Negotiations* (Washington, D.C.: World Resources Institute).

Repetto, Robert, Roger C. Dower, Robin Jenkins, and Jacqueline Geoghehan (1992). *Green Fees: How a Tax Shift Can Work for the Environment and the Economy* (Washington, D.C.: World Resources Institute).

Rutledge, Gary L., and Mary L. Leonard (1992). "Pollution Abatement and Control Expenditures, 1972–1990." *Survey of Current Business* 72(6): 25–41.

Sample, V. Alaric, and Dennis C. Le Master (1992). *Assessing the Employment Impacts of Proposed Measures to Protect the Northern Spotted Owl* (Washington, D.C.: Forest Policy Center).

Sanchez, Roberto A. (1990). "Health and Environmental Risks of the Maquiladora in Mexicali." *Natural Resources Journal* 30(1): 163–186.

Scholl, Russell B., Raymond J. Mataloni Jr., and Steve D. Bezerganian (1992). "The International Investment Position of the United States in 1991." *Survey of Current Business* 72(6): 46–59.

Schor, Juliet B. (1991). *The Overworked American* (New York: BasicBooks).

Schumpeter, Joseph (1939). *Business Cycles: A Theoretical, Historical, and Statistical Analysis of the Capitalist Process* (New York: McGraw-Hill).

Scott, Robert (1997). *Accelerating Globalization? The Economic Effects of Climate Change Polices on U.S. Workers* (Washington, D.C.: Economic Policy Institute).

Sutherland, R. J., N. Richards, M. Nisbet, D. Steinmeyer, R. Slinn, M. Tallett, and R. J. Fruehan (1997). *Impact of High Energy Price Scenarios on Energy-Intensive Sectors: Perspectives from Industry Workshops.* (Washington, D.C.: Argonne National Laboratory and the Department of Energy).

Tietenberg, Thomas (1992). *Environmental and Natural Resource Economics* (New York: HarperCollins).

Tuchmann, Thomas E., Kent B. Connaughton, Lisa E. Freedman, and Clarence B. Moriwaki (1996). *The Northwest Forest Plan: A Report to the President and Congress* (Washington, D.C.: USDA).

U.S. Department of Agriculture, Forest Service, U.S. Department of the Interior, and Bureau of Land Management (1990). *Economic Effects of Implementing a Conservation Strategy for the Northern Spotted Owl* (Washington, D.C.: USDA).

U.S. Department of Energy (1997). *Annual Energy Outlook 1998* (Washington, D.C.: Energy Information Administration).

U.S. Department of Labor (1994). *Clean Air Employment Transition Assistance*

Grants as of June 30, 1994 (Washington, D.C.: Employment and Training Administration, U.S. Department of Labor).

U.S. Environmental Protection Agency (1998). *Survey of Environmental Products and Industries* (Washington, D.C.: U.S. Environmental Protection Agency, Office of Policy Planning and Evaluation).

———— (1995). *The U.S. Environmental Protection Industry: A Proposed Framework for Assessment* (Washington, D.C.: U.S. Environmental Protection Agency, Office of Policy Planning and Evaluation).

———— (1993). *International Trade in Environmental Protection Equipment* (Washington, D.C.: U.S. Environmental Protection Agency, Office of Policy Planning and Evaluation).

———— (1981). *Economic Dislocation Early Warning System: 2nd Quarterly Report* (Washington, D.C.: U.S. Environmental Protection Agency).

U.S. General Accounting Office (1991). *Some U.S. Wood Furniture Firms Relocated from Los Angeles Area to Mexico.* GAO/NSIAD-91-191, report to chairman, House Committee on Energy and Commerce (Washington, D.C.: U.S. Government Printing Office).

Vogan, Christine R. (1996). "Pollution Abatement and Control Expenditures, 1972–1994." *Survey of Current Business* 74(9): 48–67.

Warren, Debra D. (1998). "Production, Prices, Employment, and Trade in the Northwest Forest Industries, Second Quarter 1997." Pacific Northwest Research Station Bulletin PNW-RB-228 (Washington, D.C.: USDA).

Warton Economic Forecasting Associates (1990). *The Economic Impact of ANWR Development* (Washington, D.C.: American Petroleum Institute).

Webber, Carrie, and Richard Brown (1998). "Saving Potential of Energy Star Voluntary Labeling Programs." *Proceedings of the 1998 ACEEE Summer Study on Energy Efficiency in Buildings* (Washington, D.C.: American Council for an Energy Efficient Economy).

Wendling, Robert M., and Roger H. Bezdek (1989). "Acid Rain Abatement Legislation: Costs and Benefits." *OMEGA International Journal of Management Science* 17(3): 251–261.

Wheeler, David, and P. Martin (1992). "Price Policies and the International Diffusion of Clean Technologies: The Case of Wood Pulp Production." In P. Low (ed.) *International Trade and the Environment* (New York: World Bank).

Wilderness Society (1993a). "Forest Policy Baselines for the Pacific Northwest" (Washington, D.C.: Wilderness Society).

—— (1993b). "A Critique of the Clinton Forest Plan" (Washington, D.C.: Wilderness Society).

Wykle, Lucinda, Ward Morehouse, and David Dembo (1991). *Worker Empowerment in a Changing Economy: Jobs, Military Production, and the Environment* (New York: Apex Press).

Yellen, Janet (1998). "Statement Before the Senate Committee on Agriculture, Nutrition, and Forestry, March 5" (Washington, D.C.: U.S. Senate).

—— (1997). "Statement Before the House Subcommittee on Energy and Power, July 15" (Washington, D.C.: U.S. House of Representatives).

Young, Jim (1998). "Just Transition: A New Approach to Jobs v. Environment." *Working USA* (July–August): 42–48.

INDEX

191